DOUN-HAUDEN

The Socio-Political Determinants of Scottish Independence

Alfred Baird

ISBN-13: 9798634652320
ISBN-10: 1477123456

Kindle Direct Publishing

Available from: www.amazon.co.uk

Cover design by: Art Painter

*This book is dedicated to the millions of Scots who
were forced to leave Scotland due to oppression
and the lack of opportunity in their own land.*

CONTENTS

PREFACE

There is an increasingly urgent need to provide a deeper understanding of the phenomenon that is Scottish independence. Many commentators assume general policy matters remain key influencers of voter decisions on whether to support or reject Scottish independence. This may grossly underestimate and misunderstand the real complexity of the matter. Here, the author uses his academic expertise to 'ground out' an analytical framework which helps to identify, based on analysis of key environmental factors, the fundamental determinants and influences of Scottish independence.

It is argued that the framework, entitled 'The Socio-Political Determinants of Scottish Independence', permits far deeper analysis and understanding of the Scottish independence challenge. Collectively, the nine socio-political determinants which the author has 'ground out' of the data collected and analysed, help to explain and underpin the quest for, and outline the barriers opposing, Scottish independence.

Each of the determinants is analysed using appropriate and relevant theories as well as supporting data. It is argued that this work represents a new, comprehensive, robust, and scientific way to approach the subject of Scottish independence. It is an approach that has arguably never been taken before in any of the growing mass of literature concerning the subject of Scotland's independence, and hence represents an important and unique contribution offering new and provocative insights into Scotland's quest for liberation.

"The poverty of the people, national oppression and the inhibition of culture are one and the same thing. After a century of colonial domination we find a culture which is rigid in the extreme, or rather what we find are the dregs of culture, its mineral strata. The withering away of the reality of the nation and the death-pangs of the national culture are linked to each other in mutual dependence."

(Frantz Fanon)

CHAPTER 1:
INTRODUCTION

Introduction

For those interested in the study of society and politics, living through the Scottish independence referendum in 2014 and the debate prior to that, and its aftermath since, was and remains an intense experience. For those with an academic background, such as the author, it has often been necessary, and important, to seek to develop a better and deeper understanding of what independence means for the Scottish people, and for Scotland as a country. Independence is a multifaceted and complex phenomenon, which often seems to be reduced to rather crude and simplistic notions of how better or worse off Scots might be.

Within the author's academic and research background, which is to do with the study of organisations, businesses, and globalized industries and the generally dynamic internal and external environments within which they operate, compete, and expand or contract, a common approach has been for researchers to develop analytical frameworks which help focus and structure in-depth research and analysis of any specific issue or phenomenon under investigation. This is the approach taken here which, it is argued, is necessary in order to adequately explore, analyse, understand and explain the social and political phenomenon that is Scottish independence. Here a theoretical framework-based research approach provides guidance to, and serves to strengthen any research work (Ravitch and Riggan 2017). Any statement of theoretical assumptions then allows for these assumptions to be critically evaluated.

The essence of a theoretical framework is the question or problem to be addressed, which in this instance is Scottish independence, as well as the approach used to answer this question or solve the problem (Lederman and Lederman

2015). This requires a thorough review of the literature, which is what the author has sought to achieve, as reflected in the extensive bibliography contained in this book. References include theoretical as well as empirical literature, and identification of some of the gaps in this literature, hence this book, which aims to fill as much of that gap as possible. Inevitably, other researchers will in due course come up with other approaches to study the same question or phenomenon, and that is the role and function of research, to extend knowledge.

The theoretical framework which the author has developed over a period of several years, has effectively been 'ground-out' from the data and information drawn on concerning the subject matter or phenomenon in question (Glaser and Strauss 1967), which is Scottish independence. This framework is entitled: 'The Socio-Political Determinants of Scottish Independence', reflecting the nature of its content and aims. The overall structure of the framework is considered to include key socio-political environmental variables which influence and impact on the subject or phenomenon of Scottish independence, and hence determine and influence any outcome in this regard (i.e. Scottish independence, or not, as the case may be).

This approach is therefore rather different to most other contemporary works concerning the subject of Scottish independence. Often the question of Scottish independence is argued from purely economic and/or political perspectives (Hassan and Mitchell 2013), with historical aspects also to the fore (Devine 2012). Sometimes an economic and political comparison with other countries may be the focus, for instance with an emphasis on federalism and devolution as constitutional alternatives to independence (e.g. Keating and Laforest 2018). Few writers, though, seem to get close to what we might call the 'nitty-gritty' issues such as identity and belonging (e.g. Henderson 2007; Riddoch 2013); although again, even here, there is a need to widen the theoretical and analytical net to include other environmental pressures and influences. The determinants of Scottish independence remain many and varied, reflecting this environmental complexity, and the wide-ranging structured analysis and findings presented here.

Whilst other contemporary approaches are all perfectly valid in their own way, they often miss some of the essential though perhaps less evident socio-political factors and significant influences at play, in what is a multifaceted phenomenon. There are also certain 'touchy' socio-political areas which most writers and researchers have tended to avoid, for one reason or another. This includes aspects such as colonialism, nationalism, demographic change, culture, language, and ethnicity, and the impact these environmental factors have on the quest for Scottish independence. This necessarily demands a more comprehensive and holistic approach, taking account of the many different environmental factors and influences involved in, and ultimately determining, such an outcome or phenomenon as Scottish independence.

It is argued here in this book that one of the most significant environmental influences impacting on Scottish independence is language, and more specifically the Scots language. Although the book is written in English, throughout the text the reader will see interspersed numerous small pieces of text written in the Scots language. These Scots language inserts are intended to emphasise particular points discussed within the main text and to help reinforce the contention in the book that the Scots language is a fundamentally important factor or variable in the context of Scottish independence, in the telling of Scotland's story and, crucially, in helping form the identity of the Scottish people, much as any people's or nation's mother tongue would (or should) be considered important.

There is, in addition, the pivotal relationship between language and culture which, together, help form identity, and these relationships are explored in some detail. Language and culture have not thus far really featured much, if at all, in any scientific analysis on Scottish independence, which is a curious omission.

Also considered as an important influence here is the English language and a hypothesis explored is that the Scottish independence question reflects, to a large extent, a cultural and linguistic divide between Scots speakers and Anglophones, much as there are language divides in Quebec and in Catalonia or indeed wherever there is a demand for self-determination of 'a people'. In this context, relevant socio-political theories are explored such as cultural imperialism, linguistic imperialism, internal colonialism, cultural hegemony and more.

These and other environmental factors and variables investigated and analysed are reflected in the main title of the book, 'Doun-Hauden', which in the Scots language means 'oppressed'. When a people are oppressed this effectively means they are held down and therefore prevented from achieving their full potential, resulting in the continual under-development of a people and their nation. The Scots term 'doun-hauden' itself well illustrates the uniqueness of (the Scots) language in its ability to amplify meaning through language; for a people who remain 'doun-hauden', or 'held down', this conjures up an altogether different and rather more violent and expressive image than merely 'oppressed'.

Many people, not least people in Scotland, may not automatically view the Scots as an oppressed or 'doun-hauden' people in their own land. However, the structured analysis and discussion presented throughput this book, based on the grounded theory analytical framework, as developed by the author, and applied and discussed with reference to a range of relevant theoretical works relating to each area or environmental variable, highlights numerous examples and areas of life, society, institutions, governance, culture, language etc. in which the Scots are indeed oppressed and hence 'doun-hauden' within the UK union. At times this oppression is by Scots themselves, for example, through 'Appropriated Racial Oppression' (or 'internalised racism'), a condition which is closely related to the Scottish 'Cultural Cringe'. In addition, there is strong motivation for some Scots to assimilate within a supposed 'higher order' Anglophone culture, although more often this is a consequence of externally imposed forces and influences, as reflecting Scotland's colonial reality, the UK 'union' being something of a political charade. In this context any quest for Scottish independence may therefore be considered a necessary and rightful pursuit in order to finally put an end to the longstanding social and political oppression suffered by the Scottish people and their nation; a people and nation who, it is argued, on the basis of the evidence presented, remain oppressed, or 'doun-hauden', and therefore unable to fully develop as they might naturally otherwise be expected to do.

This theoretical framework-based analysis therefore adds a new scientific dimension to the general literature on Scottish independence. Reflecting this, the findings presented should and will doubtless be considered as radically different to what has gone before. What is offered here is a new, science-based, and therefore no holds barred approach and perspective aimed at explaining what is really happening to Scotland and to the Scottish people in the context of their quest for independence, and it is neither pretty nor for the faint hearted; colonialism, which the UN describe as 'a scourge' (i.e. a punishment), seldom is.

There is, in effect, a constantly changing socio-political environment within which the question of Scottish independence needs to be considered. The many pressures and challenges (or variables) highlighted within the structured framework as presented are continually changing and, in turn, this means that the opportunities for and barriers to independence may also strengthen or weaken, depending on the socio-political environmental circumstances at a given point in time. Only through fully understanding the nature of the different key socio-political pressure points can those who wish to see an independent Scotland really hope to overcome the challenges faced. In this regard, it is argued that the framework offers an important strategic analytical tool for decision and policy makers, for researchers and commentators, students and analysts, as well as being of interest to those who are more generally drawn to the subject of Scottish independence and the self-determination of 'peoples'.

Scottish independence in and of itself is a radical and hence a challenging quest and this demands a robust and detailed structured appraisal and understanding of the environmental pressures involved. This book tells it as it is and, in the great spirit of Scottish egalitarianism and enlightenment, what is written is believed to be both honest and true, based on the evidence presented, reflecting the literature on the subject and supported by discussion and analysis of a wide range of relevant theoretical perspectives.

There is no attempt here at hiding from the tougher questions and issues still holding down Scotland and its people, as so often has tended to be the case with those looking at the issue of Scottish independence, the latter perhaps mostly from a unionist and Anglophone perspective. In this regard the development and application of a robust analytical theoretical framework has helped facilitate what is arguably a deeper and more rigorous science-based analysis and evaluation of what might be considered the brutal realities concerning the quest for Scottish independence.

CHAPTER 2: CONTEXT AND METHODOLOGY

Context

Adeterminant is any factor or factors which decisively affects the nature or outcome of something. That Scotland and its people are not yet enjoying their own national independence must be due to some determinant, or perhaps a range of determinants. But what are these determinants? And, more importantly, once identified, how might such determinants be overcome if Scotland is to become an independent country again?

Boris Johnson MP, in his inaugural Prime Ministerial statement to the House of Commons on 25th July 2019, stated that: *"independence is about our self-respect"*[1]. He was of course referring to Brexit and the UK's exit from the EU, however, the same message could just as equally apply to any nation and its people, including Scotland. If independence is about self-respect, what does this mean for Scotland and the Scottish people who remain devoid of independence, and hence by implication are 'dependent'? Does this imply that the Scots are lacking in self-respect until such time as they are independent? Within the UK 'union' many Scots supporting independence would argue this to be the case, and that Scottish independence is, at least in part, about self-respect.

As John McGrath[2] once said of Scotland and the Scots, there is a 'fine line between altruism and being mugs'. Not many countries and peoples freely give away their sovereignty, as Scotland's 'No' voters arguably did in 2014, and with it they also gave away Scotland's lands, seas, and key social institutions, in the process leaving their people disenfranchised, and their nation stateless and 'unrecognized' by any other country. The Scots are certainly big on altruism in denying and blocking, or so it would seem, their own independence, and through this rejecting the prospect of their own nationality and citizenship, in the process giving away their sovereignty to England's Tories to do with Scotland as they please. Or are the Scots simply mugs, as McGrath implied? Inevitably the reality is more complex than this, and that is essentially what this book aims to investigate and explore in more detail.

By the time you read this book Scotland may or may not be an independent state. More likely it will not be. Quite possibly Scotland may have ceased to exist in any meaningful sense, much as it arguably did in 1707, with the new 'devolved' parliament shut down or at least further diminished by its larger neighbour and their ever loyal 'little helpers' in Scotland. Scotland might then be like a zombie nation; breathing, sort of, but not much happening 'upstairs'. A nation and its people wandering rather aimlessly, led predominantly by forces from elsewhere, namely Westminster and its almost 600 MP's representing other nations and 'peoples'. A Scotland run, some might argue, by an increasingly Anglophone meritocratic elite, many of whom its larger neighbouring country regularly dispatches northwards to 'help manage' Scotland and its social institutions, as appears to have been standard practice over the past couple of centuries.

Despite prevailing socio-political 'realities', the 'inalienable' right to self-determination of Scotland's people is, or should be, by implication, a matter for the Scots and them alone. But who are the Scots today? Are all the people living in Scotland 'Scottish'; or, to use the more politically correct term, are they all 'Scots'? Do all the people living in Scotland even consider themselves to be 'Scottish', and do they all have any desire to be 'Scottish' now or in future? What about those 'Scots' still holding to their own national identities, be that English, German, Welsh, Polish, Spanish or whatever? What is the make-up of Scotland's population today, and how does national identity influence the way 'Scots' and other 'nationals' living in Scotland vote on the question of Scottish independence? These are all valid questions when discussing matters of such importance as Scottish independence and national self-determination.

Moreover, how rapidly is Scotland's population changing, also considering the fact that Scotland is one of few countries with no control over its own immigration? Is independence less to do with national identity or the self-determination of 'a people', and merely about how better or worse governance would be for Scotland's residents, each of whom, by virtue of their residence, or so we are told, have a 'stake' in the nation? Conversely, is independence, as the UN maintains, not really about the self-determination and hence liberation and decolonisation of a defined group of 'people' based on established criteria? These are just some of the questions this book seeks to address.

> *Deceit haes aye bin the main unionist tuil sae faur as Scotlan's fowk an naition is concernt; thayr'e mooths appen an deceit fa's oot.*

Supporters of independence would claim that Scotland does not see much in the way of democracy from being a 'part' of the UK 'union'. Scotland does not vote Tory, yet Scotland invariably gets Tory governments (blue or red) forced upon it, the latter based in a parliament sitting in another country's capital city. Almost two-thirds of Scotland's voters opposed Brexit yet they and Scotland have had Brexit forced upon them. Scotland has voted several times for an SNP majority in Scotland and to hold a second independence referendum, yet that has been refused by those whom Scots do not vote for, yet who aye rule over them. Most Scots do not want nuclear weapons in Scotland, yet that is likewise forced upon the Scots. It is believed that a majority of 'Scots' (or at least those born in Scotland) voted for independence, yet still the Scots have a 'union' forced upon them and the right to enjoy their own Scottish nationality and Scottish citizenship denied, not least by perhaps as many as a million or more people from other countries and cultures and national identities who happen to live in Scotland, and who were given the right and opportunity to vote 'No' in order to block Scottish independence. Do these 'No' voters really desire to hold a Scottish identity when they voted to reject and prevent the existence of Scottish nationality and Scottish citizenship in 2014? Why is this, and is it right that 'peoples' from other nations and hence those holding to other national identities should be able to influence and prevent Scottish independence, to reject Scottish citizenship, and therefore to block the self-determination of the Scottish people?

Scotland is a nation that, in some respects, seems to have been stolen from its own people and is controlled within the UK 'union' by a people (or rather an 'elite') and ideology mostly from another country – England – the latter reflecting a different culture and language, and whom most Scots do not vote for and who many Scots still appear to have relatively limited or at least questionable cultural or linguistic affinity with. These elites propagate and impose on Scots a supposed British 'one-nation' and with that a 'British' (i.e. Anglophone) culture and language; however, an increasing number of Scots now see through this 'cultural illusion' and falsehood which is perhaps more accurately defined as cultural and linguistic imperialism.

Politically, many Scots no longer differentiate between the three main British 'unionist' political parties of Labour, Tory and Libdem after that same pro 'one nation' British axis 'conspired' in the No campaign group 'Better Together' to interfere in and hence to influence and thwart Scots of their right to self-determination in 2014. All three main British political parties act as essentially British 'one-nation' Tories given their political case and campaign is based on continued British hegemony and British (Anglophone) national rule over Scotland.

As far as many Scottish 'nationalists' are concerned, Scotland is therefore being oppressed ('doun-hauden', in Scots) as well as exploited through this British Anglophone 'one-nation' cultural imperialist and nationalist hegemony, as if Scotland were some powerless colony and not an equal nation and kingdom in joint union with another nation as per the Treaty and Act of Union which created the UK joint parliament and administration in 1707.

Does this ongoing undemocratic political reality not simply reflect sustained material breaches of that Treaty and its jointly constituted (UK) parliament insofar as Scotland is concerned, and should that not be considered enough to end the 'joint' administrative and political arrangement that is the UK? What is the constitutional and legal reality of Scotland's place in the UK union? Who ultimately holds Scotland's sovereignty and how can they, or should they, assert it? And, while Scottish MP's and others legally tested the sovereignty of Westminster to withdraw or to block the withdrawal of the UK from the EU (Brexit), why has no Scottish 'nationalist' MP thus far tested in a Scottish court Scotland's sovereign right to withdraw itself from the UK union, the latter a similarly treaty-based entity?

Reflecting on Westminster's Brexit shenanigans, it almost seems, from a Scottish perspective, as if 'they' (i.e. the Westminster 'village') are often discussing politics in a foreign country. It all appears so 'un-Scottish'. Perhaps this is because debates in Westminster often have little or nothing to do with Scotland, certainly culturally and linguistically, and as evidenced by the absence of any Scottish Ministers in the Brexit 'war' cabinet of Mrs. May when the latter was Prime Minister. Yet, in 2014, two million people in Scotland still voted in favour of this continued, remote, and yes 'alien' leadership and rule over Scotland. They also voted for Scotland to be, well, to be nothing, effectively. They voted for Scotland to be ruled over by what also seems an alien political philosophy from another land – i.e. England – given that England's 533 MP's (effectively 82 per cent of UK 'sovereignty') may do as they wish with Scotland and its paltry 59 MP's (the latter amounting to just 9 per cent of UK political 'sovereignty'), or so it would seem. In 2014, 'Scots' therefore voted for Scotland to be just another region of Britain with 9 per cent of UK decision making power; in other words, they voted for Scotland to be a meaningless minority. They voted for Scotland to continue to be, arguably, a powerless colony run by what is effectively an 'administrative Power' and an elite from another country.

Which raises the question, what is Scotland's constitutional status today? After the supposed 'union' of 1707, Scots were kept in check through the deployment of English troops garrisoned throughout Scotland, whilst Scottish troops were invariably sent to fight Britain's imperial and colonial wars overseas in far off places. This, plus abnormally high levels of Scottish emigration and the slaughter of many Scots during further major wars, most notably WWI, kept the numbers of young men in Scotland down and rendered Scotland's remaining, diminished, shrunken and powerless communities defenceless against exploitation by the Anglo-Scots 'toadies' in league with the power elites; some regard the Scottish Tories as the continuation of this toady class.

Did the Scots never realise that English garrisons were placed all over Scotland to keep the natives in check? Scotland was occupied militarily for rather a lengthy period after 1707 and to some extent this remains the case today, with prevailing uncontrolled demographic trends also playing a role in major population change and in resulting changes in political preferences. Which raises another important question, and that is, politically does Scotland not present the essential features of a colony, rather than that of a sovereign state-party to an international treaty-based union? In referring to independence supporters as 'chippy' Scots (a BBC journalist's description) this implies an allegedly inferior people (i.e. the meaning of 'chippy'). Is this how British Anglophone institutions view the Scots - as an 'inferior' people?

Aince fowk lairn Scots, pikkin up local dialects o the leid is nae bather, ee'n in Shetland! Its aw Scots efter aw. Yet bairns an aw Scots fowk preventit fi bein taucht tae read an screed an unnerstaund thair ain mither tung is aye nae doot cultural doun-hauden.

Despite external British institutional opposition to independence, today many Scots claim that independence is not only inevitable, it is getting ever closer. Some Scots may wish that this were so, and many have been voting and hoping for independence since the 1970s, and before. But what's the plan? Where's the strategy? How and when is independence going to happen? And, crucially, what is stopping more Scots from voting for independence? In other words, what are the essential determinants of Scottish self-determination and hence Scottish independence? This book, it is argued, offers the answers to this vital question.

The present so-called 'Scottish Government' and its supposedly SNP 'nationalist' political leadership depend, it seems, on having another dubious UK sanctioned referendum to secure Scotland's independence, as if that were somehow the only legal and constitutional way for a sovereign Scotland to exit the UK union. There seems to be numerous problems with that solitary 'strategy'.

To begin with, all 'peoples' have the right to self-determination, as embodied in Article I of the Charter of the United Nations, and this includes the peoples of England, Wales, Northern Ireland and Scotland. In Scotland, the question is about the right of the 'Scottish people' to self-determination. Yet in a referendum on Scottish independence, residents in Scotland from other UK and EU and indeed many other nations, each inevitably holding to their own national identities, are given the right to vote against and hence to block, as they wish, the self-determination of the Scottish people. In other words, other 'peoples' are given the right to prevent and to negatively influence the 'inalienable' right of Scots to secure their own self-determination. Is this right?

What do other countries do? Are such 'open' residence-based voting rights reciprocal? What is the UN position on this? Does Scotland's resident-based franchise not contradict and serve to undermine this 'inalienable' right?

> *Scots are aye a doon-hauden fowk an laund; nae leid an nae (bona fide) naition an a cultur on the wey oot juist lyke ony daft wee colonie.*

Self-determination, the key word here being 'self', does not mean that people from other countries and therefore people holding to numerous other national identities should be given the power to prevent or influence the 'inalienable' right of the Scottish people to their own self-determination simply by virtue of their having an address in Scotland. This would further imply that residents who are from other countries will also be permitted to vote on the self determination of 'the people' from whence they came, be that in Turkey, Italy, Finland, or England or Wales or wherever. That cannot be right, and in most other countries the national voting franchise does not permit such an outcome, more especially in the case of national elections and referendums.

The rather open or universal Scottish franchise uniquely based on residence, which is not reciprocal, is what has become known as 'civic nationalism'. 'Civic nationalism' sounds awfully nice, but in practice it could and possibly will prevent self-government for the Scottish people in future, much as it arguably did in 2014. In reality, 'civic nationalism' can only really occur once independence is achieved whereby a newly independent country may thereafter offer its citizenship to those from other nations who wish to apply for it and who therefore desire to hold it.

Scotland's 'civic nationalist' SNP Government appear to be offering a (Scottish) national citizenship prematurely, because it does not yet exist, and will not exist until Scots create their own national citizenship through first becoming an independent State. And, moreover, it (i.e. 'Scottish' citizenship) is being offered to a great many people who are rather obviously rejecting it anyway; 'No' voters clearly do not wish to be 'Scottish' in terms of citizenship or nationality, and they also seek to prevent those who do want it (e.g. the Scots themselves!), from having access to it.

Much of this perhaps seems a little academic so long as the position of Westminster and the UK Government, as in early 2020, remains simply to refuse a second Scottish independence referendum anyway. The aim here is clearly to hold Scotland firm in the British, or rather, the English parliamentary majority grip. That in turn should mean there is a need for Scotland's 'nationalists' to have a Plan B this time around. That Plan B could be, for example, to deploy the majority of Scotland's MP's elected in a General Election to end the 'union' in the same way it began. That has always been regarded as constitutionally 'sufficient', at least many Scots believed it to be so. As did previous UK Prime Ministers, including Margaret Thatcher and John Major, who often taunted SNP MP's in this regard to first secure a majority of Scotland's MP's in order to 'claim' independence. That is until a referendum (and with it a dubious wide-open residence-based franchise) was thought to represent some sort of democratic 'gold standard', although perceptions of what is and isn't 'democratic' differ.

This results in the present constitutional and socio-political impasse insofar as Scotland's quest for independence is concerned, generating the need for in-depth research-based works such as this to identify and explore, in sufficient detail, and arguably for the first time, the *real* socio-political determinants of Scottish independence.

Methodology

Given the above brief background and context, a key

objective of this work is to investigate and endeavour to explain the reasons why Scotland is not yet independent and hence to identify the main issues and challenges that need to be addressed and overcome if Scotland is to become independent again. Thus, the purpose of the research is to establish the determinants of Scottish independence. To achieve this, it is first necessary to identify the key socio-political environmental influences that determine, and which, by implication, also serve to prevent and stand in the way of Scottish independence. This is no easy task.

The methodological approach employed has involved 'grounding out' a theoretical framework from analysis of the data collected and evaluated (Glaser and Strauss 1967). This, in turn, has revealed and helped the author select key headings for the applied framework that have been developed during the research. Each of these headings are then used to structure the main chapters of the book, within which further discussion and analysis of relevant theory and other related perspectives is provided.

These key headings are presented in the figure below and are encompassed in the overriding theme and sub-title of the book, which is collectively considered to be: 'The Socio-Political Determinants of Scottish Independence'. As a 'determinant' is a factor which decisively affects the nature or outcome of something, it is asserted here that these determinants are each highly significant in serving to influence the subject or phenomenon in question, which is Scottish independence. Moreover, it is argued that, collectively, in a holistic sense, and reflecting their interconnectedness, the determinants depict for the first time the comprehensive nature of the challenge and phenomenon that is Scottish independence.

Here Silver's (1983) definition of theory seems appropriate, in that theory offers a unique way of perceiving reality, as an expression of profound insight into some aspect of nature, thereby giving a different and a fresh perception of an aspect of the world. In this context the component parts, or 'building blocks', of a theory reflect the relationships, constructs and propositions made. In this regard the theoretical framework developed by the author offers a positive movement based on concrete experiences, to provide for a level of informed and structured description (Anfara and Mertz 2015).

Anfara and Mertz (2015: p. 15) define a theoretical framework as: *"any empirical or quasi-empirical theory of social and/or psychological processes, at a variety of levels (grand, midrange, explanatory), that can be applied to the understanding of phenomena"*. The 'Socio-Political Determinants of Scottish Independence' analytical framework developed as presented therefore provides for a structured methodology which can be applied to help analyse, discuss and better understand the phenomenon and dynamics of Scottish independence.

The Socio-Political Determinants of Scottish Independence

A wide range of criteria are explored in the framework. Aside from culture and language, the effect of demographic change is also considered; it is, after all, people who vote and where they come from, their cultural and linguistic influences (and prejudices), and sense of belonging, matter a great deal when it comes to the question of preferred national identity, and in their rejection and hence blocking of another (e.g. alien?) national identity, as the case may be. It remains that Scotland is a country which has no control over its immigration and this inevitably also has an impact; in this sense Scotland's population is effectively out of Scotland's control, or at least it is not under the control of the Scottish people, as it would be after the country secured independence.

Detailed analysis of the admittedly politically 'touchy' subjects of colonialism and nationalism further help to elucidate the reality of Scotland's position and status, or rather its predicament, whilst also identifying and exploring some common misconceptions, not least through illustrating numerous examples relating to the ongoing exploitation and oppression of the Scottish people. As might be expected in any colonial context, the strategic control over key social institutions in Scotland looms large; whosoever controls these institutions controls the nation and its resources, its people, and even their culture and language, as well as its ultimate destiny.

The constitutional status and position of Scotland is also explored, taking account of recent Brexit related court case outcomes which, paradoxically, serve to demonstrate the legal simplicity of a signatory state party withdrawing 'itself' from a treaty-based union. The important issue of self-determination and options in that regard are probed and analysed. Crucial in this connection is the definition of what exactly comprises 'a people' and the 'inalienable' right of that 'people' to self-determination, and the role of the United Nations, the latter highly relevant in the context of

'Decolonisation' and independence which, it may be argued, are one and the same thing.

A range of theoretical perspectives associated with each of the framework determinants are presented and discussed. This includes, for example, in the chapter on ethnicity, the theory of 'Appropriated Racial Oppression', which comes into play, as one might expect, with ethnically discriminated and oppressed peoples. Also referred to as 'Internalised Racism', this is not a term we hear much about, if anything, in the Scottish independence debate. But we will hear more of it in this book, not least because internalised racism theory helps in part explain Scotland's constitutional dilemma brought about through the way some Scots tend to vote, based on their attitude towards their own ethnic group, which is also influenced through the dominant role and actions of elites holding power.

It seems evident from this analysis that the predicament Scots and Scotland faces is therefore multi-faceted. That is, there are multiple key environmental pressures holding Scotland back from achieving independence and thus enjoying true nationhood. Traditional political thinking suggests a need to focus primarily on important areas of general policy, such as the economy, pensions, defence, and currency etc., as the way to influence people's minds and opinions on independence. Yet, is the question of Scottish independence from the British 'union' not also, and perhaps fundamentally, a choice of national identity too? That choice, and how national identity is influenced and formed through culture and language, suggests a somewhat deeper analysis to be necessary, one that has been lacking in the literature thus far. This book and its developed theoretical framework aim to fill that gap.

Culture and language are found to be critical factors and influences. Throughout the text, examples of the Scots language are inserted to help illustrate the effectiveness of the Scots language in explaining issues and perspectives rather differently and distinctly from the English language.

The purpose of this is in part to reveal and explore also the richness and distinctiveness of the Scots language as the very basis of Scottish culture and identity, as well as the influence of language on people's thoughts and decisions, and to demonstrate the fundamental purpose of language as the way a people communicate their thoughts and understanding of the world around them.

> *A brawlike scance tae gie fowk juist eneuch feel for whaur we are culturally an whaur we shuid be. Thon Scottish 'Cultur Meenister an 'Language Meenister' shuid baith hing thayr'e heids in shame, an aw thon Anglophone ceevil servants and schuil teachers anaw for their ill-willt an preventin Scots bairns fi lairnin thair ain Scots leid.*

The evidence presented suggests that a key divide in the independence debate may be at root linguistic, and that it is predominantly between Scots speakers who mostly tend to vote 'Yes', and Anglophones who mostly tend to vote 'No'. This, to a large extent, reflects the similar nature of secession arguments in Quebec, in Catalonia, and elsewhere (e.g. Ireland) where language differences are clearly evident in matters of national identity and self-determination.

Constitutionally, Brexit may seem a necessary precursor to Britain's (or rather England's) independence, in which Scotland may either be fully dissolved (i.e. integrated) or become independent. Scots need to make their choice, assuming they are given one – to continue to be ever more integrated within the UK, which essentially means to be Anglophone dominated, culturally and linguistically, also in terms of external political control, or to be independent. Based on recent political events and other evidence presented here it can be argued that there is scant evidence of any UK political 'union' in practice; rather, Scotland may more readily be defined as holding the key features and characteristics of a colony, which would imply the alleged 'union' is merely a political con trick played out on Scots.

Furthermore, there remains numerous misconceptions about what is the primary focus within the Scottish independence debate. For instance, Scottish independence is not about 'nationalism' per se; rather, Scottish independence is about self-determination, and with that it is about liberation, freedom and, yes, it is also about decolonisation. Moreover, it is hardly the fault of independence supporters that 'unionists' seek to promote a British 'unionism' that is itself a trans-national nationalist political ideology, and arguably one of the more aggressive and exploitative forms of nationalism.

Here, so-called British 'unionism' (i.e. trans-national nationalism) depends upon and is therefore primarily about oppression, through occupation, exploitation, cultural and linguistic imperialism, and hence the subjugation of neighbouring countries and peoples (i.e. the 'Celtic Periphery'). Scottish independence clearly has no such oppressive 'nationalist' objectives, yet is often portrayed by a dominant unionist MSM (mainstream media) as 'nasty nationalism'.

> *Am awfu gled tae see fowk are mair connectin leid wi cultur an naitionhood. Thay SNP shuid tak thon Scots leid 'bull' (i.e. Scots Language Act) bi the horns – fowk wad shuirly walcome thon, as wi the 'Gaelic Language (Scotland) Act 2005'. Gie us equality anaw, no afore time tae.*

Independence is arguably never merely a matter of Scotland being better or worse off economically, far less about what currency might be used. A more in-depth analysis here suggests the Yes/No decision on independence is far more related to the protection and projection, or alternatively the diminishing and removal of Scotland's culture and language, and where language plays a key role in defining national identity. British/Anglophone ('No') or Scottish/Scots ('Yes'), appears to be a key dividing line, which is clearly a linguistic determinant. Unionist Anglophones in Scotland, it might be argued, would mostly still vote for a 'one-nation' Britain even if Scotland were the richest country on earth, which it may well have been at one time in the not too distant past. Independence may therefore be at root a cultural and hence ethnically and linguistically determined decision, much as it is elsewhere, from Quebec to Catalonia and beyond, to the many new nations that have been established over the last century and more.

Collectively, the framework's nine socio-political determinants, which the author, using his research skills and expertise, has 'ground out' of the data and information analysed during this research, help to explain and underpin the quest for, and outline the barriers opposing, Scottish independence. Each of the determinants is presented, analysed and explored through application and discussion of a wide range of appropriate theories and supporting data which help to support and strengthen the findings (see Annex I).

This book therefore represents an innovative, robust, scientific contribution to the subject and study of Scottish independence which provides for many new and provocative insights. Moreover, if the quest for Scottish independence is to succeed, it is each of the determinants identified which will need to be addressed, not least given that these determinants also represent the main barriers to independence.

CHAPTER 3: CULTURE

What is culture?

Culture is what we know as the holistic social world and its products. The strongest feature of our culture is social organisation, and hence the way in which our society is structured. Culture may also be defined as *"the sum of social knowledge, organisation, forms of life and social products"* (Spiers 2019). Culture is therefore a whole lot more than the 'arts', or the *'airts'* even.

> *Cultur is juist the wey we dae awthing, an Scots fowk shuid bi able tae dae awthing thay're ain wey, ayeweys respectin wir ain cultur an oor Scots langage.*

Moreover, culture represents *"the way of life, especially the general customs and beliefs, of a particular group of people at a particular time"*[3]. Culture is also considered to be the sum of attitudes, customs, and beliefs that distinguishes one group of people from another. It is important to note here that culture is *"transmitted, through language, as well as through material objects, ritual, institutions, and art, from one generation to the next"*[4].

There seems to be a cultural chasm reflecting different cultural priorities and beliefs between pro-union and hence British and Anglophone vested interests and what we might term the 'typical' Scottish independence voter. People in Scotland clearly vote rather differently from people in England, the latter demonstrating a far greater preference for the Tory Party.

Yet, the paradox remains: why do so many Scots still deny their own nation its rightful place and existence in the world? When rejecting their own Scottish nationality and citizenship, and instead voting to remain part of the UK 'union' and hence

'British', this allows a mostly foreign Tory 'toff' hierarchy to continue to control Scotland. That the Tory party cares little for Scotland seems rather obvious given its many past policies. Indeed, even Winston Churchill is reputed to have once described the Tory or Conservative & Unionist Party as:

> "*A party of great vested interests, banded together in a formidable confederation; corruption at home, aggression to cover it up abroad; the trickery of tariff juggles, the tyranny of a party machine; sentiment by the bucketful; patriotism by the imperial pint; the open hand at the public exchequer, the open door at the public-house; dear food for the million, cheap labour for the millionaire.*"

(Roberts 2018: p. 92).

Are Scots 'No' voters simply that deeply afflicted by the 'Scottish Cultural Cringe' that they have no confidence in their own people, or 'thair ain fowk', preferring to be ruled over even by England's Tories? The Scottish Cultural Cringe, according to Beveridge and Turnbull (1989), relates to the Scots believing of their own people as being too inferior even to run their own affairs. This cultural and psychological sense of inferiority also reflects the way that much of England views the Scots, with Scotland being perceived as receiver of, and dependent upon England's largesse.

The Cultural Cringe psychological condition is arguably created and perpetuated by the almost continuous pro-union MSM and its institutionalised propaganda and associated symbolic machinery, all Anglophone, dragging what remains of Scottish culture and confidence ever downward. The question remains, was the 2014 'No' vote therefore not influenced predominantly by cultural factors, and hence not nearly so much by economic or other everyday 'policy' matters as some commentators and analysts appear to believe? What really is the effect of the UK political 'union' on Scottish culture and the Scottish national psyche?

Cultural Imperialism

Since the UK union was estabished in 1707 it can be argued that Scotland has suffered from what is known as cultural imperialism, which is also referred to as cultural colonialism. This involves unequal relationships which favour the more powerful civilisation and its culture, hence where the power lies here is the pertinent feature (Tomlinson 2001). Cultural imperialism involves imposing and promoting the culture and language of the powerful entity onto the oppressed people and society. The definition of cultural imperialism seems to fit Scotland's predicament rather well:

> *"Cultural imperialism is the practice of promoting the culture or language of one nation in another. It is usually the case that the former is a large, economically or militarily powerful nation and the latter is a smaller, less affluent one. Cultural imperialism can take the form of an active, formal policy or a general attitude."* [5]

Cultural imperialism may therefore take different forms, including government policy on such matters as language, dress, and attitudes, with the broad goal to enforce and reinforce what is a (alien) cultural hegemony. Public media is usually the main vehicle employed in what is known as *'the penetrative process'*. For this to happen on a sufficient scale (e.g. nationally) usually requires the media (especially broadcasting) to be 'captured' by the 'dominating/penetrating power' (Schiller 1989). Schiller developed the term *'packaged consciousness'* to describe this process, maintaining that major media corporations can "*create, process, refine and preside over the circulation of images and information which determines our beliefs, attitudes, and ultimately our behaviour*".

Scotland's (or any nation's) enduring difference ultimately

rests in what remains of its own culture (in which language forms the basis), which in Scotland's case is inherently strong and distinctive such that core parts of it persist. This is despite centuries of ongoing 'Britishing' (or rather Englishing) and indoctrination through British state propaganda processes and its endless symbolism which form a large part of cultural imperialism. This includes primarily the fact that Scotland's (colonial) leaders have consistently refused to allow Scots to even teach or *lairn oor ain Scots langage tae Scots bairns in schuil* ('learn our own language to Scots children in school'), the latter a basic and fundamental human right denied. With language itself comprising the foundation of culture this means Scots are essentially deprived of a major aspect of what would be their natural cultural development.

What remains of Scottish culture today has aye been welcoming and emphasises fairness and equality, yet therein perhaps also lies arguably the Scots main weakness, which is their naivety, *tho wir nae feardies* ('although we are not scared'); it is perhaps this naivety and a trust in the goodness of others, entirely misplaced in this instance, that has allowed Scotland to be mercilessly exploited by another very different, repressive and alien culture. In this context independence may be viewed as casting out a repressive and imperial domineering alien culture, allowing the Scottish culture to flourish unhindered, and for Scots to culturally develop freely, naturally, and never again be subject to cultural prejudice, domination, discrimination and oppression (i.e. 'doun-hauden').

Scotland's ongoing perceived national 'failures', oft repeated and reinforced by the British Anglophone MSM – e.g. culturally, socially, sporting, economically, politically, nationally, internationally etcetera - reflects the timidity and inertia (and cringe?) at the heart of its current cultural and institutional leadership, which includes Scotland's political classes and other institutional elites. Indeed, such a statement could easily form Scotland's epitaph, and cuts across numerous policy areas including that of Scotland's virtually non-existent film industry and various other less developed cultural areas (literature, music, song, dance etc), and this with a self-proclaimed 'competent' and 'nationalist' SNP administration in 'power' (well, devolved at least) for a decade and more.

> *Langage is the verra foonds o cultur an awthegither is shuirly Scotland's ki tae independence. Gie Scots fowk bak thair ain naitural leid (an thay're culture wi it) an thay'll shuirly want thair ain nation bak anaw, swith-lyke tae.*

We might ask, then, what the point is of a Scottish Cabinet Secretary responsible for 'Scottish culture', currently Fiona Hyslop MSP, who arguably to a significant extent does not even understand (*unnerstaund*) never mind promote actual bona fide Scottish culture? What hope for Scottish culture when Scotland's political and institutional cultural leadership (the latter rather more heavily Anglophone than Scots speaking) are incapable, it seems, of even drafting a Scots Language Act, with language forming the basis of any culture?

An entrenched feeling of national inadequacy (i.e. *Scotland's too wee, too puir, an too stupit tae dae onythin bi itsel*) is arguably strongest amongst 'No' voting (often self-proclaimed 'proud') Scots, though 'nationalists' when 'in power' tend to similarly hold back. This, it seems, may be largely due to the absence of teaching Scots to read and write in *thair ain langage, thair ain mither tung*; in this connection many Scots remain unable to fully respect even *thay're ain Scotis cultur*. 'No' voters in particular often therefore exhibit the 'Scottish Cultural Cringe' as a result; there is a specific explanation for this unfortunate psychological condition, which we will get to later.

In this regard 'elite' Scots 'No' voters are perhaps rather like the well-known comedian and actor John Cleese so eloquently described this Scottish 'class' as: *"obedient retainers desperately seeking social status"*[6]. In Scotland, higher social status is primarily a function of and is reflected in one's speech, i.e. the language used, which in elite circles tends to be Anglophone, not Scots; the higher one ascends in the social stratosphere, the more Anglophone (and hence less Scots) one tends to become.

As state broadcaster, the BBC remains the dominant purveyor of the Anglophone cultural and imperial message, with language being the essential ingredient influencing Scots' cultural thought and beliefs and determining their resulting 'packaged consciousness'. However, an Anglophone institutional Scotland also looms large in its wider cultural and linguistic influence, from over a thousand schools, to the many universities and colleges, to the hundreds of public bodies, law courts, government departments, major commercial organisations, and the Scottish Parliament itself, etcetera and ad infinitum.

Those Scots (and others) throughout Scotland's elite signing up in their droves to a dominant Anglophone culture accept all this, and more, in order to maintain their one-nation 'Britain', and Scotland's culturally 'subaltern' place in it. Most of the immense oil wealth from the North Sea would not alter the Scottish 'elites' Anglophone cultural mindset as far as Scottish independence is concerned, and it didn't. Culture, it seems safe to say, is therefore a far more powerful influence on national identity than mere economics.

Linguistic Imperialism

Because the formation of culture is also dependent on language, if there is any desire to respect and maintain (or even change!) a culture, one needs to begin with addressing the language itself or, in other words, to consider 'the way the story is told'. A 'Scots Language Act' would therefore seem to form an essential start in this regard, as was demonstrated with the Gaelic Language (Scotland) Act in 2005. A Scots language policy and Act would therefore ensure that Scots were not only able to speak in the Scots language, as many still do today, despite its institutionalised repression, but that Scots would also become literate in the language they speak, i.e. Scottish people would then be able to read and write in *thair ain mither tung langage as weel.*

> *Scots arena taucht thair ane leid, fer if we waur, we wid shuirly want wir ane nation bak, swith-lyke. Thay SNP shuid hiv gied Scots fowk a Scots Language Act lang afore noo, tae remuive thon creenge fer guid. Thay didna.*

Learning their own language would also assist Scots in overcoming the ongoing cultural oppression and lack of confidence in their own people and nation (i.e. the Scottish Cultural Cringe), thereby permitting Scottish culture to flourish naturally, much in the way culture develops in most other free and independent nations. Language, it would seem, must therefore be a key factor and influence in the context of Scottish independence, which is the focus of the next chapter. The very existence of the 2005 Gaelic Language Act confirms that the Scottish Parliament has the power to bring forward a Scots Language Bill and pass an Act. Which means Scots need to ask the question – why has the SNP 'nationalist' government not yet done so – and, indeed, why has the Scottish Government refused to meet this most basic and fundamental of Scottish human rights, the right to one's own language (*richt tae wir ain leid*)?

Of course, English could continue to be taught in Scotland, much as it is in many other former colonies and countries, where it is still taught as what is often referred to as an 'administrative' language. This is also the case in other European nations, in the European Commission, and at the UN etcetera, albeit where indigenous languages are properly respected as well – unlike here in Scotland and the UK where the Scots language is not respected, but instead is actively blocked from being taught, by state institutions themselves.

In this sense, the 'responsible' state educational institutions in Scotland simply refuse to teach the Scottish people to read and write in their own Scots language, which many still speak day and daily, though are prevented from being fully literate in due to the absence of even basic formal learning opportunity and formal recognition of the language.

> *Scots Langage Act? Aa widna haud ma braith oan thon fi thay SNP heid bummers.*

The inevitable consequence of this 'policy' is a confused and distorted (i.e. Anglo-Scottish) culture, leading in turn to a confused and therefore relatively easily indoctrinated people, many Scots (i.e. 'No' voters) lacking even in the self-confidence to believe they can run their own nation's affairs. This also relates to reinforcing the important cultural distinctions between 'Britishness' and 'Scottishness', which in turn heavily influence critical actions such as, for example, the voting preferences of Scots. If 'nationalist' politicians really wished to increase the 45 per cent 'Yes' vote from 2014, they would be well advised to bring *forrit* a 'Scots Language Act', *swith-lyke tae.*

The SNP should not be surprised at the popularity of such an initiative amongst 'Yes' voters, though they would of course expect Scotland's Anglophone elites running most of the institutions of Scotland to object, strongly and robustly, as they invariably always have done when it comes to the natural projection of Scottish culture and Scots language in the past. The essential point here is that cultural strategies can and should be at the forefront in the drive for positive political and constitutional change through self-determination, providing for a necessary cultural renaissance within formerly oppressed colonial territories (Fanon 1967).

British Anglophone Tory 'one nation' ideology is thus enforced on Scotland through a policy of cultural imperialism. Just as most Scots do not vote for Tory ideology[7] and did not vote for the Tory policy of Brexit either[8], their language rights are similarly ignored.

The often tortuous (for Scots speakers) English language is forced on Scots bairns, by law, and the law meanwhile refuses (i.e. prohibits?) *Scots bairns fae lairnin thair ain mither tung in schuils*. This is raw cultural imperial coercion at its worst, and indeed it represents British nationalist cultural coercion. Is there really any difference here to the enforcement not so very long ago of the Russian language onto Polish or Finnish speakers and with indigenous languages forced underground? Thus, an alien political, ideological, and social British-Anglophone culture, in which language forms the basis, is forced onto Scots who are given little choice, far less respect in the matter. The consequence of this is clearly a diminished and confused Scottish culture and people, the latter relatively easy to demean and diminish and stereotype in a cultural and linguistic anti-Scottish sense. Meanwhile, the widespread prevalence of Anglophone dominated social organisations and institutions in Scotland serve to limit opportunities for Scots speakers, through elevating a dominant and controlling Anglophone cultural elite.

Culture is also about 'the way we do things', aspects which can and do endure even in midst of, or despite, ongoing sustained socio-political oppression, however subtle, or not, that persists. If the Scottish Parliament has shown anything since devolution, and more especially since the SNP formed the government, it is that Scots do things differently and want to do things differently, and Scots for sure want to do things very differently than their neighbours across the border; 'their' culture and way of doing things is their concern, Scotland's culture should be a matter for Scots, but it is not. A dominant Anglophone culture and 'way of doing things' continues to be imposed on Scots via an Anglophone elite and Anglophone dominated institutions, and this reflects cultural imperialist oppression.

Tae forfaut yer ain langage is tae forfaut yer ain cultur, an yer ain naition tae. Aye, thare's nae sic thing as Scots cultur withoot oor ain Scots langage, an nae sic thing as a Scottis naition aither.

The ongoing refusal of state authorities to ensure that the Scots language is formally taught (taucht tae aw Scots bairns an aw fowk) in Scotland is itself cultural discrimination and an infringement of a basic human right, the right to one's own language. Respect for equality and human rights requires that Scots must have a Scots Language Act – and not least to belatedly follow the Gaelic Language Act of 2005. Until this happens there is clearly no respect for the Scots language, only weasel words from Ministers and their mainly Anglophone officials and public quangos within the devolved UK predicament Scotland still finds itself in. Public institution's inertia and pontification on this matter is generally based around spurious excuses for non-action such as the well-trod 'there's so many Scottish dialects' 'fallacy', as if this were somehow unique only to the Scots language. The discernible underlying view of public officials here is invariably that Scots is merely 'bad English', or 'the language of the gutter', or 'not valid'; these are arguably racist anti-Scottish perspectives on the part of Anglophone elites, which have become rather standardised and accepted offhand rebuttals from those in 'authority'.

Anybody would struggle to put this better than the author James Kelman after he won the Booker Prize for his novel '*How Late It Was, How Late*' in 1994, and when he said: "*My culture and my language have a right to exist.*" The Scots language may well have a right to exist, but this also requires a law to ensure the language does fully exist in any meaningful sense and, crucially, that it is taught to future generations.

It remains rather curious to say the least that Holyrood MSP's and a supposedly 'nationalist' Scottish Government 'in power' for a decade or more has yet to comprehend the essential relationship between Scottish language and Scottish culture, or indeed to appreciate the fundamental influence of a nation's language and culture on national identity and hence its role in the Yes/No decision on Scottish independence.

Scots refer to the Scottish Cultural Cringe[9] often without appreciating (or perhaps even realising) that this 'condition' is primarily due to the inferior and discriminatory way the British state, the British media and the many British Anglophone run social institutions (including in Scotland) continue to mis-treat and disrespect Scotland's culture and language. Cultural imperialism serves to alienate Scotland's people and diminishes their natural prospects for full and free cultural, linguistic, socio-economic, and indeed national development.

Scottish literature, which forms a key part of culture, is similarly oppressed ('doun-hauden') when and so long as the Scots language remains so constrained. *'The Panopticon'*, Jenni Fagan's 2013 novel[10] about life in a care home, is partly written in Scots. Although Fagan said that she had been warned that writing in Scots would harm her chances of being published, she didn't hesitate: *"I talk in Scottish every day so it's not unusual to also write in it,"* she says. *"I am not sure why people writing in their own language is even an issue any more."*

> *Langage is the verra foonds o cultur - oor wey o thinkin an daein stuff.*

And yet, the reality remains that the Scottish people continue to be prevented from learning to read and write and to use their own language properly through the oppressive actions of the British state and its Anglophone dominated institutions and elites (including the 'devolved' Scottish Government), primarily via the refusal to teach the Scots language in schools. Even Scottish authors such as Fagan, Welsh and others seem unable to write as accurately in Scots as they might otherwise be able to do with even just a little basic education and knowledge of the language. Scottish literature is inevitably constrained and doun-hauden as a direct consequence of the Scots language not being taught. Scottish literature is essentially a literature still waiting to happen and so long as Scotland remains within an Anglophone-dominated UK union it may have a very long wait.

However, it is not only in literature terms that a diminished culture is oppressed or 'doun-hauden'. Lectures given by Sir Harry Burns, the former Chief Medical Officer of Scotland, discussing the unfortunate reputation of Scotland as being the "sick man of Europe", suggested the desperate health primarily of men in Glasgow – due to substance abuse, violence and mental health issues – by explaining that the statistics are very similar to those of aborigines who have become dislocated from their culture. This is what the destruction of the industrial and manufacturing economy did to many people and communities throughout Scotland and what the neoliberal policies (of Westminster and Holyrood) continue to do today. This seems further related to what the former trade union leader Jimmy Reid famously described as the 'alienation of the people'; that alienation, coupled with the Anglophone and institutionalised ridicule of their Scots mither tung, represents no less than the Imperial Roman overlord turning down of the thumb to signal the end of a people and their deemed to be 'worthless' language and culture, the end of their very way of life, and ultimately the end even of their nation. Ongoing cultural and linguistic imperialism renders the Scots as therefore a culturally deprived, diminished, de-humanised and alienated people in their own land – much like the experience of numerous other indigenous peoples such as the Maori, the Australian indigenous people, Bushmen, and native North Americans.

The actions of a senior civil servant formerly in charge of the Scottish Parliament administration, Sir Paul Grice, reflected rather well this Anglophone cultural oppression and alienation in his taking of legal action leading to the ultimate eviction of members of the public who sought to camp nearby the Holyrood Parliament until such times as Scotland became an independent nation again[11]. Many Scots will remember the similar encampment of activists that existed during the 1980's and 1990's outside the former Royal High School building on Calton Hill in Edinburgh, the latter providing a rallying call for a Scottish parliament, and which continued to exist until a Scottish parliament (albeit devolved) was created. Such protests are welcomed by Scots who support independence but are clearly opposed by unionist Anglophone elites heading up Scotland's institutions, the latter invariably using their positions to seek to block Scottish independence.

Cultural Hegemony

Cultural imperialism related oppression of Scots and of Scotland by an Anglophone elite and its artificial social constructs seems aptly reflected in Gramsci's theory of cultural hegemony, which is defined as:

> '..the domination of a culturally diverse society, by the ruling class who manipulate the culture of that society—the beliefs, explanations, perceptions, values, and mores—so that their imposed, ruling-class worldview becomes the accepted cultural norm; the universally valid dominant ideology, which justifies the social, political, and economic status quo as natural and inevitable, perpetual and beneficial for everyone, rather than as artificial social constructs that benefit only the ruling class'. (Buttigieg 1992)

The initial theoretical application of cultural domination was as a Marxist analysis of 'economic class' (i.e. its base and superstructure), which Gramsci developed in order to understand what he termed as 'social class'. Here, cultural hegemony proposes that 'the prevailing cultural norms of a society, which are imposed by the ruling class (or bourgeois cultural hegemony), should not be perceived as in any way natural and inevitable, but rather need to be recognized as artificial social constructs in terms of the established institutions, practices, and beliefs, et cetera. Gramsci concluded that the philosophic roots and objective of this artificial social construct was to act as instruments of social-class domination.

> *Sae lats blether a wee bittie mair oan thon Anglophone 'cultural hegemony' that haes snared Scots an thay're laund.*

Scots might consider here the British Anglophone elite culture as similarly nothing other than an artificial social construct imposed on Scots by a ruling Anglophone elite. Nor, clearly, should Scots accept that this imposed social construct is in any way natural or inevitable. Ultimately, an elite Anglophone social structure acts as a form of cultural control and represents the main force of national and colonial oppression, intended to keep the Scots 'doun-hauden' in their own land.

The imposition on a people of a culture reflecting a particular 'class' of people is a phenomenon referred to as 'enculturation' (Bourdieu and Passeron 1990). In this the cultural capital of elites differs from that of the working class. The latter have a culture imposed on them which is not their own and which makes them feel inadequate and inferior. This suggests that an Anglophone elite culture imposed on Scots is the basis for the 'Scottish Cultural Cringe'[12]; the latter relates to the sense of cultural inferiority among Scots brought about in response to Anglocentric cultural domination.

Scots are made to feel inferior primarily because an elite Anglophone culture is imposed upon them, the basis of which is (English) language. Cultures necessarily create power structures which are dominated and controlled by a cultural elite. Thus, an Anglophone elite dominates Scotland and the Scots, with most Scots and the Scottish nation itself suffering oppression and inhibited socio-economic development as a consequence.

Part of this in some respects is the Scots own (subconscious) doing and may be explained through Fanon's (1967) theory of 'inferiorisation'. This relates to the process whereby an indigenous population comes to internalise the dominant culture and narrative of the coloniser at the expense of their own native, local, traditional culture. This may also be described as 'self-colonisation'. Hence the life possibilities of many Scots are quashed not by their lack of ability or knowledge, but through their sense of 'inferiorisation' due to Anglophone enculturation, which is effectively creating a lack of belief in themselves and others like them, and even in their perceived inability to govern themselves and run their own social institutions. A major consequence of this internalised sense of inferiorisation is a lack of socio-economic opportunity for Scots, which they accept, if not expect, due to Anglophone cultural and colonial elite domination and control over social institutions and resources.

Cultural domination depends amongst other things on symbols, and descriptions of the world expressed in language are symbolic models of the world (Spiers 2019). Language itself is a symbolic system for representing the world as we see it; hence an elite Anglophone culture will tend to view the world quite differently from a Scots speaking culture, and that should seem rather obvious. There are many notable British Anglophone (political) symbols such as the poppy, monarchy, union flag, Churchill, Dunkirk etcetera. Symbolic events include the numerous and often lengthy televised commemorations of everything and anything possible to idolise under the British meme. Although social diversity, economic variety, and political freedom appear to exist, because most people see and experience different life-circumstances they are incapable of perceiving the greater hegemonic pattern created when the lives they witness coalesce as a society. The cultural hegemony itself is manifested in and maintained through the existence of minor, different circumstances that are not always fully perceived by those living the culture.

Bourdieu used the term 'symbolic violence' to depict actions which support the legitimacy and domination of social structures imposed by cultural elites. However, 'respect' and 'understanding' of such things as symbols are quite different matters. As the world football association FIFA noted, to countries outside the UK the British poppy is regarded as a 'political symbol'[13]. Many people in the UK still do not seem to understand this or appreciate the views of other European states on the poppy's use and purpose as a political symbol. In terms of the poppy and its symbolic role in commemoration, there is another word used to describe the rounding up of millions of people and sending them to their deaths over a prolonged period, but it is not 'sacrifice'. Here as in so many other areas of life, respect without understanding remains ignorance. And so it is, arguably, with cultural hegemony, where many Scots continue to doff the cap to a supposedly 'superior' Anglophone unionist elite, without really understanding why they do so, far less having an appreciation as to how an Anglophone culture and structured society came to be so heavily weighted against them.

Illusion of Culture

The Scottish folk singer Dick Gaughan, referring to Gramsci's theory of cultural hegemony, suggested that *"the ruling class maintains cultural control, or control of the culture"*[14]. Gaughan argued that it is not easy for a small group of people to control a society *"by brute force alone"*, so they need another approach. Gaughan maintains that: *"...the primary tool by which the ruling class keeps itself in power...is (through) 'an illusion of culture', the idea that there is one culture that is shared by the society as a whole*". According to Gaughan, this cultural illusion extends to music and all the arts, *"though its very basis is language"*, i.e. the English language.

Historically, musicians and artists depended on patronage from wealthy individuals and institutions and that 'bought' their allegiance. As more of Scotland's elites became Anglophone and pro-union, so the arts have tended to follow suit as personal development and reward depended on it. To make a living from performing, Scottish artists had to conform, and those who did not conform were left marginalised and excluded. We can see this with many artists who focused on the Scots language and Scottish culture including Gaughan himself, and Michael Marra, Hamish Henderson and Alasdair Gray; many Scots today don't even know who these very fine artists are. Clearly, Scottish artists performing and producing material in the Scots language were and still are 'doun-hauden' and hence their opportunities are and remain limited within an Anglophone dominated and controlled social and cultural hegemony.

Gaughan further noted that working-class music has tended to be produced at grassroots level by those without formal training. In contrast, bourgeois middle class orchestral composition was treated 'differently' and which, by the 20th century, had rendered *"composed music as an intellectual pursuit"*. The 1960's so-called 'protest songs' often described the 'bad things' that were happening, such as poverty, wars, etcetera. However, and as cited by Gaughan, the American folk songwriter and singer Woody Guthrie noted: *"I am out to sing songs that make you take pride in yourselves and in your work."*

Gaughan notes here that, regarding music and across the arts generally, there is a need to: *"...draw the distinction between what is propaganda, what is sloganizing, and what is actually progressive content"*. In this respect people often underestimate the role that music and the arts can play in the quest for constitutional change through their cultural role and influence. Here the linguistic influence seems critical, as anyone listening to Dick Gaughan's rendition of Scots songs such as Hamish Henderson's awesome 'Freedom come aw ye' would appreciate[15].

Yet, even today, policy making still tends to ignore the significance of Scottish culture and language insofar as the Scottish independence debate is concerned. The First Minister's 'Growth Commission' report published in May 2018 seemed just like another White Paper setting out the usual policy and governance reasons in support of independence. But it entirely missed a crucial point; if the Yes/No decision on Scottish independence is at root cultural and language and hence identity based, then it is highly questionable how effective any general policy or economic arguments will be in 'changing minds'. Here we might conclude: 'it's not the economy, stupid'; rather, it is more to do with the 'illusion of culture'.

Culture and Identity

International diplomats and UN sources claim that communications technologies and other efforts are often used to distort cultures and falsely elevate one culture above others, which fuels a false superiority of some racial or religious groups[16]. This may even threaten international peace and security and undermine the positive contributions of a culture of dialogue. Racism in some regions may increase in a crude and dangerous fashion due to any resulting 'apartheid' system. A state can create a racial separation 'wall' and build a racial entity that excludes others, usually under a mantra of the importance of the elevated culture in which language forms a critical role. There is plenty of evidence of this kind of elitist Anglophone cultural behaviour active in Scotland and its resulting social apartheid (e.g. private schools, elite universities, public bodies, courts, broadcasting etc.) with

Scots speakers excluded and held back from what might otherwise be their natural growth and development into positions of authority in social institutions within Scotland (The Social Mobility and Child Poverty Commission 2015).

On the fundamental question of national identity, in any referendum on Scottish independence and hence dissolution of the UK union it might be anticipated that many people will ultimately vote depending on how British/Anglophone or how Scottish/Scots they are, or consider themselves to be. A 'peoples' culture, never mind their preferred national identity, cannot be changed by mere economics or political promises on this and that. Both 'Yes' and 'No' voters may accept and reject policy aspects of any Growth Commission or think tank report, but they will still tend to cast their vote the same 'national' way when it comes to the matter of their national identity, which is what any vote on Scottish independence is really about, and this aspect remains primarily culture and language determined.

Politicians in Scotland do not appear to appreciate what happened with the Brexit vote. Pro-Brexit voters did not need any White Paper or tome of policy promises, far less any post-referendum 'plan'. The Brexit outcome clearly did not depend on any 'plan' as none existed. For many the vote was largely based on the question of identity and the issue of Scottish independence should be expected to be similarly determined.

Hamish Henderson's research and writings tracked a path of sorts through the Scottish literary landscape, highlighting linkages between Scottish literature, folk songs and poetry, and thus the Scots language, and the connection with national identity, in search of a Scottish political literary culture (Gibson 2015). Tradition is important in this context, conveying as it does a constant process over time and helping preserve a culture that binds people together.

Similar to Fanon (1967), Henderson (as noted in Gibson 2015) maintained that a peoples' national cultural inheritance was important in reproducing and sustaining the nation and this could also be a positive source for internationalism and socialism. This is totally unlike (British Anglophone) cultural imperialism as the latter involves removing and hence replacing a national culture, i.e. the Scottish culture. Henderson's cultural-political principles, with an emphasis on Scottish literature, Scottish folk songs and poetry, combined with egalitarian internationalist socialist political ideals, helps go some way to clarify the question surrounding the main components of Scottish identity today. In this sense the egalitarian, centre-left-leaning propensity of thought exhibited by mainstream Scottish political culture and discourse is reflected in and in large part determined by this tradition within Scottish literature, song, poetry and hence national culture. In this context the Scots language is fundamental, not least as illustrated by Robert Burns, Scotland's national bard and which, among his many works is the undoubted international anthem of the entire world, 'Auld Lang Syne'.

In terms of 'national political culture' and hence the way people vote, England broadly seems predominantly right of centre, whereas Scotland is predominantly left of centre, although the UK as a whole was once described as a 'deferential civic culture' primarily emphasizing the importance of class and regionalism (Almond and Verba 1963). This nevertheless reflects the fact that England and Scotland remain two different countries which can be distinguished by their distinct national political cultures. England seems most unlikely ever to become a socialist republic, its Anglo-Saxon culture exemplifying status and wealth, much like its outdated parliament in Westminster. Scotland's more socialist credentials are there in Holyrood for all to see with differential and more egalitarian policies to match. Scotland's problem remains, however, in that the Anglophone elites running most of its social institutions and major businesses today are either part of, or have bought into, our larger neighbour's imperialist culture, which keeps most Scots 'doun-hauden' and prevents

Scotland and its people from really developing as they should, i.e. naturally.

Yet, how do people develop the perception of their own national identity? At the end of the day people are essentially products of their culture. The Scot is a Scot whether in Dundee or Durham, Broxburn or Birmingham. Similarly, the Englishman is still an Englishman in Montrose (or Mumbai) as surely as in Manchester. EU economic migrants may think of themselves as neither Scots nor English: the family and cultural ties to Alsace or Silesia or Liguria remain firm and Scotland may be just an economic or academic waypoint. The lukewarm desire of most EU citizens and more especially English people living in Scotland to help create, far less to hold Scottish national identity and Scottish citizenship, given their predominant 'No' vote in 2014, surely reflects their perspectives and priorities as to their own national allegiance which, by implication, is not to Scotland, and hence not to be 'Scots'.

> *Thares nae want o guid Scots wirds in mony Scots sangs tae tell wir naition's yairn in a wey Scots fowk unnerstaund fineweel. Juist a peety maist bairns an fowk in wir kintra irna taucht Scots langage at aw - mony can speik Scots yet canna read an screed it sae weel, so irna fully literate in thair ain leid. In ither wirds, we discriminate agin wir ain fowk an thay're aye doun-hauden in thay're ain laund.*

In terms of identity, culture really does matter, a lot, and turning your coat on one's own identity is never a trivial matter. Pro-independence voters seemed pretty-well maxxed out in the 2014 referendum and since then polls suggest limited scope for growth unless they can turn the Brit 'No' population[17]. Cultural preferences and influences associated with an individual's national identity are also impacted by demographic change and this issue is considered in a later chapter. If, as some assume, the 'Yes' vote is maxxed out, then 'the choir already believes' as it were. Culture is very difficult to change, as is reflected in the opinion polls stasis.

Asking those from a non-indigenous culture to alter their

national identity to the identity of another national culture is a big ask; Scots cannot simply assume that everybody living in Scotland wants to be Scottish because the 'No' vote emphatically tells us many of them did not. Essentially, those who are not Scottish or don't consider themselves to have a Scottish identity appear to be the least likely to wish to trade in the identity they already have for a new Scottish citizenship and Scottish nationality. The related matter here of defining the correct criteria for 'a people' seeking self-determination and Scotland's irregular residence-based national voting franchise is considered in subsequent chapters.

National Culture

Every culture is first and foremost national. Oppressed peoples', according to Fanon (1967), must fight for the survival of their national culture which in turn means a fight for the liberation of the nation. Here a national culture requires the efforts of a people to create and keep itself in existence, which means that national culture is "*at the very heart of the struggle for freedom*" and hence for colonised and oppressed peoples, national culture also reflects the reality that "...*the rhythm of the people and that of their rulers are not the same*" (Fanon 1967: p. 44). The 'natural rhythm' of the Scots is not therefore Anglophone; the latter is no more than an illusory culture, an artificial cultural construct imposed on Scotland by Anglophone unionist elites.

Colonial domination is rather merciless in that it seeks the cultural obliteration of those nations and peoples it oppresses. This is usually achieved through introducing new laws and institutional arrangements, which negates any national reality, by the banishment of natives (and Scotland has suffered plenty of that, see chapter on 'Demographics'), and by enslaving the colonised people. Efforts are made to ensure the colonised people acknowledge and accept their cultural 'inferiority' (i.e. through Appropriated Racial Oppression, or the 'Scottish Cultural Cringe', see chapter on 'Ethnicity'), to accept the 'unreality' of their nation, and even in some instances to question their own 'biological structure' and hence their confused and imperfect character (e.g. the 'Scottish stereotypes'). A (Scottish) national culture under colonial domination is thus a contested culture whose destruction is sought in systematic fashion. According to Fanon (1967), attempts to cling on to the national culture (including language) are viewed by the occupying power (see chapter on 'Colonisation') as a refusal to submit. The national culture under colonial rule becomes condemned to secrecy and hence obscurity, turning into a *'clandestine culture'*.

In this sense national independence becomes a priority to secure national liberation which is a prerequisite for the continued existence of nothing less than an entire national culture:

> *"...the colonial situation calls a halt to national culture in almost every field. By the time a century or two of exploitation has passed there comes about a veritable emaciation of the stock of national culture. It becomes a set of automatic habits, some traditions of dress and a few broken-down institutions. The poverty of the people, national oppression and the inhibition of culture are one and the same thing. ...what we find are the dregs of culture, its mineral strata. The withering away of the reality of the nation and the death-pangs of the national culture are linked to each other in mutual dependence. For culture is first the expression of a nation, the expression of its preferences, of its taboos and of its patterns. In the colonial situation, culture, which is doubly deprived of the support of the nation and of the state, falls away and dies. The condition for its existence is therefore national liberation and the renaissance of the state. The first necessity is the re-establishment of the nation*

> *in order to give life to national culture......the conscious and organized undertaking by a colonial people to re-establish the sovereignty of that nation constitutes the most complete and obvious cultural manifestation that exists. If culture is the expression of national consciousness....it is the national consciousness which is the most elaborate form of culture. National consciousness, which is not nationalism, is the only thing that will give us an international dimension. ...it is national liberation which leads the nation to play its part on the stage of history. It is at the heart of national consciousness that international consciousness lives and grows. And from this two-fold emerging is ultimately the source of all culture."*
>
> (Fanon 1967, published in Bhabha 1994: p. 46-51)

People of indigenous and hence ethnic culture, in which language holds a critical influence, form an overwhelming majority of the pro-independence voters in Scotland, as is likewise the case in Catalonia, Quebec and in numerous countries that have previously secured independence from an 'administrative Power'. The ongoing integration of Scotland within the UK implies that the anti-independence vote on the other hand tends to be made up rather differently and will be substantially boosted and may even perhaps be made up predominantly by those of non-indigenous culture and language, the latter primarily Anglophone. What the Scottish Government continue to advocate via its (highly exceptional) open franchise voting system based on residence rather than the global norm (parental descent) seems therefore more likely to increase the anti-independence vote, as it arguably did in 2014.

Ultimately people vote on the basis of their emotions and in this they are clearly influenced by their dominant cultural affinity, heritage, and national identity, much as researchers at Cambridge Analytica have found[18]. Those voters with a more dominant British cultural heritage and affinity and therefore holding to a British national identity and emotion will tend to vote against Scottish nationhood, citizenship and independence. Hence the reason Britain's MSM are feeding the Scots wall-to-wall union flags and 'Great British' this and that TV programmes and narratives all day every day, much as they have done for many years. Cultural imperialism initiatives of this nature are a key tool used to maintain the union and are employed to the full via all forms of available communication media (Edwards and Cromwell 2018). Mere party-political policies seem of little consequence. Hence Brexit was won not because it was based on (any) policies as such; Brexit won based on national emotion (Dorling and Tomlinson 2019). The desire for nationhood is itself a cultural emotion (Fanon 1967) which means that **Scottish independence is similarly dependent on cultural emotion**.

A supposedly 'inclusive' or 'civic nationalism' constitutional referendum on Scottish self-determination with the voter franchise based on residence assumes that the Scots must also invite people from other nations and cultures (and hence those holding to other non-Scottish national emotions) who simply happen to have an address in Scotland at a given point in time, to vote in order to create a new Scottish nationality and citizenship. However, many people holding to other national identities might be expected to have little national, cultural, or emotional interest in, far less desire for Scottish nationality. Indeed, many of those from other nations and cultures and hence of other national cultures may prefer quite the opposite, as we know from the 2014 result, and may take the opportunity to reject the offer of Scottish citizenship hence blocking the self-determination of the Scottish people.

Is this active blocking of the right of Scots (by voters of other national cultures and emotions) to self-determination and to thus enjoy their own Scottish nationality and self-government not in itself a rather oppressive colonial and bigoted act? Moreover, whilst the UN is opposed to any external interference in the self-determination process of a 'people', the Scottish referendum franchise appears to invite such external interference via an irregular open franchise based on residence.

In Quebec, immigrants from Rest of Canada tend to integrate primarily into the Anglophone community, and rather less into the Francophone community. The vote for secession in Quebec is linguistically and hence culturally divided. Similarly, the propensity of Scots to vote for independence is twice the level of those from rest-UK, which suggests a linguistic and national cultural divide also exists in Scotland. Of the two million 'No' voters in 2014 perhaps half or more may therefore have been culturally and linguistically 'British' and 'Anglophone' (McIntosh 2015). Conversely, those whose national culture is Scottish, and particularly Scots language speakers who consider their identity to be Scottish, seem far more likely to vote for Scottish nationality, Scottish citizenship, and Scottish self-government (i.e. independence). Any referendum on Scotland's withdrawal from the UK union and hence on Scottish independence is essentially asking people to choose to alter their national identity (and with that their national culture) from 'British/UK' to 'Scottish'. It is not asking voters to choose between right-wing or left-wing policies, or for this party of government or that; a constitutional referendum is not a national election. Essentially, in a referendum on independence, Scottish residents are being asked if they wish to create and to hold to a Scottish national identity and with that a Scottish citizenship, or alternatively to block Scottish national identity and thus to force Scots to remain British 'nationals'. Scottish independence is not therefore a question of political ideology, it is a question of national culture and this implies it is about national identity and emotion, which is also determined by language.

> *A Scots Language Act wid be juist braw an is necessar onywey*
> *if respectin oor human richts anaw - 10 year efter thon Gaelic*
> *Language Act! Sae awauk fi yer doverin, Scottis Cultur an Langage*

Meenisters an muive yer bluidy airses!

In the referendum context voting preferences are therefore dependent upon the more dominant national culture (and language) held by an individual. The more culturally British and Anglophone one is, and therefore feels, then the more likely they may be expected to vote 'No' to oppose changing their national identity to 'Scottish'. And the more culturally and linguistically Scottish one is or feels, then the more likely they may be to vote 'Yes' to the national identity they already hold a sense of belonging and emotion toward. Votes for governments of right or left, and hence for different policies, will happen after a referendum, whichever way it goes, but that is not what a referendum on Scotland's withdrawal from the UK union, nor what Scottish self-determination is about. **Scottish national culture is therefore a clear dividing line and represents a key determinant of Scottish independence.**

CHAPTER 4: LANGUAGE

What is Language?

There are various definitions of language albeit with common themes. For example, language is considered to be: *"….a system that consists of the development, acquisition, maintenance and use of complex systems of communication, particularly the human ability to do so…"* (Katzner 1999). Language is certainly the normal everyday way humans communicate, and: *"Only humans use language…(and) … language has syntax, a set of rules for connecting words together to make statements and questions"* (Stevenson and Waite 2011). Language is also considered to comprise: *"..a body of words and the systems for their use common to a people who are of the same community or nation, the same geographical area, or the same cultural tradition."*[19]

Different peoples and nations and culures therefore have different languages and this is natural, as is language development. However, the natural development of a language will be inhibited if it is subjected to discrimination, domination, or removal and replacement by another language, as has occurred with the Scots language, and which adversely affects culture.

> *If Scots fowk kent thay hid thair ain braw langage, thay'd shuirly want thair ain naition bak an aw, swith lyke tae.*

Language is also: *"…a system of conventional spoken, manual, or written symbols by means of which human beings, as members of a social group and participants in its culture, express themselves. The functions of language include communication, the expression of identity, play, imaginative expression, and emotional release"* (Robins 1964). Here we might note the critical linkages between language, culture and identity, and also how language informs us about who we are and our place in the world around us.

Spiers (2019) provides important insights into the philosophy of language. To begin with, language is critical to our thoughts because we cannot think in non-linguistic ways. Language and thought are therefore necessarily related, and language is inherently social in which story telling is an important aspect. Language is used to explain our societies and to present ourselves (and our 'place') within them. Here the teaching of language forms a critical aspect of learning. The complexities of language and thought are one and the same. Narrative and hence language are therefore essential for all forms of explanation of phenomenon. Our language is thus a critical aspect of who we are, and how we think and view the world around us.

Power is an essential feature of social discourse, and language and more especially language differences between people and groups infer and determine power imbalances. Language is a tool for understanding and thinking and allows us to model the world around us symbolically (Wittgenstein 1953). We learn about and absorb our culture as soon as we learn to speak our mother tongue. Social discourse is the dominant source of our linguistic knowledge. We do not ourselves perceive the outside world; this is constructed for us via our linguistic discourse with others. Language is therefore essential for the construction of societies and culture. Social events, objects and persons are functions of status and the basis of organised institutions and cultural artefacts, within which rules are linguistically expressed. Language thus involves shared conventions of meaning and structure. Our language is therefore fundamental to who we are. Languages form our culture and identity and determines how and where we 'fit' into a society and its hierarchical structures.

Indigenous Language

Chris Maser's research into indigenous languages lend numerous valuable insights into the significance of language in everyday life and in terms of cultural development. Maser (2011) argues that: *"Of all the gifts of life, language is one of the most incredible. The tenets of society are founded on language"*. According to Maser, every human language *"is the master tool representing its own culture and has its unique construct, which determines both its limitations and its possibilities in expressing myth, emotion, ideas, and logic. As such, language is the medium with which the condition of the human soul is painted."* Thus, losing a language is like losing the soul of a people.

Language forms the basis of all unique cultures, with its own unique form and structure, meaning and expression. Maser argues that: *"for us and our children and our children's children to continue protecting the historical context of our cultural evolution, we need to protect above all one aspect of our culture that we normally neglect: that is our language."* In this respect language evolution represents perhaps one of the greatest feats of humanity. Moreover, it is language which makes culture possible. Conversely, for a people deprived of their own language (i.e. the Scots) there can be no natural culture for the people concerned, their culture effectively being substituted through an adopted or imposed culture and language emanating from and representing another people.

According to K. David Harrison, Director of Research at the Living Tongues Institute based in Salem, Oregon: *"When we lose a language, we lose centuries of human thinking about time, seasons, sea creatures, reindeer, edible flowers, mathematics, landscapes, myths, music, the unknown and the everyday"*[20]. Harrison maintains that, as languages become extinct, cultural knowledge is lost, along with perceptions and modes of expression, and the way we communicate with other speakers of the language. Critically, Harrison suggests that: *"because language is the fabric of culture, when a language dies, the demise of the culture that gave birth to it is imminent."* Scots might well ponder this thought when considering the diminished 'subaltern' role and 'invalid' status of the Scots language today under Anglophone linguistic domination, and the implications this has for Scottish culture, for Scottish identity, and for the Scottish people and nation.

Harrison goes further: *"With the loss of a language we also lose the evolution of its logic and its cultural myths and rituals—those metaphors of creation that gave a people a sense of place within the greater context of the Universe, because language represents unity within and through time. Temporal unity is the language of memory, those images of experience stored in the human psyche and passed forward from generation to generation in the form of stories, myths, and rituals."*

This implies that, **when we allow a language to become extinct, we are losing a whole facet of understanding, a facet of ourselves and of our 'place' in the world, and therefore we lose the very basis of our identity**. Indeed, the collective memory of a people (is) archived within their language as *"a memory that is part of the human hologram"*. Scots clearly need to think of the Scots language as much more than merely a supposed 'inferior' literary inconvenience in an Anglophone dominated society. If language is who we are, then, without our language, who are we? **A people without their own language is a people without their own identity**.

Language and Culture

A unique culture cannot exist without its own language to protect its history and guide its continued social evolution. Our growing blindness through the extinction of languages is exacerbated by the global spread of languages such as English, which limits the imagination and understanding within the rigid confines of its own constrained fence of intellectual logic and unnatural soundings.

When a language dies, we lose cultural identities and the richness and diversity of humanity's linguistic heritage (Duchene 2008). Lipski (2008) maintains that something more is lost as the full dimension of such loss is only fully understood by those deprived of their mother tongue: "*Imagine being told you can't use your language and you'll see what that undefinable 'more' is. I feel that I have drunk the milk of a strange woman, that I grew up alongside another person. I feel like this because I do not speak my mother's language.*"

> *Whaur's thon eejit o a Holyrood Langage Meenister, an whit's he daein fer oor langage an cultur? Naethin Aa wad say. Oor ain langage is naitural, nae fause-soondin 'bools in yer mooth'. Englis is bein garred doon bairns thrapples whither thay lyke it or no; thon's the rael fausehood, an cultural doon-hauden. Englis is aw richt, tho ma mither tung is Scots.*

Lipski (2008) argued that, since some aspects of learning language begin at birth—even perhaps in the womb—and speaking abilities begin at around one year old, language is essentially a lifetime experience. It is inevitably the case that we learn our native languages from those individuals who are closest to us, emotionally and physically. According to Lipski (as quoted in Duchene 2008), the philosophical argument behind biodiversity—that the greater the variety of plant and animal species, the more enriched our lives are—also supports the importance of a rich diversity of languages: "*Those who live around many cultures and languages tend to be more tolerant than those who don't*".

Enforced language imposition or linguistic imperialism is not tolerance, neither is being deprived of one's own language somehow 'progressive'; rather, these are oppressive, discriminatory and xenophobic acts. Language imposition and substitution may more rightly be viewed as a violent act of linguistic imperialism, leading to ongoing discrimination and thus creating conflict and inequalities between peoples, resulting in justified calls for self-determination from oppressed and colonised groups. This itself underlines the fact that **language is often the most common rationale for peoples seeking self-determination and hence liberation from oppression**.

Lipski further adds that: *"In 1940s Spain, dictator Francisco Franco banned minority languages such as Basque, Galician (his own native language!), and Catalan"*. According to some sources, children caught speaking Basque in schools would be whipped. Today, those languages are flourishing and considered co-official to Castilian Spanish in their respective regions. Such linguistic punishment (and reward for cooperation) is a common theme among imperial powers, reflecting the 'scourge' of colonisation and language oppression. In Kenya, children were whipped for speaking in their native language and rewarded for informing teachers of anyone who continued to speak in their native tongue rather than English, the language of colonial rule.

The African novelist Ngũgĩ Wa Thiong'o, recalled from his colonial education in mid-twentieth century Kenya that simply by attending school *"the language of my education was no longer the language of my culture"* (MacKinnon 2019). Such enforcement of an alien culture and language on the 'colonial child' is intended to condition the child to see the world in a certain way, and to dissociate the child from their own natural social environment and culture, resulting in what MacKinnon terms 'colonial alienation'.

In the same vein, Scots speakers have another language imposed on them which seeks to downgrade and replace their own ('invalid' or 'inferior') Scots language, the latter intentionally marginalised, and institutionally ridiculed, even today. This ongoing maltreatment is essentially ethnic and hence cultural/linguistic discrimination. Such language imposition is achieved through 'Linguistic imperialism'. Phillipson (1992) defines English linguistic imperialism as:

> *"...the dominance asserted and retained by the establishment and continuous reconstitution of structural and cultural inequalities between English and other languages."*

At root the imposition of a language and the marginalisation and simultaneous removal of an indigenous or minority language is therefore about the expression of power. Linguistic imperialism inevitably leads to inequalities in culture, in society structures, and in the more limited opportunities and hence restrictive development of indigenous language speakers and their nation itself. A central theme within Phillipson's research relates to the complex hegemonic processes which continue to sustain the pre-eminence of English in the world today. In the specific Scottish context, what language imperialism means is that Scots speakers remain structurally and hence institutionally unequal and are effectively considered a lower or inferior class of people through language. The sense of linguistic and cultural inferiority then becomes internalised and hence is accepted by the oppressed people as 'deserving'. This is further reflected in the Anglophone elite's view of the Scots language as being 'inferior' English, or not even a 'valid' language, spoken primarily by the working class and hence by 'less educated' people.

Phillipson analysed the British Council's standard use of rhetoric employed to promote the English language, and outlined some of the key tenets of English applied linguistics and English-language-teaching methodology. These tenets typically hold that:

• English is best taught monolingually (Phillipson calls this *"the monolingual fallacy"*);
• The ideal teacher is a native speaker (Phillipson calls this *"the native-speaker fallacy"*);[
• The earlier English is taught, the better the results (Phillipson calls this *"the early-start fallacy"*);

- The more English is taught, the better the results (Phillipson calls this *"the maximum-exposure fallacy"*);
- If other languages are used much, standards of English will drop (Phillipson calls this *"the subtractive fallacy"*).

According to Phillipson, those institutions who promote English—organizations such as the British Council, the International Monetary Fund and the World Bank, and others such as operators of English-language schools—use three main types of argument to back up their case for the 'deserved' domination and prioritisation of the English language:

- *Intrinsic arguments*, which describe the English language as providential, rich, noble and interesting.

- *Extrinsic arguments*, which point out that English is well-established: that it has many speakers, and that there are trained teachers and a wealth of teaching material.

- *Functional arguments*, which emphasize the practical usefulness of English as 'a gateway to the world'.

Such arguments tend to assert what English *is* and what other languages *are not*, which is basically a prejudiced assumption based on a form of British or English 'exceptionalism' and sense of 'superiority', and which implies or assumes that all other languages are somehow 'inferior' to English. Another theme in Phillipson's work concerns *"linguicism"*, which relates to the prejudice that leads to endangered languages becoming extinct or losing their local eminence due to the rise and competing prominence of English.

The key argument here is that Anglophone elites are prejudiced against other languages; given Scotland's educational history, we might add that this includes the Scots language. Phillipson (1992, p. 65) maintains that: *"Linguistic Imperialism is a sub-type of Cultural Imperialism. Linguistic Imperialism permeates all other types of imperialism, since language is the means used to mediate and express them"*.

In this regard a language that is imposed on a people with the intention to replace their own natural language, in this instance the English language imposed on the Scots, represents the essential voice of imperialism and hence the voice of a peoples' oppressors.

Linguistic Genocide

The International Congress of Linguists has declared that: "...*the disappearance of any one language constitutes an irretrievable loss to mankind...*". The United Nations Educational, Scientific and Cultural Organization (UNESCO) has responded to the threat of language loss by creating the UNESCO Red Book on Endangered Languages[21]. This is in part intended to raise awareness of mother-tongue based multilingual education (MLE) and various other related support options available.

Linguistic genocide *"relates to the extermination of a group's language or linguicide, i.e. the death of a language"* (Phillipson and Skutnabb-Kangas 1994). The process of linguistic genocide is generally deliberate with little left to chance that the oppressed language might survive; however, often such a strategy may not be entirely successful. Language is recognised as a key dimension in maintaining patterns of dominance in a society, along with class, gender and race, through the hierarchising of groups. According to Philipson and Skutnabb-Kangas: *"Linguistic underdevelopment parallels economic and political underdevelopment"*. The argument here is that a people whose language is being lost or forcibly replaced will not be able to contribute to their national development as they otherwise would have done. Scots and Scotland would appear to fall into this category of under-development, which implies that many more Scots could contribute to national development were the Scots language respected and prioritised (i.e. taught in schools etc.) and treated in the way it should be, as a national language.

> *Mebbe ane day thon Scots Langage Meenister in Holyrood micht gie us oor Scots langage bak, e'en lairn Scots bairns thair ain mither tung in scuil ken, an at lang an last gie Scots fowk equaliti wi Englis and Gaelic langages and fowk. Nocht lyke haein equaliti raither than aw Scots fowk an bairns bein doun-hauden bi yer ain pairlament, lyke juist noo.*

Hierarchisation of languages also brings with it a rejection of authentic local values and their substitution of cultural values introduced by the dominant language group, and hence the imposition of cultural imperialism. This serves to strengthen the elite language group's social stratification resulting in a segregated society reflecting class, status and power, all of which is distinguishable by language. Scottish 'society' is clearly linguistically structured thus with an elite Anglophone hierarchy reflecting these key aspects of power and control. This in turn limits potential for social mobility among those subsequently placed lower down in the system, i.e. Scots speakers, due to language difference.

Language is not the only indicator of cultural distinctiveness, but it is well established that the basis of any culture, and arguably its most critical feature, is the language that underpins it. There is therefore a unique and irreplaceable connection between culture and language:

> *"The languages we speak provide us with the words and concepts to describe the world around us, allowing us to verbalize certain values easily. Anything we as a cultural group value will surely have a known and easily understandable term. Being a native speaker of our mother tongue brings with it more than just the ability to communicate, it brings with it the ability to understand why someone thinks and acts as they do".[22]*

Our language therefore helps us to understand others, and the way they act, including the way they vote, and why. Language also influences the way we interpret things and determines the way we see the world around us. Indeed, the *Sapir–Whorf hypothesis* states that the way we think about and view the world is determined by our language (Anderson & Lightfoot, 2002; Crystal, 1987; Hayes, Ornstein, & Gage, 1987). Here it may be hypothesised that the more Anglophone a person is, and hence the more British they feel in terms of identity and emotion, this being a reflection of their culture, then the more likely they will be to oppose Scottish independence. Conversely, for Scots language speakers, and more especially those who feel Scottish in terms of national identity and sense of belonging, the greater the likelihood is that they may be expected to be supportive of Scottish independence.

Yet, despite the importance of language, the Scots still ignore and do not even teach their own Scots language when it seems rather obvious from the literature that *"culture and language are undeniably intertwined"*[23]. To a large extent the scientific evidence and perspectives relating to culture and language help explain why Scotland clearly does things and 'thinks' things very differently from other countries within the UK, and particularly England. And, moreover, as "... *cognitive research suggests that language profoundly influences the way people see the world*"[24], we can accept that language and culture would make Scots respond to wider global challenges differently than their much larger near neighbour. The propensity for imperial powers to wage war and enter into and even foster international conflicts might be a good example here. Whereas Britain (or rather England) has a long history of engaging in armed conflicts and diplomatic disputes with other nations, often to protect or further its imperial and colonial interests, the Scottish consensus remains rather more attuned to seeking alternative peaceful solutions, more akin to its Nordic neighbours. This suggests that language is a great deal more than merely a utilitarian means of communication, and not least because language "*.. influences our culture and* *even our thought processes*"[25]; hence language (and culture) inevitably influences and indeed determines the way a people act and behave.

Whilst invariably giving an impression of respecting human rights, some western countries often act to prevent indigenous minorities from learning their own languages in schools. The 'major powers' have tended to block efforts to give minorities more protection, for instance the failure to approve Article 3 of the UN Draft Convention for the Prevention and Punishment of the Crime of Genocide, which also referred to cultural and linguistic genocide. Phillipson and Skutnabb-Kangas maintain that granting linguistic rights to minorities would help to reduce conflict potential instead of creating it. They further suggest that the alternative approach, if not the opposite to linguistic genocide, is the granting of linguistic human rights. Clearly in this respect Scots are, and remain, deprived of their linguistic human right – the right to their mother tongue – which is the Scots language.

Language and Identity

The importance of language (and culture) in influencing and determining our identity, and the way we view the world around us, should not be underestimated:

> *"We understand things, events, ourselves and others through a process of interpretation, which occurs in language. This is how language, culture, and identity intersect. We make sense of our surroundings and interpret our experiences through the languages we speak, creating a culture-specific lens through which we view the world. When a language dies, however, that particular lens shatters."*
>
> (Pamela Serota Cote, in: Wallace 2009)

In this sense many Scottish people may be expected to hold primarily to a Scottish national identity based largely on their Scottish language and culture. However, those Scots and others who are more or wholly Anglophone may be expected to hold to a more British/Anglo identity, which is likewise based on the influence of their dominant (Anglophone) culture and language, and which is not Scots per se. Clearly our identity is therefore in large part linguistically determined. This further implies that those who do not or cannot speak much or any Scots language might be least likely to hold to a distinct Scottish identity.

Perceived 'wisdom' is that, as a matter of practicality in an increasingly global world, the use and existence of fewer languages is not only less work, in terms of learning and maintenance, but is an advantage. However, this is not done because language is *separate* from culture. On the contrary, efforts to stamp out regional languages (such as 'Scots') and instill one, unified 'national' language (i.e. English) are undertaken because language is so inextricable and *central* to culture (and hence to identity). Given that regional native or tribal languages may be viewed as a threat to 'national' loyalty and identity, a national language doesn't just make trade and communication easier, it also helps build another, unified, 'national' identity, with identity being linguistically and culturally determined. Instilling such a (i.e. foreign) language into the minds of a people (i.e. linguistic imperialism) essentially gives people another identity which is not their own natural or national identity.

Looking at language as only a practical or commercial tool clearly misses the central importance of language with respect to culture, personal narrative and identity, which then makes it merely a political tool. The effective subjugation and attempted removal of a minority language, such as the Scots language, is clearly politically motivated. In this respect, continuing efforts to diminish, remove and replace the Scots language reflect an intent on the part of the British state to make the Scots feel more 'British' in terms of 'national' identity, and by implication to make them feel less 'Scottish'.

The prevailing Anglophone linguistic policy in Scotland is thus anti-independence oriented.

We can only understand things, events, ourselves and others through a process of interpretation, and this occurs through language. The diversity of our languages represents the richness of our expressiveness of Being; language tells us 'who we are'. This is how language, culture and (national) identity intersect; it is also why the loss of a language is such a concern and why minority language rights remain such an emotionally charged issue in many countries around the world. Because language discloses cultural and historical meaning, the loss of language is a loss of that link to the past. Without a link to the past, people in a culture lose their sense of place, purpose and path.

The loss of language therefore undermines a people's sense of identity and belonging and place, which uproots the entire community in the end. When a people become incorporated into the dominant language and culture that has subsumed them, they have then lost their heritage and culture along the way. This is where the Scottish people are currently rapidly headed, to an unknown destination with the only certainty being that, as things stand, they will be without their own Scots language, and with their language gone so will their culture and heritage and identity be gone too. This in turn implies that, without their own Scots language, a 'Scottish people' may not exist in any meaningful (i.e. cultural) sense, and their sense of identity will disappear.

For a language to be revived, there must be a population left to learn it, and a strong desire among the young people to revive that connection with their heritage. In Brittany, which was subsumed into France only after the French Revolution, the language became endangered not because of low population numbers, but because national administrations insisted that French be the only language spoken or learned (Wallace 2009). In the late 1970s, a movement was established to revive the Breton language, which bears more resemblance to the tongue of Brittany's Celtic settlers than to French. Language immersion schools now teach the language to children wishing to learn Breton as well as French, and other cultural revival efforts in Breton music and dance have accompanied the language movement. To some extent this mirrors the ongoing Gaelic language revival in Scotland and Ireland. However, compared with recent Gaelic language initiatives in Scotland, the Scots language appears to have been singled out for rather more extreme 'treatment' by Scotland's Anglophone institutions, doubtless due to its potentially far greater political significance vis-a-vis the question of Scottish independence.

The result has been positive for Bretons. The shame (or 'Cultural Cringe'?) at being Breton has receded, much like the African-American "Roots" movement reduced the shame at being black by offering a narrative story and pride that the children of slaves had lacked. A high rate of alcoholism and depression has receded and, as Pamela Serota Cote observed[26]:

"...*every Breton I spoke with who has learned the language as an adult said they feel now that they have been able to close the gap and heal those past wounds of shame. Many described finally discovering their roots by learning the language. One Breton said that the language 'completes the whole.'*"

Learning one's mother tongue properly provides for a kind of 'healing' function within the linguistically oppressed situation. In instances where the language wanes not because of physical extinction, but because of *cultural subsumption*, as is the case with Scots speakers, the loss of a language is a far more personal tragedy, at least to those within that culture. For someone inside a lost or dying culture, a language can be like the memories of parents and grandparents--not required any more, or even convenient, ostensibly for efficiency of operation in a modern, globalized 'progressive' world, as if that were all we should be concerned about; yet, language is absolutely essential for our sense of roots, security, identity, pride, continuity and wholeness.

What is lost to us when a language finally goes silent? Charlie "Red Hawk" Thom, a medicine man and ceremonial leader, suggested that English goes in one ear and out the other but it never touches the heart. Karuk, his own indigenous peoples' language, he says, *"begins in the heart and moves to the mind"* (Johnson 2019). *"The wisdom of humanity is coded in language,"* according to Lyle Campbell (quoted by Johnson), director of the Center for American Indian Languages, who goes on to say that: *"Once a language dies, the knowledge dies with it."*

Johnson refers to Caleen Sisk, the spiritual leader and the tribal chief of the Winnemem Wintu tribe—and a last speaker of the language that sustains her people's identity. For a hundred years, the tribe has been fighting with the U.S. government over its territory along the McCloud River, next to Mount Shasta, which they consider their birthplace. Loss of land and loss of language are connected, says Sisk. *"This land is our church"*. In what has become known as 'The Silent Genocide', loss of Aboriginal Languages has been avoided in many cases because these communities are not letting go of their language or culture willingly (Prodanovic 2013).

A Scots Language Act? A winna haud ma braithe!

The death of a language is also considered as a process by which the fluency of a language in a given speech community dissipates over time, eventually resulting in the complete loss of speakers of the language. The central premise of language death is that language is no longer a self-sustaining entity; essentially, language will only exist when there is a community willing to utilize it. For a given language to thrive in a community it must have the social infrastructure, and most especially the teaching of the language to younger generations, to do so. Ultimately, languages are considered at risk of dying when they are no longer transmitted or taught to younger generations.

This is clearly the case with the Scots language whereby the state, in the form of the 'nationalist' Scottish Government, is refusing to formally teach the language to younger generations of Scots. As the number of fluent speakers declines, possibilities for transmission decline as well, eventually resulting in the death of the language. Do Scots really wish to see the death of the Scots language? Does the SNP Scottish Government really wish to kill off the Scots language? It appears so, given the state has refused to formalise teaching of the Scots language in schools.

The cause of language death is therefore largely attributed to the marginalization of indigenous and minority communities and the subordination of their languages, which is generally promoted by state authorities. Globally, indigenous peoples are shifting towards the economically and culturally dominant languages of their regions (Muehlmann 2008). This is the direct consequence of *language subordination*, in which the speakers of a culturally dominant language in a particular area or nation marginalize the speakers of minority languages (Lippi-Green 1997, p. 68). As a result of marginalization, speakers of minority languages feel inclined to assimilate to the social standard, which is the English language in Scotland's case, primarily in order to increase their social mobility.

Language is not therefore simply a means of communication, as many opponents of the Scots language tend to argue when they advocate that only English should be formally prioritized and taught in Scottish schools. Language defines a person's cognitive perception of reality. When a language is lost, the knowledge contained within it is lost as well. ***"Language is resoundingly more than a mere means of communication; it is the means by which humans can claim diversity and define their identity"*** (Shaw 2001). In a time of rapid globalization, the quest and need to preserve our languages is also an effort to preserve ourselves and our diverse heritage and culture (Nettle and Romaine 2000, p. 23).

The causes of language loss mostly date back to the treatment of Aboriginal peoples by colonial powers. In 1763 the Royal Proclamation allowed the Crown to take over Canada's First Nations land through treaty (First Peoples' Heritage, Language and Culture Council 2010). This was followed by the Indian Act in 1876 which removed Aboriginal people from any political decision-making process. Thus, the Aboriginal communities that were required to foster language transmission were forcibly dismantled. Furthermore, residential schools that began operating from the 1840's to the 1990's forced younger generations of Aboriginal language speakers to assimilate culturally and speak English. It is this forced assimilation that has been largely to blame for Aboriginal language loss in Canada and elsewhere. Scotland appears little different in this respect concerning the 'imperial' Anglophone linguistic treatment meted out to both Gaelic and Scots language speakers, and which one might also argue came about through a treaty entered into with England and resulting 'educational' policies imposed on what were and remain, in British 'national' terms, minority peoples.

Can Scots be considered an 'aboriginal' people? Aboriginal is defined as a people 'inhabiting or existing in a land from the earliest times or from before the arrival of colonists. Aboriginal is also the term for 'indigenous' or 'native' people'. From this it may be argued that Scots are native and may indeed be considered aboriginal insofar as Scotland is concerned. It might also be argued, in the case of Scotland, that the arrival of colonial rule, bringing with it cultural and linguistic imperialism, occurred primarily since the 1707 'union', though some evidence of the Anglophone 'enculturation' process exists since the 1603 Union of the Crowns (Ross 2008; Devine 2012).

> *Aye, maist Scots spikkers weel ken whit ye mean aboot bein 'mou-ban' (i.e. articulate). Aw Scots bairns ir aye still telt tae spik 'properly' (i.e. the English language), an aw dominie's an maisters in wir schuils hae tae hiv Higher 'English', yet nane o thaim teachers hiv tae ken ony o oor Scots langage. Scotlan is juist lyke ony ither*

auld colonie, langage-wise, A wad sae.

Research confirms that Aboriginal language communities are marginalized by the mainstream society and tend to assimilate in order to increase their social mobility (Kirkness 1998. P. 96). Furthermore, there is a common thread in discourse on the issue suggesting that the political infrastructure currently in place to 'ensure' the maintenance of Aboriginal languages is greatly lacking. Kirkness (1998) urged that: *"Legislation to protect Aboriginal Languages......must become reality now, because the opportunity to save our languages becomes more remote with each passing generation"*. Aboriginal languages are also a fundamental right and freedom. The framework for such a recommendation was established in the *United Nations Declaration on the Rights of Indigenous Peoples Resolution*. Article 14 states that Aboriginal languages should be treated as fundamental rights that the government has an obligation to protect (Kirkness 1998, p. 99).

As more and more languages become extinct, linguists are realizing that they contain a type of knowledge that is far beyond merely a different set of words and grammar. According to Thurman (2015): *"the consequences of losing a language may not be understood until it is too late. When you deprive a kid of his language at the sponge time of life, the most precious learning years, a bond is broken"*. First Nation communities have introduced 'immersion classes' in order to preserve their languages since the passage, in 2006, of the Esther Martínez Native American Language Preservation Act. The Act provided funding for language survival and restoration programs from pre-school through college.

For 'peripheral' or minority languages to survive they must find a way to coexist with what some call the "bully" languages. According to David Harrison: *"The ideal of stable bilingualism is a given. Nobody wants these communities to remain isolated"*. Moreover, a mother tongue is a human birthright and should not be deprived. Nevertheless, British institutions, and that includes the 'devolved' Scottish Government, appear to take a different view insofar as the Scots language is concerned. That view is not unlike other trans-national States who likewise consider ethnic languages as a threat to their hegemony, and deploy measures to suppress them and the identity of minorities in what remains a clear violation of linguistic human rights.

Language Oppression

Language subordination means Scots who primarily speak the Scots language may often be considered as less 'articulate' than Anglophones, which is ethnic prejudice. This readily relates to the North American situation where language differences are drawn upon in the complicated race politics there, and often by use of that one word, "*articulate*". Articulate is a rather dangerous word to use as it is all too frequently employed to describe black people with an air of condescension, in that it is almost used as if being articulate was somehow a surprise (Clemetson 2007). In such a way linguistic discrimination leads to racial or ethnic discrimination, which is the same outcome for indigenous Scots speakers in Scotland. Language discrimination results in numerous negative consequences including intellectual, social, health and economic oppression.

And therein lies the undercurrent and basis of the long established 'Scottish Cultural Cringe', or 'creenge' in Scots, a psychological condition reflecting the lack of confidence Scots speakers often have in themselves, in the Scottish people, in their nation and its potential, reflecting the longstanding institutionalised cultural discrimination they face. For at root this is what language oppression and language subordination is – ethnic discrimination. And, like North American and aboriginal racism more generally, Scots speakers also suffer from ridicule and exclusion as so ably portrayed by that single solitary word - articulate. To be 'articulate' in Scotland one must be able to speak 'proper' English, and Scottish people must therefore become Anglophone in order to advance themselves within an Anglophone elite culturally dominated society that controls Scotland and its institutions. Meantime, the indigenous Scots language is made out to be reflective of a rather less articulate individual, or so the prevailing institutionalised Anglophone 'wisdom' goes.

This linguistic and cultural tragedy manifests itself in various ways, and invariably negative for Scots speakers. For instance, the Scottish Government has culture and 'language' Minister's, a multitude of civil servants, numerous cultural quangos, endless directors of education in local authorities, and self-proclaimed *'warld cless'* Scottish universities, yet none of these supposedly *'bricht mynds'* appointed to run Scotland's myriad social institutions and paid well in return, would appear to appreciate the Scots language at all. Those institutions responsible for language and culture in Scotland are essentially killing off both, by ignoring the Scots language, which they seek to 'haud-doun'.

A 'Scots Language Act' is therefore essential not only to provide for fairness and equity with the Gaelic and English languages, but also to meet that most basic of human rights – the right to one's own language. It is not a complicated matter to organise adequate numbers of qualified Scots Language teachers and to educate graduates with the necessary linguistic knowledge. Yet without an official, taught, legally enshrined Scots language provision there is only the English language ingrained in the minds (or 'garred doon the thrapples', i.e. forced down the throats) of Scottish people, and with it a diminished, distorted and ever withering Scottish language, culture, heritage, and national identity.

> *Thon langage garred doon bairns thrapples in schuil isnae whit thair uised tae et hame. Whan Scots bairns staert the schuil Englis is a furrin leid.*

English would of course still be taught as an 'administrative' or official language, as is the case in many other countries and especially in former colonies, but always with the indigenous languages brought to the fore, not disregarded and 'doun-hauden', as is evident with the Scots language. The absence of legislative action by the Scottish Government on the critical matter of the Scots language is nothing short of continued cultural oppression and ethnic discrimination.

Scots speakers are discriminated against (from birth) in their own nation and are thereafter continually disadvantaged throughout life by prevailing Anglophone language policies, language resources, and language infrastructure of the state. This inevitably has strong linkages to the so-called 'attainment gap'. To put it another way, under-privileged indigenous Scots, many of whom live in poverty, mostly speak Scots, whereas those in control of Scotland's authorities, establishment, and institutions (including key communication mediums such as education, broadcasting, media etc) do not; the latter are primarily Anglophone, not Scots speakers. This linguistic and cultural segregation and divide reflects and represents ongoing cultural and language discrimination, and its consequences include institutionalised socio-economic constraints placed upon the Scots speaking population.

Robin McAlpine of Common Weal made the point that: *"There will be no Scottish independence if there is no increase in Scotland's collective confidence in itself both as a cultural entity but more importantly as a functioning, modern nation state"* (McAlpine 2016). While such reflection on the lack of national confidence is, in the event of a 'No' vote, inarguable, the raising of the capability of a people to even achieve statehood above that of culture is questionable. Here, even McAlpine, a supporter of Scottish independence, does not appear to appreciate the function and significance of language as a critical factor in the development of a 'peoples' culture and identity.

In the recent past many traditional Scottish rhymes and songs provided children with a useful understanding of the Scots language and its meanings. The Scots language offers plenty of options in terms of singing, counting games, rhymes, stories, etc. which are still well used in many Scottish households but are not quite so common in today's state-sanctioned Anglophone nurseries, far less in primary schools where only English prevails. Indeed, many teachers in Scotland today are unable to speak the Scots language, and there is no requirement for teachers recruited from outside Scotland to be able to speak or understand the natural national language of the children they teach; teachers in Scotland merely require to be qualified in English,some now also in Gaelic, but none are required to know the Scots language.

Evidence from the extensive language/culture literature confirms that it really does matter what language one learns as a 'mither tung'. The absence of a properly learned Scots language leaves a significant cultural and linguistic gap in the makeup of today's Scotland and in the Scottish people which materially influences perceptions of their own national identity as well as an entrenched feeling of cultural inferiority for many. Scotland's predominantly Anglophone decision makers, particularly educationists and those within responsible state institutions, appear to be tasked to ensure this language oppression continues.

Language 'Shift'

It should seem rather obvious that Scotland's enduring cultural difference (with any other 'peoples') rests in the Scots language, which continues to exist, despite the lack of any formal teaching. Some 1.6m people still speak Scots, according to the census in 2011, though arguably this should be many more, and would be were the language taught. That it is just 1.6 million people (28.6 per cent of Scots) is a consequence of centuries of ongoing Anglophone domination, cultural assimilation and language 'shift' whereby the English language has replaced the Scots language.

> *If Scots want tae hiv a Scottis cultur an identitie, thay hiv tae mak shuir oor bairns an aw ither fowk ir taucht tae read an screed in Scots, as weel as spik it anaw. Yet whaur is oor Scots Language Act, Cultur Meenister? Withoot oor ain mither tung thar's nae Scottis cultur nor Scottis naitional identity, an thar's nae Scottis naition naither.*

The assimilation process has been so successful that not only has Scotland's Anglophone leaders consistently refused to allow Scots to even teach their own language to Scots children in schools, a basic human right denied, even the current SNP 'nationalist' governing administration has largely ignored and played-down the Scots language. One would think that the Scottish Government itself was ashamed of the Scots language.

The entrenched feeling of inadequacy (i.e. 'Scotland's too wee, too poor, too stupid'[27]), an attitude perhaps more prevalent amongst 'No' voting Scots, seems in part due to the refusal to teach Scots to read and write in their own language and hence not to fully respect their own culture. Many 'No' voters arguably suffer more from the Cultural Cringe, viewing the Scots language as no more than poor English, a stance that Scotland's Anglophone educational authorities and social institutions tend to reinforce. Outside the educational establishment, the BBC and the wider MSM are arguably the dominant purveyor of the Anglophone message drilled into Scots. To this might be added the all-pervading influence of institutional Scotland which looms large, from Scotland's schools, to the universities, the law courts, to the myriad of government institutions, and the parliament itself.

Scots are therefore discriminated against in their own nation, deprived of their own mither tung, and thereafter continually disadvantaged throughout life by the prevailing colonial Anglophone language assimilation (or language 'shift'), resource allocation, and prejudiced policies of state authorities. Inevitably this discrimination has linkages to the 'attainment gap' in that under-privileged indigenous working class Scots for the most part speak Scots, and most 'Yes' voters speak Scots, whereas Scotland's social institutions and establishment and hence Scotland's elites (including those running key institutions across government, education, health, broadcasting, courts, business etc) tend to be Anglophone and unionist. The attainment gap clearly reflects this cultural and linguistic divide which to some extent also mirrors the pro and anti-independence divide.

Scotland's language divide, a consequence of linguistic imperialism and 'enculturation', reflects institutionalised (Anglophone elite) cultural and linguistic discrimination. This results in what the late Jimmy Reid referred to as the 'alienation' of the Scottish working class; virtually all of the working class Scots in Scotland are Scots speakers. The consequences of alienation involve very real life-long socio-economic constraints imposed on and suffered by a great many Scots speakers who also often remain objects of ridicule by Scotland's Anglophone elites simply because they speak their own mother tongue Scots language, something few of the elite themselves are able to do, or do competently.

> *Noo thon wid be a Scottish cultural nirvana, tae feel an think in oor ain mither tung. Whaur is oor Scots Leid Act, Cultur Meenister? Langage is a human richt efter aw.*

Paradoxically, it is Scotland's Anglophone elites, many if not most of whom are not Scottish, who remain largely ignorant of and unable even to speak Scots in any significant measure, or at all. However, it remains in the personal and hegemonic interest of the Anglophone elites running Scotland's social institutions to ensure that this linguistic and cultural discrimination and segregation continues, and hence that the Scots language should not be formally taught to the Scottish people.

Scotland's Anglophone elites maintain that there are several Scots languages and raise other dubious excuses as to why the Scots language should not be taught to Scottish people. Yet without doubt 'A Scots Grammar' (Purves 1997) exists, as does a 'Scots-English Dictionary' (Ross and Smith 1998), and there are many other sources of information on the Scots language, not least even 'The New Testament in Scots' (Lorimer 1983). As the Scots-English Dictionary itself states: "*...language is one of the factors that serves most effectively to define and unite a nation*". This also suggests that the refusal of Scotland's Anglophone dominated state authorities to teach the Scots language is wilfully intended to create disunity amongst Scots and to render Scottish identity confused (e.g. 'British <u>and</u> Scottish'?) and diminished, whilst seeking to develop in Scots minds, through the medium of English language, a 'superior' British identity and British cultural mindset.

Language is clearly one of the main symbols and educational vehicles for cultural assimilation, and which influences beliefs and behaviour, i.e. how people think and act, and even how they vote. The British state has long experience in applying an English language policy to assimilate culturally diverse peoples throughout its imperial and colonial history. Scotland has not been exempted from this process; indeed, arguably Scotland was, and remains, at the very forefront.

It is not so very long ago that British linguists and educators promoted what was known as the '*verbal-deficit perspective*' which proposed that anyone who did not use standard English was verbally deficient, had less prospect of academic advancement, and did not even have a 'valid' language (Bernstein, 1971). The verbal-deficit perspective has since been found wanting though its impacts arguably continue to be felt, more especially among working class Scots speakers. The 'theory' proposed that the way language is used within any particular societal class affects the way people assign significance and meaning to the things about which they are speaking. Littlejohn (2002, p. 178), in reference to Bernstein's work, stated that *"people learn their place in the world by virtue of the language codes they employ"*. Moreover, the code that a person uses essentially symbolizes their social identity or class (Bernstein, 1971). In this context, the Scots language has been diminished and scorned as the language of a backward and lower order people, just as Gaelic was once regarded (Bunting, 2017).

> *Aw thay soor-face't creetics o Scots langage canna haurdly pit a pickle o wirds thegither in Scots. Thay're juist no interestit in lairnin hou tae read an screed in Scots. Maist fowk comin tae wirk in Scotlan dinnae e'en hiv tae lairn hou tae spik Scots. Thon's nae bather tae efter a wee bittie lairnin.*

Wittgenstein (1953) argued that 'objects in the world are reflected symbolically in language', suggesting that language gives us a picture of a fact or of a particular state of affairs. The meaning of a sentence is really a proposition and it is language which allows us to express such propositions. However, language alone does not give us the truth, for that we need to first compare the propositions with the state of affairs in the world as we see it.

Our own language therefore provides us with a picture of how we as a 'people' see the world. Our social structures and institutions are also language created and therefore the domination of English within Scotland's social institutions reflects what is effectively an Anglophone linguistic control mechanism and socio-cultural imbalance which often excludes Scots speakers and promotes and hence elevates Anglophones. Because we cannot think in non-linguistic ways, this means we use narrative to create and explain our society and its purpose. An Anglophone narrative essentially determines and dictates Scotland's society, values and purpose in Anglophone terms, not in Scots language terms.

Scots therefore need to ask themselves the question, what would Scotland be like if a Scots language narrative determined and defined Scotland's society and purpose, instead of an English/Anglophone narrative? And, moreover, how would a Scots language narrative then shape and influence the identity and life chances of the Scottish people?

A wid imaigine wee bairns in schuil wid bi fair awa lairnin Scots wirds an sangs alangside Englis wirds an thon wid mak for muckle betterment ower aw an mair unnderstaundin o wha we are an oor ain cultur. Mair pouer tae yer elbae, an aw ithers that wid taucht Scots tae Scots bairns an fowk in Scotlan's scuils an aw whair else.

Language is the expression of thought in symbolic form (Spiers 2019) which means that language is the symbolic system we use to represent the world around us. Today, however, there is still no protection nor proper learning provision made for the Scots language in Scotland. This is like saying there is no protection nor proper learning provision made for the Danish language in Denmark, or for the Norwegian language in Norway, and so on. In many countries such disrespect for a peoples' own language would be unthinkable, yet in Scotland it appears to be the accepted norm, or at least it is for the Anglophone elite in control of Scotland's institutions and who set the educational agenda. Westminster and Holyrood have thus far refused to prioritise the Scots language or ensure that Scots is taught in Scotland's schools, unlike English and more recently Gaelic, with the latter languages protected and taught by statute. Meanwhile, the Scots language receives little if any respect and is not required to be formally taught to anyone in Scotland, the indigenous language remaining subordinate and forgotten about even relative to several other languages taught in schools. The Scots language remains ignored and left to wither, and with that will inevitably wither Scottish culture and Scottish identity, and in turn the Scottish nation itself.

Efter ten year in pouer whaur's oor 'Scots Language (Scotland)

> *Act', Holyrood? Tae be taucht an lairn oor Scots langage is oor
> human richt, naw? Yet Holyrood aye daes naething aboot oor
> Scots langage. Gaelic spikkers haes thair Act, yet whaurs the Scots
> Langage Act?*

According to the Open University, as it announced a new online Scots language course in late 2019, the Scots language is described as *"a crucial and integral part of Scottish culture and identity"*[28]. Similarly, in a study into the influence of language on national attachment, Madeiros concluded that: *"it is linguistic perceptions that directly determine national attachment"* (Medeiros 2017). Medeiros found that, in terms of support for Quebec independence, being a Francophone, compared with an Anglophone, had a strong and significant, at $p < 0.01$, influence on supporting Quebec independence. There seems little reason to believe the situation is any different for Scots speakers and Anglophones on the question of Scottish independence. The critical influence of language as a determinant of national identity is self-evident and is confirmed by empirical evidence.

Clearly, language 'shift' constitutes a key element in any cultural imperialism strategy with the objective being to replace the supposedly 'inferior' and 'non-valid' indigenous language by elevating and prioritising the language of a cultural hegemony and elite. It is therefore rather obvious that the Scots language is singled out and is not taught in Scottish schools and hence is intentionally removed from the Scottish people for socio-political control purposes. The prevailing and long-established language 'shift' policy (i.e. prioritising and elevating the English language whilst denigrating the 'Scots' language) is intended to diminish the notion of or desire among the Scots to hold to an implied 'subordinate' Scottish identity as far as possible, and hence to instill and promote a greater sense of belonging to a supposedly 'superior' British identity and thus ensure Scots accept and adhere to British 'exceptionalism'.

Language and Self-Determination

Historically, the rise of the nation-state in the 19th century led ethnic diversity to be perceived as a threat to the national unity of enlarged 'countries', and to evolving imperial constructs and so-called 'union's', however defined. Linguistic diversity is presented as a potential hurdle to what might be promoted as the need, at least insofar as hegemonic elites are concerned, to maintain something akin to a serene national social environment devoid of social unrest. Any recognition of cultural diversity, through such things as language rights and institutional autonomy, is often portrayed as a 'slippery slope' that leads to the detachment of minority group members within the 'country' or 'union', ultimately leading to calls for secession.

Although groups can be differentiated by different types of social markers, one factor always stands out, and that is language. Not only are most enlarged 'countries' multilingual, the overwhelming bulk of groups in conflict are separated along linguistic lines. Scotland is no different in this respect, being part of a multinational and multilingual state, the UK. Independence and hence the 'separation' of Scotland and England would therefore provide an opportunity to reverse the longstanding oppressive language-based 'colonial' regime by freeing and hence elevating the Scots language whilst reducing (or replacing) an Anglophone hegemony and its related linguistic controls.

> *Thon SNP MSP's shuid be black-affrontit. Ye cannae hiv ony 'equal and fair society' withoot lairnin yer ain leid.*

In a similar vein, the issue of Quebec and Canada is frequently presented as a divide between a Francophone Quebec and an Anglophone Rest of Canada (RoC), two groups with differing social, political and indeed cultural interests and identities. Although the share of Francophones in Quebec has slowly been declining, it nevertheless was a mother tongue of 79.1 per cent of people and spoken at home by 87.1 per cent. In terms of English in Quebec, it was the mother tongue of 8.9 per cent of Quebecers and 19.2 per cent spoke it at home. Scotland seems rather different with, according to the census, just 1.6m Scots speakers (28 per cent) and hence some 4.0m Anglophone speakers (72 per cent). That the divide in Scotland is also language based seems well reflected in the fact that some 1.6m Scots voted 'Yes' to independence in 2014.

Francophone Quebecers' attitudes towards Canada have multifaceted origins, however, the main determining force remains language. Although the 'Quiet Revolution' led Quebec towards a so-called 'institutional completeness' permitting social interactions to take place in French, non-Francophones must nevertheless be attracted towards joining the Francophone community in order to cement its dominant social status. This is not the case in Scotland where the dominant elite social status is largely maintained by the Anglophone community, not by Scots speakers.

In Quebec, English institutions and services are protected by the Canadian constitution and supported by the federal government. Moreover, a large portion of Anglophone immigrants and their children continue to integrate into Quebec's Anglophone community rather than its Francophone counterpart. Some evidence of this lack of cultural and linguistic integration is apparent in Scotland too, where Anglophone communities have formed in specific areas of the country, such as certain rural regions, on islands, as well as in areas within towns and cities.

The linguistic tensions between Francophones in Quebec and Anglophone RoC have clearly influenced national attachment. This dynamic particularly plays out in the debate surrounding secession, which has defined the political context in the province since the 1960s. Studies have repeatedly demonstrated a strong relationship between Quebecers' perception of French language in Quebec and their support for secession. In this respect there appear to be several similarities between Quebec and Scotland in terms of voter perceptions, for example:

• Being a Francophone, compared with an Anglophone, has a significant, at $p < 0.05$, and negative influence on feelings towards Canada. This finding appears to reflect a similar divide between Scots speakers and Anglophones regarding the UK.

• Women in Quebec are shown to have statistically more positive feelings towards Canada than men, as in Scotland where more men than women support independence.

• Age has a negative statistical effect on support for independence. Older Quebecers support secession less. There is a similar outcome in Scotland.

• Social ideology displays a negative and significant, at $p < 0.05$, influence on support for secession. The more socially conservative a Quebecer is, the less they support Quebec's independence. This also corresponds with what occurs in Scotland with those on the Anglophone Conservative right and higher income middle-class professionals generally supporting the 'union', i.e. British control.

Identification with Quebec, unsurprisingly, shows a positive and significant, at $p < 0.01$, relationship with support for secession. In a province in which language has historically played an important role—and continues to do so—on socio-political relations with Canada, it is notable that it is not who Quebecers are linguistically but rather the beliefs that they hold regarding their language that more accurately determines their attachment to Canada. Similarly, in Scotland, those who least value the Scots language, such as Anglophones and Scots suffering from higher levels of the 'Cultural Cringe' remain least supportive of secession/independence.
Findings from the Quebec research therefore reflects identity

as very much 'ethnic' driven rather than 'civic' (Henderson 2007). This suggests the 'civic nationalism' rhetoric of Scotland's political leaders does not adequately explain identity in the sense of belonging; identity in the context of independence relies predominantly upon ethnic 'markers'. Rather, it is socialization and resultant shared understanding which determines national identity based on ethnicity, in which culture and language play a crucial role.

More generally, the fate of languages is an incontestably important factor in any socio-political debates undertaken within multilingual countries. Linguistic issues have for several centuries shaped the socio-political landscape globally. However, the importance of linguistic factors in terms of socio-political control of countries has not received the required empirical nor political attention in Scotland. Exploring the influence of perceived linguistic threat on national attachment is clearly an area requiring more research in Scotland.

Enculturation, or the imposing of an elite class (and hence also the culture and language of that elite class) on a people is essentially what an Anglophone unionist elite have done and continue to do in Scotland. Unlike Quebec, where the elite is predominantly Francophone, Scotland's elite class is predominantly Anglophone. If Scotland were more like Quebec this would mean that Scotland's elite class would be predominantly Scots speakers, not Anglophone. This distinction is important because it suggests that Scotland, being controlled mostly by an Anglophone elite, is more akin to a colony (than Quebec) in that the indigenous language community in Scotland are invited to fill few elite positions, which is dominated by Anglophones and with many of the latter recruited as a matter of course from outwith Scotland.

Whit aboot ma human richt tae hae ma ain leid? Whaur is oor Scots Langage Act? Efter aw, langage is the basis o cultur. Nae langage, nae cultur, nor juist a gey thrawn an bauchelt ane. Mebbe we shuid aw bi ca'd Anglo-Scots an bi duin wi it?

We might refer here even to relatively recent times when British educationalists did not even consider Scots to be a 'valid' language and the clear implication this must have for the Scots speaking community, who must likewise be deemed not to be 'valid', especially when it comes to filling high level positions in institutions. The different reality in Scotland is also due to the ongoing refusal of the state to educate Scottish children in the Scots language, their mother tongue; in Quebec the French language is compulsory as is English in a dual language or multilingual state. The Charter of the French Language (*Charte de la langue française* in French) is a Quebec law that also makes French the usual language of business in Quebec. Recruitment in RoC for jobs in Quebec, especially professional and public positions, require applicants to have a knowledge of the French language.

There is no such Scots language requirement for Scottish managerial and professional positions which as a matter of course are mainly advertised in the London press; applicants for these posts need have no knowledge or understanding of the Scots language, and indeed applicants only speaking Scots may be considered to be at a disadvantage. In other words, in practice an Anglophone elite considers Scots not to be a 'valid' language, and hence not worth learning or needing to be learnt, and so not worth bothering about in the slightest, for posts in Scotland.

Here Scots perhaps need reminded of Edwin Muir's claim that a Scot couldn't pen poetry of real stature in English because we *feel* in Scots but *think* in English. For the poet, Scots words vastly alter the possibilities for expression. What Scots need do is *feel* and *think* in Scots to be true to themselves. And the only way for Scots to feel and think in Scots is by first learning to read and write in Scots, which is something they are prevented from doing in an Anglophone linguistic dominated society.

Language is further impacted by significant movement of people to a country, and in the case of Scotland this is primarily English speakers (mostly from England but also from various other countries) when taking posts in or retiring and moving to Scotland. Hence an Anglophone elite dominates Scotland's social institutions, with no perceived need to understand, far less any inclination to learn Scots; there is simply no statutory requirement for anyone coming to work (or live) in Scotland to be able to speak and understand the indigenous language as is a standard requirement in other countries, and in Quebec. Only an understanding of English is deemed a necessary qualification for top posts in Scotland unless, that is, one applies for a position in Bòrd na Gàidhlig, the principal public body in Scotland responsible for promoting Gaelic development, where, interestingly, the ability to speak Gaelic is considered essential[29]. Many Scots language speakers may still have problems being understood by, or being able to understand an English speaker, but such issues are ignored, reflecting the colonial balance of power in favour of the replacement language, and the disregard for the indigenous Scots speaker.

It therefore seems clear that Language, as the basis of culture and identity, will inevitably have a major influence in any Yes/No decision on Scottish independence. Cambridge Analytica, who focus on psychographics to influence voter behaviours, suggest that people vote on their emotions and in that regard culture, heritage, language and hence identity have a very large part to play. Yet, despite such rather obvious linguistic influences, in Scotland few if any political commentators or analysts ever mention language as being of importance, or even as being an issue in the debate on independence. It therefore appears that the political classes, and especially those on the pro-independence side, really need to better understand the extensive scientific evidence on this matter.

Linguistic similarities are clearly associated with positive emotions that tend to draw people closer to those who speak the same way. As Scotland's elite is dominated primarily by Anglophone speakers this implies that many Scots speakers will naturally be excluded from Scotland's elite groups. Bourdieu's theory of 'enculturation' explains this phenomenon, and particularly where the class of an elite is imposed on a people emphasizing linguistic differentiation and bias. Language is therefore a 'public phenomenon' but it is also a powerful socio-political tool, and perhaps the most powerful tool (aside from e.g. military occupation) for successful domination over another people.

Given the significance of language, the question as to why the political leaders of the pro-independence side of the debate, not least the SNP Scottish Government, have thus far ignored the Scots language as an obvious dividing line between pro and anti-independence voters remains unclear. Tragically, the lack of educational provision of the Scots language means the ability of virtually all Scots to read and write in their own mother tongue remains woefully inadequate and, for the most part, non-existent. This remains something of a cultural catastrophe as well as a violation of human rights.

Perhaps most curiously of all, the SNP Scottish Government, which has been 'in power' since 2007, has demonstrated so little interest in bringing forward any 'Scots Language Bill'. This lack of political will or action on Scots language policy is considered to be because the SNP fears any Anglophone MSM backlash and media onslaught that might ensue with the inevitable shouts of 'parochialism', and the 'barefaced cheek', should any Scot dare to suggest that Scottish people might actually learn their own language! This would almost be funny if it were not quite so tragic, given that language is clearly a key driver for national self-determination.

Language Policy

Considering the political reality, and the colonial-like Anglophone unionist control over its key institutions, Scotland may understandably need to be independent before Scots ever see any sign of a Scots Language Act, despite the fact a Bill could be voted through Holyrood now, much in the way the Gaelic Language Act was passed more than a decade ago. Indeed, such an Act will be necessary in order to respect the human right of Scots to learn their own language. The Scottish people meanwhile remain in the rather ridiculous position where an allegedly 'nationalist' Scottish Government is infringing the human rights of all Scots by refusing their own people the opportunity to learn their own language.

Scots langage is raither mair nor jist Englis wirds.

The Scottish working class are basically all that is left of 'Auld Scotia' in linguistic terms. They are the heart and soul of Scottishness, Scottish culture and the Scots language. They also comprise the great bulk of the pro-independence vote and thus tend to have fewer uncertainties about their identity than many bourgeois Scots. Further up the elite class ladder one proceeds, the more Anglophone any discourse tends to become. Jimmy Reid's 'alienation' of the working class comes to mind, with language differences and ongoing language discrimination a key determinant of an individual's expected social and economic progress in what remains an Anglophone-dominated Scotland. In other words, Scots speakers are aye 'doun-hauden' in Scotland.

Are the SNP leadership really that worried about what the British Anglophone MSM might say if the Scots language were taught in Scottish schools to Scottish children? Or is the blockage here perhaps from within Whitehall's Anglophone unionist civil servants who are still 'managing' Scottish Government departments on behalf of the Scots, and who will no doubt be arguing: '*Scots langage - naw Meenister, ye cannae dae thon*'?

Given that Language forms the basis of culture and identity, this implies that the Scottish 'Cultural Cringe' may be directly linked to the absence of any formal teaching of the Scots language. Culture (and language) determines how we view the world, especially when it comes to critical matters such as national identity. Scots might well remain surprised, shocked even, that the SNP has yet to realise that the Scots language, and with that Scottish culture, are fundamental political tools of independence, yet they remain tools left sitting in the toolbox, unused and ignored. 'Philosophy' is itself the study of knowledge and yet some Scots seek to block and prevent the learning of their own language (often for pedantic reasons) which is knowledge itself and much more. According to Spiers (2019) 'Language is the expression of thought in symbolic form' and 'our descriptions of the world expressed in language are symbolic models of the world'. The Scots language therefore explains how Scots view the world and why they view it differently from those in their larger neighbouring nation and from other peoples and nations elsewhere. Language is what helps to explain why the Scottish Parliament does things differently from Westminster, reflecting Scottish culture and the Scots 'way of doing things'.

This means that we do not formally teach the Scots language at our peril. If we do not respect our own language then we do not respect our own people or their culture, never mind their human rights. For these reasons and more, Holyrood must deliver a Scots Language Act with all the resources necessary to implement it properly, much in the way this has already been done for the Gaelic speaking community through the Gaelic Language Act.

> *Sel confeedence in yer ain cultur is a maun gin Scots are tae wun full statehood. Mebbe the SNP think o oor leid in the same wey as thon monarchy – ower pernickitie.*

Current language policy in Scotland for schools involves the '1+2 language learning' approach, where the first and mandatory language taught is English and children also learn a first additional language in Primary School and then a second additional language in Secondary School[30]. The main additional language taught in Primary Schools is French (offered by 88% of schools), and there are 8 different language options offered in Secondary Schools of which Spanish is the most popular. However, none of the required additional language offerings under the 1+2 policy at Primary or Secondary involves the Scots language, the latter is intentionally excluded by Scotland's state educational institutions.

For many years, university Degree and Master's courses have been taught in English in numerous countries (e.g. Norway, Germany, Netherlands, Dubai, Singapore etc), however the indigenous languages in these countries are also taught by law to their own people. Unlike these nations, however, in Scotland many Scots are still under the impression that English is their only language and that the Scots language is not even a language but a slang speech of the gutter and of the working class, much in the way the unionist MSM publisher DC Thomson depicts Scots and the Scots language in its cartoons, 'Oor Wullie' and 'the Broons'. This is also the stereotypical way British broadcasters generally depict the Scots language in TV programmes such as 'Still Game', 'River City', and 'Rab C Nesbitt'. Meanwhile a plethora of Anglophone 'British' productions (e.g. Downton Abbey) emphasize the language of the better off elites, and educated intellectuals, with casts reflecting 'upper class' English accents.

And yet, for now at least, the working class in Scotland still speak Scots despite not being formally taught their own Scots language. The Anglophone elite class in Scotland, aided via cultural reinforcement by Anglophone social institutions such as private schools and elite universities, the MSM, and key public organisations, seek to prioritise and apply only the English language and hence they ignore and demean the Scots language. This institutionalised discrimination and bias serves to limit opportunities for socio-economic progression of Scots speakers and helps explain the attainment gap. Scots speakers are effectively 'doun-hauden' through institutionalised language discrimination and bias within Scotland.

The Scots term for 'manager' is 'heid bummer', which admittedly does not sound over complimentary and is not intended to be, reflecting the Scottish cultural tradition never to be too impressed by an individual's status, no matter at what social 'level' they may be. Hence Scots language is rather more than just English words; indeed, 'language is the expression of thought… and our description of the world… expressed in symbolic form'. Language thus reflects social knowledge. Often the meaning of Scots words and phrases will differ from English (or other) language 'equivalents' reflecting differences in culture (e.g. the causal-cultural theory of reference and meaning; see Spiers 2019). By refusing to formally teach the Scots language to Scottish children, the Scottish people are therefore deprived of this unique cultural knowledge (and language), whilst social institutions imposing a single (Anglophone) non mother tongue on Scots is no more than 'enculturation' (Bourdieu), and cultural and linguistic imperialism.

> *A wad jalouse we'd tak mony mair independence votes wi a weel thocht throu Scots leid act. Efter aw, equalitie maunna be exclusive tae issues o race an gender alane.*

The imposed language and hence prevailing and ever strengthening Anglophone culture of Scotland's elite hegemony (i.e. senior managers and professionals, or indeed 'heid bummers') ensconced throughout the Scottish public and private sectors, serves to hold back any real move towards equality in Scotland, given that prevailing institutionalised practices primarily excludes Scots speakers. Moreover, as most of Scotland's senior managerial positions are and have historically been advertised outside of Scotland in the London metropolitan press, the consequence of this is that many of Scotland's 'top managers' are not Scottish and hence many are not and will not be Scots language speakers. This further implies that a great many professionals active in and leading Scottish institutions will tend not to know very much, if anything, about Scottish culture or language. And, with the balance of Scotland's elite tending to be 'Anglo Scots', whose depth of understanding and use of Scots language is likewise often limited, for example due to private schooling, family influence, privileged backgrounds etc, in line with the findings of the 'Elitist Scotland' Report (The Social Mobility and Child Poverty Commission 2015), this serves to create an extensive Anglophone elite running and controlling most of Scotland's social institutions.

Throughout the wide range of professional contexts across education, health, government, business and more there is not only often a language mismatch, but also a cultural and identity mismatch. Essentially, those who make most of the decisions on behalf of Scots do so from an Anglophone-hegemonic elite, linguistic and cultural perspective, which by its nature is also British (or English) and hence unionist, and which tends to be, for the most part, devoid of and distant from Scots language and culture. There remains in this comprehensive 'enculturation' process, therefore, a general ignorance on the part of an Anglophone meritocratic elite about their host people, i.e. the Scots, or of their language, culture and indeed often their nation too.

Fowk wad bi content if juist the ane Scots langage wis taucht in oor scuils and uni's (wi a regional 'gust' aye), raither than nane at aw. Thon wad be movin forder fi whit wi hae the noo – i.e. naething?

The 'enculturation' process that many Scots are forced to endure in Scotland reflects the dominant cultural capital of elites, which differs markedly from the working class; this differentiation is primarily linguistic and therefore cultural, which also reflects a different identity and sense of belonging. In this the Scots working class have a culture and language and identity imposed on them by elites which is not their own (it is British and Anglophone) and which makes them feel inadequate. A direct consequence of this is the 'Scottish Cultural Cringe' which is a language based psychological impediment suffered by Scots (speakers) resulting in a lowering of confidence and self-esteem. Culture necessarily creates and maintains power structures and social boundaries which are based around language.

Language reform is therefore vital to ensure equality for Scots, many of whom will never find equality (or 'attainment') in a society dominated by Anglophone cultural capital and the bias of Scotland's elite class which is institutionally imposed on them, and by an ever-increasing Anglophone elite, many recruited from outside Scotland, and who remain ignorant of Scottish culture and language. Scotland is therefore similar to Quebec in the sense that culture and language is the main differentiator when it comes to the question of identity and independence. However, unlike Quebec which has a Francophone elite, the elite in Scotland are not Scots speakers, they are predominantly Anglophone and hence hold more toward a British identity, with much of Scotland's Anglophone elite drawn from rest-UK on a continuous basis supplementing the elite positions filled by Anglophone Scots. In this Anglophone elite hegemony dominated environment the Scots speaking Scot is generally consigned to a subordinate, marginalized position.

Inevitably, languages will tend to die off where state education authorities steadfastly refuse to formally teach them by law in schools and where the policy of an 'administrative Power' (e.g. over a colony) is to assimilate a people through forcing upon them a single common 'national' language, which is not their own, but the language of the 'administrative Power'. Many former British colonies, today now independent states, adopt the approach whereby they teach English as an 'administrative' language; however, the population is also given options to learn a mother tongue, e.g. in Singapore, Kenya, Dubai, India, etcetera. Singapore, with a population similar in size to Scotland, teaches English and also offers its people one of three indigenous language options, Malay, Tamil or Mandarin. A Scotland where English plus the Scots and Gaelic language were taught would therefore seem little different in this regard.

It appears to be the prevailing political view that Gaelic is a greater social cause and hence more deserving than the Scots language. According to census data there are some 1.6m Scots speakers in Scotland, yet only about 50,000 Gaelic speakers. Gaelic language has been given its own Act of Parliament, a TV station, a language degree, Primary school and Higher national qualification, a language regulatory Board and some £50m of public money every year, equivalent to about £10,000 per speaker. Conversely the Scots language has received none of these benefits or institutions nor pro-rata public spending. In comparison with Gaelic, the Scots language has received nothing of any real substance. A key question, therefore is, why is Gaelic perceived to be a much greater and deserving political cause than the Scots language?

> *Ane wee 'Scots Language Center', aw fine an guid, yet thon isnae ony substitute fer a Scots Language Act tae dae whit wis duin for Gaelic. If Gaelic haes £50m a year, hou muckle siller is oor Scots langage wuirth?*

The answer to this is most likely that Gaelic is not perceived as a political threat to the UK 'union', given the relatively small number of speakers, whereas Scots language is spoken by a great many more people. Still, if only 1.6m Scots speak Scots, this implies that the bulk of Scotland's population of 5.4m people today do not speak Scots, they speak primarily English, or perhaps many are simply not aware they speak Scots. This is not surprising given the role of the state and its refusal to formally teach the Scots language in schools.

Anglophone elites in Scotland continue to claim that 'a problem' with teaching the Scots language relates to the range of Scots dialects in Scotland, as if this were some sort of unique debilitating feature. This is simply a red herring as a standard Scots language exists despite regional differences in dialects. Ulster Scots as the name suggests is a dialect of the Scots language, as is Doric Scots, or Shetland Scots, or Orkney Scots, or Lowland Scots, or Glaswegian Scots, or Ayrshire Scots or Dundee Scots. But they are all part of the Scots language. The same regional variations in dialects is a common feature in many if not most languages, not least in England where there are geographically distinguishable linguistic differences in English language evident between, for instance, Northumberland, Merseyside, London, Devon, Cornwall and so on.

Fundamentally, though, the English language is not the Scots language, and both are quite different languages, reflecting unique identities and cultures. The key aspect here is that each language should be respected and treated equally, but in Scotland it is the Scots language that has been singled out for official state omission and exclusion. The Scots speaker therefore remains oppressed ('doun-hauden') and marginalised, by the British Anglophone 'one-nation' unionist elites both within and outside Scotland. For the Anglophone elites, enculturation and the linguistic assimilation of Scots is the overriding aim. However, those Scots who will not or cannot become Anglophone linguistically will suffer the inevitable consequences, which involves ongoing social, economic, and psychological discrimination and more (e.g. the attainment gap).

Ance yer intae 'Scots' its nae sae pernicketie tae lairn efter aw, an awfu eithly duin, mair espeicially if ye a'ready hiv yer mither tung in yer heid tae stairt wi!

The blocking of formal learning of the Scots language will therefore continue to generate entirely negative impacts for many Scots speakers. Even Scottish Government quotations and policy 'mutterings' on its website that are ostensibly made in the Scots language are often incorrect, reflecting that the language is not officially taught in Scottish schools or universities and therefore Scots language skills remain poor and undeveloped. Official formal Scots language teaching does not exist in Scotland's schools, which is rather convenient for Anglophone professional elites who consider that they do not then need to learn Scots when living and working in Scotland or running Scotland's institutions, and there is no compulsion for them to do so. Yet it remains that English is not the natural language of the Scots, with its strangulated vowels out of Edwardian country houses. Any natural Scots speaker trying to talk 'posh' English always sounds contorted and artificial, and probably always will. This is primarily because English is not the natural language of the Scots, it is a foreign language and reflects a foreign culture and identity. English language and culture has and continues to be imposed on the Scots, primarily to diminish the notion of Scottish identity, which is the purpose of cultural and linguistic imperialism.

Scots are clearly not alone in suffering oppression through enculturation and cultural and linguistic imperialism. The recentralisation campaign by the Spanish government is also aimed at education in Catalonia to 'españolizar a los niños Catalanes' (Hispanicising Catalan children) as the PP ex-minister Wert once reputedly advocated in the Spanish parliament[31]. Similarly, Britain has the Anglophoning of the Scots which seems little different in purpose. Language policy is a powerful political tool when it comes to perceptions and emotions surrounding national identity and imperial powers recognise this only too well.

Scots Language Initiatives

While a handful of Scots language initiatives, such as at Aberdeen University[32] are welcome, Scotland requires an authoritative Scots Language policy for all Scotland, and this needs to be delivered via a statutory regulatory process, as it is for the Gaelic and English languages. Some limited progress on the Scots language has been evident in recent years. There are now 'Scots Language Co-ordinators' in some schools, and a Scots 'Scriever' based at the National Library of Scotland. But these are relatively minor interventions. They will make no real difference to the Anglophone elite's linguistic domination over the Scots and Scotland or the subordination and marginalisation of Scots speakers.

There have been previous, though often sporadic, efforts to educate Scots in their own Scots language. According to Caroline Macafee (Aitken 1976, 2015), "...*the 1970s was probably the nadir of education in Scots, so to some extent subsequent developments have been the recovery of lost ground*". Earlier generations of teachers had participated in a middle-class culture that included Scots song and recitation as part of home-made entertainment and local amateur performance. They needed no special training to use Scots language materials like the series of three graded readers published by the firm Oliver and Boyd.

A Scots Langage TV Chennel - ane whit reflecs the wey Scots fowk spik, an tae educate Scots in thair ain mither tung, an nae tae garr anely Englis doon oor thrapples aw the time.

Macafee maintains that, by the 1970s the educated middle class throughout much of Scotland had become thoroughly anglicised in speech. That generation of teachers might have been gradually persuaded to respect the Scots language that rural and working-class children brought into the classroom, *"…but on the whole they did not have the cultural background themselves to add to it or deepen it"*, and this is even more the case today. The two major Scottish publishers of school textbooks, Oliver & Boyd and Thomas Nelson & Sons, had been taken over by external companies thus ending their publication and depriving Scottish schools of textbooks written from a Scottish perspective. While middle class Scottish teachers have become more Anglophone, today some one third of Scotland's teachers are from rest-UK, mainly England, and both groups therefore tend to have limited understanding or ability to teach Scots, which suggests there is very little Scots language expertise within Scotland's schools. This results in a continued cultural and linguistic mismatch between Anglophone's teaching and Scots speakers being taught, with inevitably a continuation of the 'Cultural Cringe', and a confused culture and identity for much of the populace, and with institutionalised linguistic barriers to attainment and socio-economic development.

> *Whit's 'Scottishness' onywey, theday, noo, an whaur's it gaein? Maist Scots fowk are ower faur culturally Anglophone, an maist Scots fowk canna e'en read nor screed in Scots langage, an oor heid bummers refuise tae e'en lairn oor bairns the Scots langage, an oor elites maistly dinnae e'en spik Scots thairsels. Scots 'cultur' is gey tak doun an hauden doon due tae thon lack o a Scots Language Act.*

A new Scottish digital TV channel introduced in 2019 presented an opportunity to do something positive for the Scots language. However, rather than speak to media vested interests about the new Scottish digital channel, the regulator Ofcom should have spoken to Scottish viewers. In Scotland there are a plethora of English language channels (BBC, ITV, CH4 etc), and a Gaelic language channel (Alba), but what is really needed for fairness and equality and respect for human rights is a Scots Language Channel. That opportunity, preferably linked to a Scots language Act (as with Gaelic), was ignored.

Clearly, the Gaelic Language Act was deemed politically

acceptable, affecting as it does only a limited speaking community in Scotland and pushed by a strong well connected and perhaps largely pro-unionist Gaelic professional lobby. A Scots Language Act focusing on millions of Scots was evidently not considered politically acceptable by Scotland's unionist Anglophone institutions within what is effectively an Anglophone-elite controlled socio-political straitjacket amid an independence-oriented environment. Any MSP promoting a Scots Language Act might also expect to be heavily criticised by the British Anglophone MSM whilst the mainly unionist and Anglophone establishment, civil service and education agencies would also seek to oppose and stymie such a policy, much as they do already and have done for many years. To the British Anglophone elite, Scots remains an 'inferior' language. So, primarily politics plus ethnic discrimination are probably the main reasons Scotland has yet to see a Scots Language Act. At the end of the day Scots language remains 'doun-hauden'. Any Language Minister at Holyrood should be black affrontit, more especially if they are a 'nationalist'.

> *Thon Gaels, thay hiv thay're Gaelic Language (Scotland) Act 2005, an £50 million public money a year, Gaelic school teachers, Gaelic Language Degrees, Gaelic TV, and thay're pullin the ledder up ahint thaim anaw. So, whits Scottishness? Aye, thon's a guid quaisten.*

Despite these challenges, are the SNP 'nationalist' Scottish Government not missing a trick here? If the Yes/No vote choice on independence is primarily dependent on one's dominant culture and identity in which language plays a major part, why has the SNP not developed a Scots language policy and passed such an Act? The anti-independence 'No' vote is arguably much influenced by propaganda and it is the language of propaganda here that is also important, with the BBC and British MSM more widely reinforcing and embedding what is a constant Anglophone, elite, unionist, and anti-independence narrative. When Labour and the LibDems joined with the

Tories in the anti-independence 'Better Together' campaign group, they were merely coalescing behind a dominant British nationalist ('one nation') Anglophone culture and identity in which any assertion of Scottish nationhood and citizenship, Scottish self-government, Scottish culture and Scots language, or Scottish identity is perceived as a threat to the British Anglophone cultural hegemony.

Some may say, why push the Scots language when 'they' speak it every day in Scotland one way or another? Yet the need is paramount, with only around a third of Scots speaking 'Scots' and few of them have ever been taught how to read or write in Scots. Language is the basis of culture and identity and influences the way a people think and act. If Scots do away with their own language, they do away with the only things that really differentiates them – their culture, language and with that their identity (and their nation) will follow.

It is perfectly possible to learn Scottish children their own mother tongue as well as 'administrative' English, indeed most former British colonies and EU states already emphasize multilingual policy as a matter of course. Teaching Scottish children their own mother tongue would also rid Scots of the 'Cultural Cringe', which would be of immeasurable benefit to the confidence and development of Scots and to Scotland.

The more that Scots talk 'Scottish', the more that Scots will also become and feel Scottish in terms of identity, and the more likely they will be to vote Scottish (i.e. independence); this is ultimately why the British state intentionally deprives Scots of their Scots language, and why it also deprived many other indigenous peoples of their languages in other colonies. English (Anglophone) cultural assimilation policy was standard practice in all colonies. Should Scots really be surprised that many people in Scotland have yet to 'twig' to the linguistic reality of colonial history, not least the SNP hierarchy who are supposed to have an interest in Scottish culture and heritage, and language, and identity, and even perhaps in independence?

E'en a bawheid like me coud unnerstaund Scots wuirds nae bather. Scots isna ower pernicketie an mony Scots fowk a'ready speik it onywey.

Language and Independence

Scots urgently need to develop a more concrete understanding of the significance of the Scots language to the Scottish independence cause and to recognise the critical importance of language for Scottish culture and national identity, as well as respecting the human right aspects of language. Scots also need to appreciate the role and impact of Anglophone cultural and linguistic imperialism and the resulting social, economic and political domination and inequalities that persist because of such oppression.

The main challenge (or rather tragedy, amidst ongoing cultural and colonial discrimination) for the Scots language is the continued linguistic illiteracy of the Scottish people who can neither read nor write in the mother tongue many still speak. There are numerous Scots dictionaries and texts on Scots grammar and usage, but so long as these are not given to Scots and taught to Scots children in schools, or read and listened to by the population more generally, then Scotland's linguistic illiteracy and cultural void will continue, with negative impacts for national identity and hence for independence.

What price Scotland's nationhood? The Scots Language itself is arguably a major part of that price. If the mass of Scots were to discover that they had their own distinct national language, which has been wilfully kept from them, leading to their exclusion from socio-economic progress, prevented from the running of most of their own social institutions, and depriving them of access to economic and intellectual opportunity, they would surely strive even more to reclaim their nation.

For those still unconvinced about the essential language, culture and identity 'tie in' and the critical connections between them, international evidence abounds. There are a great many theoretical works on the culture-language relationship[33]; there are numerous publications and books on the subject[34], and; there are even degree level courses and qualifications on the topic[35]. Culture, of course, is inevitably a great deal more than the written word. Nevertheless, Scottish culture or any culture for that matter will be greatly diminished when a text is presented in another language, albeit certain distinct cultural aspects may still be discernible. By disregarding the Scots language, in films, plays, poetry, politics and all else aside, there can really be no authentic Scottish culture. Scotland's Culture Minister is arguably wasting her time on promoting Scottish culture without first bringing forward a 'Scots Language (Scotland) Act', language being the basis of culture. Currently Scots are losing their (Scots) language, and when the mother tongue is finally lost there will be no Scottish culture, or rather nothing but kitsch, with whatever remains of Scottish identity finally withering away. A nation dependent on little more than kitsch is clearly not worth its nationhood, which is where Scotland seems to be heading at the present time. All Scotland has for now is a dominant overbearing (imposed) British Anglophone unionist culture masquerading as a sort of pseudo-authentic Anglo-Scots culture, overseen by an institutionalised Anglophone elite most of whom know little or nothing about the Scots language, culture or identity, and care even less.

Scotland remains a nation and people subjected to the long-term negative effects of cultural and linguistic imperialism and therefore desperately in need of a Scots Language (Scotland) Act to kickstart an authentic and differentiated Scottish cultural and linguistic renaissance. A Scots language policy is vital to remove the Scottish Cultural Cringe for good, which is at root a linguistically determined psychological impediment, and to instil in the Scottish people a renewed confidence and pride in who they are, and their place in the world, also providing a remedy to the ongoing attainment gap. **Language is a fundamental determinant of identity** and this aspect, which has been largely ignored in Scottish political discourse, is crucial in the context of Scottish independence. Language is also fundamental to the future development of the Scottish people and nation. Any vote split on independence is and will continue to be divided linguistically as is the case in numerous other examples where self-determination is proposed and may be prevented by an artificially imposed language divide. In Scotland, the social hierarchical and political divide is predominantly between Anglophone 'No' voters holding to a British identity, and Scots language speaking 'Yes' voters holding to a Scottish identity. This implies that **the Scottish independence battleground is in large part linguistically determined**, hence any strategy for Scottish independence needs to place the Scots language at front and centre.

CHAPTER 5: DEMOGRAPHICS

Population Flux

The mass exodus of perhaps as many as four million Scots from Scotland over the past 300 years or so since the 1707 union with England can hardly be considered an accident, nor should this be regarded in any way as a natural, far less a positive phenomenon. What remains one of the largest single non-war population movements in Europe for a country of Scotland's size, the loss of so many people inevitably reflects one of the most negative aspects of the UK union. Whether through UK industrial practice, UK government policies, or the absence of policy, the fact remains that a very substantial number of Scotland's people saw no alternative but to leave Scotland's shores for good. In just fifty years between 1861 and 1911 a minimum of 1.23 million people resident in Scotland emigrated in this way (Anderson 2015)[36]. They were followed by almost 800,000 more by 1930, resulting in a loss of over two million people in barely seventy years, equivalent to almost half Scotland's 1901 population of 4.4 million.

These vast outflows of Scots coincided with a constant and significant inflow into Scotland of a substantial, and mainly professional and managerial class, primarily from England, who were brought in to administer and manage Scotland's social institutions and commerce. Historic census data suggests these inflows to be an ongoing process, with by far the largest ethnic migrant group into Scotland over the last 150 years or so comprising people from England. The constant outflow of Scots seems to have run its course, particularly since the 1990's after de-industrialisation in the 1980's and then creation of the devolved Scottish Parliament, the latter perhaps giving Scots more hope for the future. Nevertheless, the mass exodus of mostly working-class Scots (and hence Scots speakers) coupled with the long established and continuing 'plantation' of an English (Anglophone) meritocracy in Scotland appears to represent the defining features of Scotland's population make up over the past two centuries.

It might reasonably be concluded from this recorded population 'exchange', with the Scots working class cast out to the empire's colonies in their droves, and mainly English 'professionals' settling in Scotland, that relatively few Scots were deemed worthy of taking higher level professional and managerial positions within Scotland. This colonial form of ethnic division of labour persists even today with measurable effects on social and political dynamics within Scotland. Such outcomes are not uncommon: *"Ethnic divisions of labour in many countries are among the most persistent legacies of European colonialism"* [37]. Ethnic divisions of labour involve offering privileged higher status positions to some groups of workers, in this case Anglophone, while assigning the most onerous and lower status tasks to others, i.e. Scots speakers. The latter were also motivated to leave the country entirely due to lack of economic opportunity and through incentives offered by the state.

Despite the drastic levels of population outflow from Scotland, it has seldom been considered that, over much of the same period, there has occurred a significant inflow into Scotland of in excess of two million people, mostly from England. This is in addition to some Irish manual labour, the latter notably occurring in the later 19th century. The population inflows from England are distinctive because they feature a consistently sustained focus on those working in the professions, and which extends to the present day[38]. In other words, since the union, Scotland has imported much if not most of its managerial and professional class from England, whilst at the same time millions of mostly working class Scots left the country due to the chronic lack of socio-economic opportunities, or social infrastructure in Scotland. Scotland's division of labour and population change is thus ethnically oriented.

> *Anither mebbe mair accurat wey tae conseeder thon 'creenge' wad bi 'internalized racism' and/or 'appropriated racial oppression'. Wad ye nae gree?*

In addition to this historic population 'exchange', in recent times there has been a further unprecedented population shift over the period between 1990 and 2020. Prior to this Scotland suffered almost continuously from negative net migration of 20,000 or more per annum. Even as recently as the 1960's Scotland was still losing significant population, to England and worldwide, the former due in part to the historic lower annual unemployment rate in England, which averaged about 2%. This was consistently less than half the unemployment rate in Scotland, and with wages in Scotland also tending to be lower than those in England (Anderson 2015).

According to Anderson (2015: p. 86), historically *"Scotland's net emigration rate, controlling for the size of the population, was never less than two and a half times that of England"*. In the 1880's and during the first decade of the twentieth century, Scottish net migration loss exceeded 5.5 per cent of the population in each decade, and it remained high right up to World War One. Indeed, Scotland's net emigration flows have not just been above those of England and Wales; taking the whole period from the 1850s to 2001, and excepting only Ireland, they were markedly above those of any other country in north-western Europe. **Over the past 150 years Scotland has proportionately 'lost' more of its people than any other north-western European country.**

Scotland's dramatic population loss is therefore one of the key features, if not a direct consequence, of Scotland remaining part of the UK union. Therefore, the root cause of this abnormally high population loss, it may reasonably be hypothesised, was due to the absence of self-government in Scotland, and the lack of national policies promoting the socio-economic development of Scotland and its people. Indeed, any UK union 'policies' pertaining to Scotland's people over the period merely appear to have promoted and facilitated their emigration and hence were aimed at effectively clearing Scotland of as many Scots as possible, and meantime to partially replace them through the immigration of a meritocratic class from rest-UK, mainly England. There seems little doubt here that Scotland's population was being 'managed' (or rather, ethnically re-arranged) by the British state, though hardly in the interests of Scotland or its people.

Up to 1900 most Scots emigrating were young and single, aged between 20-30 years. This altered between 1900 and the 1960's when entire families including young children were emigrating from Scotland. This was in marked contrast with England where, by comparison, there was very little family emigration and England was subject itself to rising immigration from the new Commonwealth countries, a feature virtually unknown in Scotland. It is clear from this that Scottish emigration therefore has a totally different history from that of England, or any other country in north-western Europe for that matter, with the possible exception of Ireland.

Aside from ethnic discrimination, if not ethnic cleansing of Scots from Scotland, few if any other explanations adequately answer the question as to why Scotland's levels of emigration (or mass expulsion) should be so much higher than England's or other comparable nations in north-western Europe. The mass expulsion or managed removal (of Scots) argument coupled with significant ongoing meritocratic Anglophone 'plantation' clearly reflects cultural (and linguistic) imperialist policies aimed at creating a more ethnically homogenous (i.e. 'British) population in Scotland. The dramatic scale of Scottish population change and the quite different demographic policies and 'treatment' afforded to England suggest this was no accident.

During the same time period when millions of Scots were

literally forced, due in part to high unemployment, low wages, and resulting poverty, to look for economic salvation globally, there were numerous instances of labour displacement occurring, with skilled workers from England coming to take positions in Scotland. Watson (2002: p. 38-39) highlights areas such as mining and engineering where, in 1911, one quarter of men employed in Scotland were born in England or Wales. Already by the 19th century there were many times more English-born residents in Edinburgh than Irish-born. By 1921 there were almost 30,000 English-born residents in Edinburgh, mostly professionals drawn there by industry, the latter increasingly English-owned due to the frequent takeover of Scottish firms, also in schools and academia, healthcare, and filling government and civil service positions. Census data confirms that Scotland was (and is still today) recruiting significant numbers of its meritocracy primarily from England. Yet, at the same time, mass unemployment in Scotland was endemic. In the 1920-1939 period, unemployment in Scotland was never less than 14 per cent, and between 1929-1932 it was nearly 30 per cent. The numbers claiming poor relief mushroomed to 40 per cent in some areas of Glasgow. Wage disparities between England and Scotland continued, with Scots earning 87 per cent of the average British wage in 1931-1933, and Scots were still lagging behind English wage levels in 1950. The cost of living also tended to be higher in Scotland whilst wealth inequalities continued and Scotland remained worse off than the UK as a whole (Knox, undated). Even during the supposed 'economic boom' of the 1960's Scotland, with 10 per cent of the UK population had 25 per cent of the long-term unemployed and consequently far greater poverty levels.

> *Scots hiv thair ain leid doun-hauden, in thon gitter. Whaur are oor human richts respectit? Naewhaur!*

In terms of recent trends in immigration to Scotland,

according to the 2011 census almost exactly one person in six resident in Scotland had not been born there (Anderson 2015); this figure is probably closer to one in four or five in 2020 given a further decade of positive net in-migration since then which has also served to boost Scotland's population to its highest level ever, some 5.4 million. By far the largest group of migrants living in Scotland, according to the 2011 census, was the near 500,000 people born in England and Wales which, again based on recent trends, will likely exceed 750,000 in 2020. If we include in this an estimate for those of English and Welsh extraction this figure could double to around 1.5 million people (Knox undated: p. 5), or around 27 per cent of the population.

Such significant ongoing demographic change continues to markedly alter the composition (and identity) of Scotland's population, with total inflows from south of the border possibly exceeding a further one million people over the last 20 years alone. A sectoral analysis briefly illustrates the impact of these significant changes. In 2018, for example, almost 70 per cent of secondary teachers in the Borders region of Scotland were English, 60 per cent in Dumfries & Galloway, and up to 50 per cent in several other Scottish counties, whilst a third of teachers across all of Scotland were from England[39]. Thus, in a number of professions in certain regions of Scotland, Scots professionals are in a minority.

Given increasing numbers of people living in Scotland who do not hold a strong cultural affinity to Scotland nor any linguistically determined Scottish identity, it is not therefore so surprising that two million 'Scottish' residents voted against independence and hence voted against changing their national identity to 'Scottish' in 2014. And the prevailing demographic trend, with rising population inflows mostly from England into Scotland, does not appear to auger well for any future independence referendum. It could reasonably be argued that such ongoing and fundamental demographic changes involving a continuous boosting of the Anglophone population in Scotland, and with that a shifting cultural and linguistic orientation where fewer people have or hold to a Scottish identity, that this will inevitably serve to limit the prospect for Scottish independence in future. This means that **ongoing demographic change is a significant determinant of Scottish independence**.

Population Displacement

Scotland's 'Clearances' may be seen to reflect a wider mindset – a global imperial mindset – which also led to the Irish Famine, the Great Famine in India, and numerous other atrocities meted out by the British State between 1750 and 1900. All those atrocities indicate an imperialist thinking that, it has been argued, was genocidally predisposed in outlook. The virtual extirpation of both Scots and Irish Gaelic society, culture and language arguably qualifies as genocide. Genocide is the intentional action taken to destroy a people (usually defined as an ethnic, national, racial, or religious group) in whole or in part. British efforts to decimate the Scottish population and their culture and languages seem well reflected in Scotland's recorded population movements.

Oppressive and discriminatory actions taken towards the mass of the Scottish people more generally tend to be viewed rather less critically, it at all, though in practice this has clearly not ended, merely moving along in another period of a seemingly endless process. Post 1707, and post 1746, it started off as overt racist discrimination and oppressive practices and has over the years merely become more covert, more subtle, gradual and less noticeable, less openly acknowledged, or even discernible to most; but it is still happening, as Scotland's ongoing demographic change and other perhaps less obvious examples of discrimination indicates.

Genocide has a well-defined meaning[40] and it is entirely possible to commit a genocide without killing anyone. In the Scottish Highlands, landowners and the State actively pursued policies to destroy the culture and remove the people through the Clearances. This was achieved by the suppression of language, dress, teaching, removal of population, substitution of population, marginalisation onto poorer lands and even direct violence. The British Resettlement Act of 1851 made emigration freely 'available' to even the poorest in Scotland; under this 'incentive' to emigrate scheme a landlord could arrange passage for 'a nominee' to Australia for just £1. In Nova Scotia in the first half of the 19th century almost two-thirds of UK settlers were Scots. There is a fairly strong case that the Clearances was genocide; arguably burning people out of their homes is the same as preventing people from having homes in the first place and forcing them to move. However, the removal of Scotland's people was not solely limited to the Highlands and islands. What matters here is the intent and relative 'success' of the intent of key decision makers who were Anglophone landowners, industrialists, bureaucrats and the British state itself. It is these governing elites who forced millions of Scots away from their homeland as refugees from socio-economic discrimination, colonial and cultural oppression, poverty, and partially supplanting them with an Anglophone meritocracy.

Devine (2012) has argued, somewhat to the contrary, that the Scots 'benefitted' from British colonial policies. His thesis maintains that 'Scots' were not only 'full partners' in this grand design but were at the very cutting edge of British global expansion. Devine takes a somewhat rose-tinted and perhaps simplistic view here as he seems to lump all classes of people together as if 'the Scots' were somehow homogenous, although he does note that the Anglicisation of Scottish aristocrats actually began prior to the 1707 union and has continued more or less ever since. However, here we are talking about a deeply class ridden society over most of the period in question, firm remnants of which persist even today and continue to exploit Scotland and discriminate against many of Scotland's people. The reality is that a relatively small and increasingly Anglophone elite in Scotland became very wealthy out of the empire's exploitation of cheap and slave labour and the general theft of resources in the many lands they (i.e. the elite) stole from, including Scotland, and Ireland. The millions of Scots who left Scotland, however, were for the most part relatively poor and working class, invariably indentured, leaving an impoverished socio-economic wasteland made bereft (by its Anglophone rulers) of opportunity, decent food, or adequate housing, a situation created thus by Britain's elites who 'owned' virtually all the land and who also formed the British governments which controlled whatever institutions, if any, that were 'overseeing' Scotland. Rather than being 'beneficiaries' of British colonial policies, most Scots were and remain victims of such policies. Death rates, particularly from fever, were notably higher in Scotland than in England, much of which was explained by greater levels of poverty (Knox undated; p. 5). Infant mortality was higher in Scotland than England, due to poverty and poor housing, with a far higher incidence of child mortality for those living in single apartment houses compared with larger houses. The 1861 census found that two-thirds of Scotland's houses contained either just one or two rooms, with large cities worst off. Rents were higher than people could afford and public sector housing non-existent, with town councils run by land and property owners in their own interest. Post the 1707 union, Scotland's elites more reflected rapacious, materialistic, Anglophone priorities, emphasizing private ownership, and stressing the individual and hierarchy, than any traditional Scottish values of equality and egalitarianism, elites even casting aside the Enlightenment despite the latter taking on a higher regard internationally.

> *Daes a heid teacher fae Brighton aye unnerstaund a wee schuil bairn fae Banff? Daes e'en a jeedge fae Morningside aye unnerstaund a panel (accused) fae Muirhoose? An daes a GP fae Hampshire aye understaund an auld wifie fae Hamilton? A hae ma doots. An dae thay see Scotlan as we dae?*

Wages in Scotland were, as noted, less than in England, with agricultural wages 13 per cent less in 1907. Secondary and higher education remained the preserve of the upper and middle classes. A very large proportion of the Scottish population lived in extreme difficulties with multiple deprivation endemic. In 1867, just 10 per cent of the population received over 50 per cent of national income. Over half of female workers in the major cities such as Edinburgh were employed as domestic servants; hundreds of thousands of Scots were therefore deemed no better than servants to the professional and upper classes, the latter rapidly becoming or long since Anglophone. In 1914, the UK Government was spending around a third more per head on the poor in England than in Scotland. Scotland was a country marked by deep inequalities and a narrow distribution of wealth, with excessive numbers of unemployed men and multitudes of servant women comprising a major part of the Scottish population. National Governance at the UK level was distant and historically totally disinterested in the Scottish peoples' plight, leaving any local governance in the hands of an increasingly Anglophone landed and privileged class who presided over this never-ending cycle of poverty and despair. The mass of the Scottish people were no more than an inconvenience to their Anglophone unionist masters, and rather less a 'full partner' in anything.

In the 20th century the focus shifted to emigration of skilled workers from Scotland. Even Britain's trade unions considered Scottish emigration to be a 'practical solution' to the low wages, unemployment, and poverty in Scotland, such was the dearth of opportunity open to Scots in their own land. Soon up to half of the emigrants were skilled workers. While skilled Scots have helped develop and enrich other countries, this has been at the expense of Scotland which has largely remained a poorly developed economy with consistent social problems resulting from poverty, inequality and lack of opportunity for

Scots to progress in their own land, made worse due to the prevailing practice of importing an Anglophone meritocracy mainly from England.

Within the UK 'union' Scotland has been ill managed, if managed at all. The country, its assets and its people have been exploited, abused and discriminated against, with millions cast out, which in large part explains the pent-up desire from Scots for self-government and liberation from colonial oppression, which continues in various forms even today.

As well as seeking to escape poverty and socio-economic discrimination and oppression, Scottish emigrants were also seeking to avoid Britain's predilection for frequent wars and military incursions, and the British state's constant recruitment of a large military resource, which young Scottish men disproportionately filled in their droves. To the alienated and impoverished masses of Scots all over Scotland, for those still retaining some energy or ambition, getting themselves and their families out of Scotland by any means would seem a rather obvious imperative even until as recently as the 1980s during the Thatcher de-industrialisation and privatisation programmes which further added to Scotland's seemingly endless socio-economic woes[41]. Census data shows that well over two million people left Scotland over a period of just ninety years between 1841 and 1931, which should seem incredible given this was around half the nation's population. And Scotland was clearly being 'treated' very differently to England; for example, in the period 1921-1931 Scotland lost 400,000 of its population (8 per cent)[42] compared with a loss of only 0.5 per cent in England.

It is also false to say that Scotland was somehow a 'wealthy' society, as if it were some homogenous classless industrial paradise, or remotely close to the Scandinavian 'model'. The reality is that millions of Scots were effectively forced to leave Scotland (i.e. they had little choice, as to stay would be futile and involve continued poverty, socio-economic alienation and suffering) over a period of little more than one hundred or so years in what remains one of the largest non-war socio-economic 'refugee' movements and population clearances ever seen in Europe for a nation of Scotland's size and population.

Historically, wealth inequality in Scotland was extensive and the inequality gap has actually widened over recent decades. The majority of Scots even up to the 1960's and 1970's still lived in poverty, on poor wages or none due to persistently high unemployment, with a lack of decent food, being subject to numerous prevailing illnesses, often living in dire, unsanitary, damp, and overcrowded housing.

In 1910 there were only 4,000 students in higher education in Scotland and in 1938 just 10,000. In the 19th and first half of the 20th century higher education catered for an elite section of Scottish society[43]. Most Scots left school at age 14 or less, later increased to 16 in the 1960's. Even today, only a third of Scots are educated to degree level and much of the student cohort within Scotland's elite universities continues to be drawn from outside Scotland.

Scots need to ask themselves, what was successive British Governments' doing to make so many millions of Scots want to leave their own land, unlike in England? This 'process' of population displacement continued until well into the 1960's, with state incentives employed by the British government to aid removal and transportation of more people out of Scotland. To believe that the ongoing mass displacement of Scotland's population (combined with selective replacement) was not 'managed' or intended and planned would seem naïve; countries do not simply misplace by accident millions of their people, virtually half the population. Nor by accident do they then proceed to partially replace one ethnic group of people through importing a meritocracy with an ethnicity, culture, language and identity reflective of the colonial 'administrative Power' itself. The latter process has accelerated over recent years as the debate on independence hots up once more.

Voting Patterns

Voting preference outcomes based on national identity and sense of belonging are well reflected in Scotland today. The 'Scottish' Labour Party are no longer the main political adversary of the SNP in terms of self-determination versus the union, the Tories now taking on this role. As recently as the mid 1990's Scotland had become a 'Tory Free Zone', Scots making it thus, responding as they did to the Tories socially divisive policies. Today it appears to be changing demographics that is breathing new life into the Tories in Scotland, with some one million people from rest-UK, mostly England, settling in Scotland over just the last twenty years since devolution[44]; it is primarily this group that appears to be helping to reverse the Scots desire for Scotland to be a Tory free zone.

Analysis of political change at the constituency level in Scotland confirms this identity-motivated shift in voting preference. The census indicates that around one third of voters in Clackmannanshire, for example, come from rest-UK, and this includes around 50 per cent of the teachers who work in secondary schools in Clackmannanshire[45]. Clackmannanshire was the first constituency to vote 'No' in 2014 with over 60 per cent opposed to independence, this reflecting its significant population coming from rest-UK.

According to voting intention surveys, the majority of voters in Scotland who come from rest-UK (i.e. 75 per cent or more) tend to vote against Scottish independence[46]; this rejection of independence, it may be surmised, is a reflection of their dominant culture, language and sense of identity, which is Anglophone and British, not Scots language and Scottish. A similar phenomenon persists now across most Tory and Libdem (i.e. unionist parties and 'No' voting) constituencies in Scotland, for example: Borders, Dumfries & Galloway, Aberdeenshire, Perthshire, North East Fife, Orkney and Shetland, and Edinburgh West & South. Each of these areas today represent the cultural Anglophone British unionist vote in Scotland which has been reinforced through ongoing demographic change.

Many political commentators in Scotland and indeed the SNP appear to misunderstand or choose to ignore the nature and impact of immigration to Scotland. According to census data, most immigration to Scotland over the past century and more has been from rest-UK (primarily England), with an emphasis on the professional and managerial class (i.e. higher earners, not low wage earners). In other words, Scotland has and still does import a significant element of its meritocracy and professional and managerial class from rest-UK, primarily England. Hence, whereas lower paid manual and low skilled employment on offer in Scotland goes mainly to the Scots themselves, and to a lesser extent EU citizens, this is not the case for higher level posts most of which are, as a matter of course, primarily advertised in the London/UK press and hence aimed at the much larger rest-UK labour market. Scotland's vacant professional and managerial posts are not therefore primarily targeted at Scots, but are directed at a far larger pool of people throughput the UK, and mainly in England.

As around half a million people from rest-UK now settle in Scotland each decade, an average of approximately 50,000 per annum, according to the census, this means that some one million people since devolution in 1999, and perhaps as many as two million people over the last half century, have moved from rest-UK to Scotland. In 2016, 46,300 people came to live in Scotland from the rest of the UK (mainly from England), which exceeds the 40,400 people who came to Scotland from all other countries combined (National Records of Scotland 2017). Migration to Scotland from rest-UK has therefore been consistently higher than migration from the rest-of-the-world in most years. Scotland's population rose to the highest ever recorded level, 5.4 million in 2016, driven by in-migration (National Records of Scotland 2015). This should also be viewed in the context of Scotland's relatively stable population over the past 50 years or so. In 1974 the population had risen to 5.24 million and then reduced to just over 5.0 million by 2000. This means Scotland's population has risen by close to half a million people since 2000, an increase of almost 10%, and due mainly to in-migration from rest-UK. This represents a significant recent and ongoing change in Scotland's population, and, in addition, it is a change which has an emphasis primarily on one single origin nation, i.e. England. It seems inevitable then, that this magnitude of fundamental demographic change also brings with it a change in culture, language, politics and indeed a change in the identity and hence in the voting preference of many people living in Scotland today.

In terms of age profile, less than half (49 per cent) of migrants from rest-UK to Scotland are aged between 16-34, compared with 67 per cent from rest-of-the-world in that age group. This means that 51 per cent of those from rest UK are aged 35 and over. During the period 2001-2016 some 755,000 people moved from rest-UK to Scotland, of which almost 180,000 (23 per cent) were aged 45 and above. Although Scotland is considered to have an ageing population, migration data suggests Scotland is also importing a higher age population from rest-UK, and certainly a much higher age group than migrants from overseas. This suggests the changing age structure in Scotland towards an older population is being exacerbated by migration from rest-UK.

The distribution of migrants in Scotland also varies. In-migration from overseas is mostly concentrated in the major conurbations of Edinburgh, Glasgow, Dundee and Aberdeen. Migrants from rest-UK are more widely distributed across rural and island areas as well as mainly in the higher property value areas in the cities of Edinburgh and Glasgow. This is further reflected in the older age profiles of more rural council areas such as Dumfries & Galloway, Perth & Kinross,

Highlands, Argyll & Bute, and Orkney.

Ye cruin the pairty sang awfu brawlike. Tae taucht an gie Scots bairns thair ane leid wad shuirly mak them muckle siccar, an tak awa thon 'naitional' creenge fer guid anaw. Appen yer een aw yous Scots fowk!

The SNP Scottish Government's approach to immigration is to keep Scotland as open as possible, although Scotland holds no powers over immigration. This is based on the crude assumption that Scots are simply *"not reproducing ourselves"* (Russell 2019), which rather ignores potential policies that could be developed both to raise the birth rate, and to better manage immigration without necessarily replacing the indigenous population. The ill-informed assumption here is that Scotland needs to bring in more people to look after an ageing population. However, according to the census, Scotland is to some extent importing an ageing population mainly from rest-UK, which the Scottish Government appear to have ignored.

Scots Language Minority

Ongoing demographic change means Scots could easily become a minority in their own land given change is being driven by a far larger neighbouring country's much larger population (i.e. England). Indeed, Scots may well be, culturally as well as linguistically, a minority people in Scotland today, reflecting the census data that there are only 1.6 million Scots speakers in Scotland, less than a third of the population. Assuming current in-migration levels continue, Scots could become a minority people in Scotland by 2040, if not before. In other words, Scotland's population is both being boosted and replaced, predominantly through migration from rest-UK, mainly from England. This is not a recent phenomenon given the historic displacement of Scots from Scotland more or less since the union began, coupled with sustained in-migration of an Anglophone meritocratic class from England over the past century and more.

It seems doubtful that any other similar sized nation anywhere in Europe, or perhaps elsewhere, is subject to such large and sustained inflows of people from a single large neighbouring country. And, more especially, a people from a large neighbouring country who are being invited as a matter of course to apply for and hold many if not most of the higher paid professional positions within the smaller neighbour nation, and also to retire there. In other countries of comparable size population such as Norway, Denmark, Finland, and in Ireland too, people there might be expected to question (and oppose) any similar largescale demographic movement and/or population replacement. They might also question the rather dubious purpose of a meritocratic elite being sourced primarily from a larger neighbouring nation. The human geography reality of what is effectively a colonial type occupation circumstance prevailing in Scotland seems evident, demographic change being but one significant aspect of this.

> *Bi the wey, aw thay heid bummers in Scotlan aye recruitet fi ootside o Scotlan shuirly arna qualifee'd tae wark in Scotlan if thay dinnae unnerstaund fowk here; thay're no bilingual, like maist o us Scots fowk! Wid thon happen in Holland, Denmark, Estonia or Norway whaur aw heid bummers appointet aye hae tae hiv Englis an spik the local leid an aw? Nae chance.*

Scotland's in-migration experience therefore differs significantly from that in many other countries in that it is predominantly people from arguably Scotland's 'administrative Power' (i.e. England) who are coming to Scotland, as has been the case for the past century and more, this being oriented towards the professional and managerial classes. This is not the case in other countries where immigrants will never be permitted to comprise anywhere near a majority of the professional class. Such an outcome appears to suggest Scots are not capable of managing their own affairs, reflecting Anglophone enculturation, and a feeling of inferiority (the Cultural Cringe).

Population migration, as we know from history, is often about influencing or even replacing a culture and language, as reflected by the 'Russianization' policies implemented in Poland and other Russian and subsequently Soviet controlled states, as well as acting to boost and indeed even to replace a population. To some, migration is basically about survival and that need is expected to grow as global warming affects the environment. However, this is not the rationale for most of the migration insofar as Scotland is concerned given that the largest ethnic migrant group coming to Scotland over the past century and more, and still today, has been people from rest-UK, mainly England, and oriented towards the professional classes. That cannot be described as migration for survival. This in-migration has occurred in an economy often struggling economically and subject in the past to mass emigration of Scots workers due to lack of opportunity for them in their home nation, which is economic migration. In this sense migration from rest-UK to Scotland is on a quite different level and focus than say seasonal fruit pickers or hospitality industry workers coming from Eastern European countries.

> *Aa doot thon's ane reason Scots leid isnae formally taucht in Scotlan's schuils an maist Scots fowk noo think Englis is thair leid, cause aw oor heid bummers spik sae wir telt 'guid' Englis an naething else. Nanetheless, thars raither plain as parritch differences, e.g. 'hoo noo broon coo' an a thoosand mair Scots wirds an aw!*

Census data from 2011 indicates that the proportion of Scotland's population born in England was 9 per cent at 476,586[47]. This is likely to be understated as the census will not 'capture' everyone, and moreover it is now a decade out of date, with the census since indicating that number may now have doubled. In any case an individual's culture, language and national identity does not necessarily depend on their place of birth (Tilley et al. 2004). Other factors will determine perceptions about national identity (e.g. socialisation, parental descent/ancestry, schooling etc.). Those born to parents or a parent coming from outside Scotland will likewise often assume the national identity of the parent(s) and their extended family members, which is influenced by factors such as socialization and language. A person's national identity, culture and language are not therefore necessarily determined by place of birth.

Prevailing political correctness and neoliberal attitudes common to the SNP political leadership maintains that 'all people living and working in Scotland are 'Scots'. Much as some politicians may wish this to be the case, it is not always possible, far less advisable, to seek to enforce a 'new' national identity on people. Most people have their own ideas about their own national identity and ethnicity and hence many people living in Scotland may well choose not to be 'Scots', however that term is defined, much in the way some two million 'No' voters decided not to be Scottish in 2014; given that 'No' voters blocked the existence of Scottish citizenship and Scottish nationality, and hence rejected the idea of being Scottish in any meaningful or recognised sense of identity, the contention that everyone in Scotland is a 'Scot' seems rather rhetorical in any event. In reality there seems little in the way of substance behind it, at least not at present given Scottish citizenship does not yet exist. Moreover, would a Brit or a Norwegian or a Swede or an American etc. living and working in say Denmark necessarily regard themselves as a 'Dane'? That would seem to be a bit of a stretch. More importantly perhaps, would these same people from other countries and holding to other national identities automatically be given a right to cast a 'national' vote in Denmark in order to determine whether or not the Danish people and nation should exist in terms of having their own citizenship and nationality or in determining their own form of government? One might rightly doubt that to be the case. Which rather begs the question as to why Scotland, in its national referendum, wrongly and unnecessarily assumed all its residents to be 'Scots'?

Immigration Control

Scotland has had no control over immigration to or from Scotland for 300 years and more, since the UK union was established. Scotland is subject to free and unhindered movement of people within the UK and this has allowed a far larger UK nation (i.e. England) to boost and in part replace the population of its smaller neighbour, Scotland. This has been a gradual process over a prolonged period, and which now appears to be accelerating. Over the past 200-300 years, whilst Scotland therefore experienced a massive exodus of its people, at the same time steady in-migration from rest-UK, mainly England, has taken place.

Given the census data, and this analysis, it should hardly be surprising that around half the voters in Scotland today reject Scottish citizenship, Scottish nationality, and hence also reject a Scottish identity. A key reason for this rejection is inevitably that many Anglophone voters in Scotland are neither culturally nor linguistically 'Scottish' and hence will be unlikely to consider themselves as having a Scottish identity. Voting on the question of Scottish independence is inevitably a matter of one's preferred national identity, a decision which is heavily influenced by culture and language, and emotion.

Professor Sir John Curtice has highlighted the importance of having a 'British' identity as opposed to a Scottish identity for those who are opposed to Scottish independence (Curtice 2013), this also reflecting an Anglophone culture and identity. Curtice noted that Scots who feel they have very little British identity are more prone to vote for independence, which reflects the significance of Scots language speakers, many of the latter being less likely to opt for a British Anglophone identity. Curtice, however, does not evaluate the significance of language and culture on identity, yet these factors clearly influence the differing voting patterns of Anglophone and Scots speakers. Neither does he consider demographic change in Scotland and the impact this inevitably has on voting patterns. Like most other commentators on Scottish independence, Curtice tends to focus more on voter attitudes towards economic and other general policy factors which, given this analysis here, seems rather inadequate.

What is most significant are the population inflows of approximately one million people from rest-UK - primarily England - into Scotland over just the last two decades, adding to significant population inflows in the years prior to this also. This is not simply a minor change to a national population of 5.5 million. If it were deemed minor, then what would represent a major change? Clearly a change approaching 20 per cent of a population over just twenty years, and following on from at least a century of previous in-migration, likewise primarily from England, represents a major population change. In addition to this, people of English extraction living in Scotland will be expected to increase this number, perhaps to double the level or more.

> *Whit aboot Fife, Lothians, Borders, Stirlingshire, Ayrshire an Galloway an aw thay fowk bidin aff the Clyde – dae we no spik Scots an aw? While thon's a guid staert in Aiberdeen tae remeed a lang affront, Scotlan aye haes need o a 'Scots Langage Act' an ayeweys wull.*

Self-determination and independence is about a people having the power to deal with the fundamentals of their country, and that includes managing its population. No independent country would ever permit such a large portion, perhaps as much as half, of its population to be removed and replaced in such a way as to threaten the very existence of its people, as well as weakening its sovereignty, culture, language and identity. Yet this appears to be what has happened with Scotland since, and arguably because of, the UK union. In other words, it is the UK union itself that is ultimately responsible for ongoing dramatic demographic change in Scotland. Scotland, like any other country, clearly needs to better manage the fundamentals of its population and this can only be done through independence.

British migration 'policy' with respect to Scotland, both overt and covert, for some three hundred years, has therefore amounted to largescale displacement of Scots (speakers) from Scotland and the boosting and replacing of the population with Anglophone peoples from rest-UK, primarily England, the latter with a focus on the professional and managerial classes. The main incentive used to entice people from rest-UK to move to Scotland has usually therefore involved the promise of access to many of the best remunerated jobs; this must naturally come at the expense of the Scots themselves.

Within the UK union, Scotland's people appear to have been used and abused by the British administrative power as little more than an experiment in social and demographic re-engineering, and this is still occurring. A country does not naturally or accidentally lose between three and four million of its people, perhaps half of its population, and meanwhile have its population boosted by a professional meritocratic class from a single dominant neighbouring country?

Could anyone imagine such events happening in say, Denmark, with several million Danes shipped out to the four corners of the earth, and the ongoing import thereafter into Denmark of a German meritocracy, and with Denmark's professional job adverts placed only in Berlin newspapers, and with that the imposition of German culture and language and social institutions being inflicted on the Danes who had remained? How would the Danes feel? How should the Scots feel?

Identity Matters!

Ireland, as is invariably the case, offers a useful reflection as to the role and impact of demographic change within the UK. There is understandably some consensus in Ireland that the creation of an independent Scotland would help speed up Irish re-unification, though the latter could occur first. Unionists in Northern Ireland lost their majority in a PR (STV) system in 2017, and the Democratic Unionist Party (DUP) held on by little more than a thread at the Westminster election in December 2019. Demographics have now tipped beyond the point of no return, with four of the six counties seeing Catholics outnumber Protestants (and in the other 2 counties, Belfast City has followed suit) and with every border constituency now firmly 'green'. Overall, in every age group under 45 there is now a large majority Catholic over Protestant. The 2019 UK General Election result gave the nationalists a majority of the seats.

What is not happening in Northern Ireland, unlike in Scotland, however, is that there is very limited population inflow there from rest-UK. Even the civil service in Northern Ireland is selected and recruited in Northern Ireland, rather than in Whitehall where Scotland's senior civil servant posts are still decided and allocated. This implies that the numbers of 'unionist' or 'British identity' voters are not being boosted in Northern Ireland anywhere near the levels experienced in Scotland. These demographics all points towards Irish reunification within the next twenty years, if not sooner, whilst Scotland's independence remains uncertain due to the different demographics at work there. The breakthrough of Sinn Fein in the Irish General Election in January 2020 further reinforces the prospect of Irish reunification and the end of partition.

Ian Hamilton QC once said, 'Scotland's greatest resource is its people'[48]. But Scotland still does not deploy its people, all its people, as it should. What Scots really need to do is lift mair o thair ain fowk up, to give them all the opportunity to do well. Scotland's historical tendency to appoint most of the leaders of Scotland's social institutions and major business corporations from outside of Scotland and/or only those Scots from more privileged Anglophone backgrounds, remains arguably Scotland's biggest social and economic weakness, and is a tragedy for the many Scots who remain excluded, and the many others who were forced to leave to find opportunities elsewhere. All of Scotland's people are fundamental to Scotland's future, yet many remain deprived of the opportunities other peoples' take for granted in their own lands (Riddoch 2013). Scotland does not need to import a meritocracy, and certainly not to lead its social institutions, as if Scots were somehow inherently incapable of undertaking any of these leadership functions themselves, as if Scots were inferior. Scotland needs to respect and facilitate all the Scottish people to progress in life, rather than squeeze many of them out and succumb to the Anglophone dominated institutionalised marginalisation and discrimination and segregation that prevails, which is at root cultural, linguistic and identity (i.e. ethnically) determined.

The perception of one's own identity is clearly crucial in any referendum on Scottish independence. Census data indicates that some 83 per cent of the population of Scotland felt they had 'some' Scottish national identity, including 62 per cent who felt Scottish only[49]. This also suggests, however, that between 17 per cent and 38 per cent of Scotland's population either have no Scottish identity and/or they also have another national identity. It may be hypothesized from this that those who hold to a national identity other than 'Scottish' represent the core element of the anti-independence and hence pro-British 'No' vote.

It is not necessarily where one is born which influences and guides one's dominant culture, language and identity. Think of

Scotland's diaspora of many millions of people all around the world, a large number of whom may not have been born in Scotland, yet who retain a strong cultural affinity to Scotland and a sense of Scottishness and Scottish identity that has continued over multiple generations and even over centuries.

There are numerous reasons why hundreds of thousands of people from rest-UK should seek to make Scotland their home, aside from accessing the more lucrative professional Scottish jobs that are primarily advertised in the London press. Scotland's progressive social policies since devolution are surely attractive and highly differentiated from those in England. A wide range of progressive government policies differentiate a devolved Scotland from Westminster. This includes policies such as free care for the elderly, free bus travel for the elderly (and for under 18's from 2021[50]), free university education, free prescriptions, plus the protection of a range of public services such as the NHS and schools, sectors which have come under immense pressure and are subject to more stringent funding cuts in England. Scottish housing and land prices remain lower than in certain parts of England, and Scotland has many attractive locations in which to live, including fashionable cities and towns and rural areas with exquisite scenery and surroundings.

The rapidly changing nature of many of England's cities and towns through immigration and increasing segregation between communities with little in common (Cantle 2012) is another reason many mainly white middle class English people move to Scotland. Multiculturalism and its many cultures, faiths, identities and ethnicities is not always to their liking, as the Brexit vote demonstrated. White people have been moving in disproportionate numbers out of urban areas in England and many avoid moving to diverse areas[51]. This has now extended to the working class too, which perhaps reflects recent increases in migration from England to Scotland particularly over the past two decades. Meantime

Scotland is still predominantly white, far less multicultural than England, and is also largely Anglophone as well, hence Scotland may seem a 'natural' home especially for the more mobile English professional classes, and now also for the working class.

Historically many of those coming from rest-UK to Scotland are from the professional and managerial classes, including retirees, who tend to be more mobile, have higher spending power, and a greater likelihood to send their offspring into higher education. Multiculturalism in England's cities and towns has clearly accelerated this movement to Scotland. These groups will also have a greater propensity to vote than less privileged social groups and a tendency to vote on the conservative right, i.e. Tory or LibDem. Scotland therefore offers an attractive destination for this group with no immigration controls nor language requirement, and a less multicultural or segregated environment. To an extent Scotland also seems to be importing an ageing population, for which, paradoxically, the Scottish Government maintains it needs to increase immigration levels even further in order to care for an ageing population.

The main conclusion from this is that, aside from the more obvious cultural, heritage and language and hence identity factors determining the way people vote, Scotland's differentiated progressive policies coupled with the absence of any control over immigration into Scotland from rest-UK or elsewhere would appear to be facilitating sustained immigration from rest-UK and hence a strengthening of the anti-independence 'No' vote. Further evidence of this phenomenon has been the lack of any significant shift towards 'Yes' in the opinion polls since 2014, coupled with the strengthening of the Tory/unionist vote in a number of Scottish constituencies that have significant resident populations comprising people from rest-UK, i.e. Anglophones who have the greatest propensity to hold to a British identity and therefore to vote 'No' to block Scottish citizenship and

Scottish independence.

Those advocating Scottish independence cannot simply ignore such fundamental demographic changes, particularly within the UK context which, on current trends, will render Scots a minority people in Scotland. This inevitably significantly influences and hence determines any future independence referendum result. In simple human geography terms, Scotland is being subsumed by its larger neighbour through uncontrolled population boost and replacement. This is made more critical, politically, and for independence, given Scotland's irregular voting franchise based on residence, coupled with the absence of immigration controls in Scotland. The essential features of ongoing population change reflect Scotland's colonial reality within the UK 'union' arrangement, as evidenced by its historic, extreme, and arguably intentional population displacement combined with a longstanding, significant and constant replenishment of an Anglophone meritocracy. Such uncontrolled demographic change implies that Scotland and the Scottish people continue to be 'doun-hauden', rendered powerless so long as they remain unable to properly manage their own nation, its population, or high-level national affairs generally. These are matters of national strategic importance, hence the existence of immigration policies in all other countries, which can only be properly addressed through Scottish independence.

CHAPTER 6: COLONIALISM

Is the UK really a 'Union'?

Under the 1707 Treaty of Union agreement there appears to be, in practice at least, no Scottish veto on anything the UK government or its parliament may decide in relation to Scotland. A majority of Scotland's 59 representatives elected to Westminster may vote as they wish on any matter, however, the near 600 MP's from other nations in the UK, of which 533 MP's (82 per cent) represent constituencies in England, will always hold sway. There is arguably therefore no 'union' as such. Politically, Scotland within the UK appears to exhibit more the characteristics of a colony than a member state of a union. Moreover, the UN defined Ireland, ostensibly likewise once a 'member' of the UK union, to be a 'former colony', and Scotland seems little different.

When former UK Prime Minister Teresa May came to Scotland on the 28th of November 2018 to sell her (or rather England's) initial Brexit deal to the Scots, who had voted to oppose Brexit, she looked every part a foreign dignitary representing another place, and another country – i.e. Scotland's 'administrative Power'; she was not visiting Scotland as a Scot, for she is not, but rather as one of those controlling the Scots and their land. Indeed, there were no Scots even in her Brexit 'war cabinet', the group of high-level people making decisions about Scotland's future. So, with no Scottish veto can there really be a UK union?

Naw, ye dinna fin mony braw braid Scots spikkers gettin heid bummer joabs in Scotlan. Hoo no?

Colonial servitude is not exactly an attractive proposition for any nation and its people, which explains why so many former colonies have decolonised. A fundamental problem with the

UK 'union', for an increasing number of Scots, is that the supposed 'union' is increasingly viewed as a charade, a fraud even, and Scotland is demonstrably treated as a mere colony, one of the last few remaining territories under the control of a rapidly decaying imperial power, which to all intents and purposes is England. Does Scotland and the Scottish people really have, or desire, a future in such a one-sided political arrangement?

Colonial Reality

Three principal areas in which colonial discrimination against a people may occur are language, leadership (and control), and land ownership. In terms of language, as we have seen in previous chapters the Scots are prevented from learning thay're ain leid by the British state (which includes the devolved Scottish 'Government'), with only English garred doon Scots bairns thrapples (i.e. forced down their throats). Hence the reason many Scots themselves regard their own mother tongue, and perhaps those who speak it, as inferior, or 'not valid'; they are programmed to think this way because they are told from early on in life (i.e. via British state education, media etc.) that so-called 'proper' English is the 'correct' way to speak, and necessary to get on in life, whereas Scots is considered, not least by Anglophone educationalists, as not being a 'valid' language, and one must assume therefore that those who speak it are not considered 'valid' either. The term 'validity' implies that the Scots language is neither legal nor officially acceptable, within Scotland.

In terms of leadership, more or less all high-level jobs in Scotland have for a very long time been advertised primarily in the London metropolitan press. As England's population is some ten times larger, this helps explain why many if not most of Scotland's leaders across several hundred of its social institutions and major businesses are not Scots. If they are (Scots) they will more likely tend to be 'Anglophone Scots' from the more privileged backgrounds, as the 'Elitist Scotland?' report discovered (The Social Mobility and Child Poverty Commission 2015). Scotland does not, of course, advertise its low paid job opportunities in the London press; for these jobs working class Scots speakers, or EU migrants will do just fine.

A third area of discrimination is in respect of land, Scotland still suffering from perhaps the most concentrated land ownership in Europe. Being deprived of the opportunity to share more equitably in Scotland's abundant lands (and seas) led to millions of Scots being literally forced to leave Scotland in order to make a decent living for themselves elsewhere, while most of those remaining were left impoverished and bereft of opportunity. Scots today still suffer from the earlier land grabs of elites and the loss of common land. Wightman (2013, p. 411) notes that: *"most land reforms around the world have taken place in response to political upheaval – be that a revolution, decolonisation or the overthrow of a dictator"*. Scotland clearly has some way to go in this regard and the devolved Scottish Government land reform agenda remains lacklustre with no restrictions on the amount of land any individual can own[52]. This suggests that Scotland's decolonisation may be a necessary prerequisite for proper land reform to take place.

With language, leadership and land, the external control and abuse of all three serves to discriminate against Scots so long as Scotland is controlled by Westminster's elites and their acolytes. These essentially imperial controls over language, leadership and land reflect Scotland's continued colonial status and the inevitable outcome when a people lose or give away control (i.e. sovereignty) of their nation, its assets and its people, to an administrative and/or imperial power to do with as it pleases.

Economic Decline

Scots tend not to be aware how weak the UK is today, especially economically, thanks to the British MSM tendency in depicting 'alternative' realities. The UK remains very much in a long-term socio-economic decline phase, as Professor Michael Porter wrote over two decades ago in 'The Competitive Advantage of Nations' (Porter 1998). Signs of decline are all over the place. Porter alluded to many weaknesses in the UK, not least high energy prices, crumbling infrastructure, inadequate regulation of monopolies (and the then soon to implode financial sector), and lack of global competitiveness. The already widening gap between imports and exports then has demonstrably widened ever further since[53]. Forever harking back to the nostalgia and myths of supposedly 'great' British glories of the distant past is a further sure sign the UK is in decline and has little to offer today. The overseas colonies are gone, with barely only 'cash cow' Scotland left to sook dry since the loss of Ireland's rich and cheap agriculture, and no longer any need to extract a massive low-cost coal resource from Wales to fuel Britain's long since departed industries.

The British MSM feed the Scots myth upon nostalgic myth about 'how great we used to be', from shipyards (now derelict), to the 'Enlightenment', Sir Walter Scott, Conan Doyle, WWI 'heroism', to MacIntosh, folk who invented this and that, defeating the 'Nazis' etc. ad infinitum. In other words 'Unionists' sell Scots a supposedly 'glorious past' narrative, one in which they conveniently forget to mention the almost four million Scots who were forced to leave Scotland since the union began in order to find a decent economic existence for themselves elsewhere, primarily because there was none to find in Scotland.

'Isn't Scotland too poor to be independent', we often hear unionists and even Scots-unionists ask? That over three hundred years of UK union has made Scotland whatever it is today escapes their notice. Yet Scotland's 'territory' contains two thirds of the UK's Exclusive Economic Area (EEA), more coastline than other EU states, most of the EU's oil and gas and now renewable energy, and most of the EU's fisheries. Scotland is, however, lacking in many things it could and perhaps should have, were it independent, such as a naval base or three, ultra-modern seaports to facilitate trade, more advanced infrastructure, and at least some regulatory 'control' over monopolies and their high prices inflicted upon the country by its 'administrative Power', which makes Scotland uncompetitive. An independent Scotland might be expected to have at least two or three strategically positioned coastal naval bases (covering east, west and north coasts) plus coastal patrol vessels stationed around the coast, none of which currently exists, within the 'union'. Within the UK union, military bases in Scotland across all three main services – land, sea and air - have been decimated – aside from the nuclear submarines at Faslane which no other country in the UK wants to house.

Scotlan's aye a wee haud doon colony, nae doot aboot thon.

Scotland's trade and hence economic growth is held back by an urgent need for port reform and modernisation which, unfortunately, even the SNP 'Growth' Commission[54] failed to notice. Most of Scotland's international shipping operations ended due in part to the lack of investment in the major Scottish central belt ports necessary to cater for modern and larger ships introduced since 'contanerisation' of world trade. Compared with port infrastructure today in Denmark, Norway, Ireland, Finland, Estonia, Poland etc., Scotland resembles a less developed nation dependent on outdated Victorian port infrastructure. It should seem rather obvious why trade performance remains lacklustre within the UK 'union'. Scotland is simply not competitive, due to poor infrastructure and high energy costs, and neither does Scotland have an adequately funded state-owned National

Investment Bank[55] (only £2bn investment over ten years?) helping to 'support' trade like many other nations enjoy.

Scots are also told that Scotland couldn't withstand 'its share' of UK debt. Yet colonies post-independence are not expected to inherit the debts incurred by an administrative Power, just as a former colony would not necessarily expect to be adequately compensated for its loss of assets and resources (and people!) over the period of its colonisation and exploitation by an administrative Power. How much has Scotland lost since the union was created due to exploitation of its lands, seas, resource and people? How does Scotland quantify the loss of 3-4 million of its people? What has been and remains the opportunity cost of the UK union to Scotland? Why does much of Scotland today more resemble Murmansk Oblast than the Mid-Norway region?

Unionists may say that the Scots should not feel bad because they remain the one area of Britain which the Romans never conquered and occupied. The irony seems to be lost here in that the British (or English) empire went a lot further than the Romans insofar as the 'taking' of Scotland was concerned; constant military invasions over several centuries leading to its post 1707 domination, followed by the displacement (removal?) of some three-four million Scots shipped off to overseas colonies, the inflow of an Anglophone ruling professional class still ongoing today, in addition to the extensive economic exploitation of resources. This is not a 'union' legacy, it is a colonial legacy.

The question might be asked, are not those Scots living in England also colonists? But Scots hardly dominate England in anything like the same way Scotland is dominated. There is no Scottish based 'administrative Power' holding sovereign rule over England, whereas England's 533+ MP's and its many more peers in the House of Lords can do as they wish with Scotland, and they do as they wish, frequently. And Scotland does not impose Scottish cultural and linguistic imperialism on England or any other nation. A real 'union' of nations involves its member countries retaining a veto over decisions it may not agree with and respecting the language and cultural rights of 'member' nations. Scotland has no veto in the UK 'union' charade and its peoples' cultural and linguistic rights are overridden in the ongoing quest to enforce the 'Britishing' of the Scots.

Internal Colonialism

Unionists, and even some Scottish nationalists, refuse to regard Scotland as a colony; it does not form part of the British 'family of nations' narrative. Constitutionally and therefore legally, of course, Scotland is not a colony, being one of two signatory party kingdoms/nations to the UK Treaty of Union. However, politically and therefore in any practical sense Scotland does appear to demonstrate the key features of a colony (Baird 2017), and this also reflects empirical research into what is referred to as 'internal colonialism'.

Rogues galore in thon sclave tred tho, wi mony o wir ruling 'elite' faimlies nae doot aye yet walthie acause o it - maist o thaim noo prood Scots-Unionists tae nae doot. Thon jubous chancers wid mak sclaves oot o onybody, e'en thir days, an thay dae tae, whit wi law pey, hie hoose rents an a widenin walth gap.

Internal colonialism differs from classical colonialism on the basis that there is no forceful takeover by a foreign entity. The definition of Internal colonialism fits Scotland rather well in that: *"the established society is characterized by group inequalities, cultural imposition of the dominant group, cultural disintegration of the oppressed group's culture, and cultural recreation of the oppressed groups as defined by the dominant group"* (David 2008: p. 120). Internal colonialism therefore encapsulates Boudieu's 'enculturation' as well as Fanon's 'inferiorisation' and Gramsci's 'cultural hegemony'. In this sense, by and large, working class Scots speakers are viewed as inferior; they are considered to speak an 'invalid' language and hence are deemed an 'invalid' people and, for the most part, are regarded as incapable of reaching high status. The cultural standards, language and beliefs of the dominant Anglophone group continue to be imposed on the oppressed group with the essential message that assimilation to the dominant (Anglophone) culture brings with it benefits and access to resources. This internalized sense of inferiority results in the oppressed group, in this case mainly working class Scots speakers, developing what is referred to as a *"colonized mentality"* (Fanon 2004), which involves internalising and accepting their oppression as somehow deserved.

Naw, sclavery isna duin, cultural owergang neither. Thon sclave-maisters aye haud Scotland doun in aw weys.

Internal colonialism theory contends that ethnic and cultural divisions within a state are not removed in the course of its development or industrialisation, they remain and indeed may fester (Hechter 2017). This is because of the institutionalization of a 'cultural division of labour'. Division of labour is imposed by the ruling group and it associates deprivation not with membership of an oppressed and exploited social class, but **with membership of an oppressed and exploited ethnic group or race**. Thus, according to Hunter (1977), the top jobs, the high wages, and the social status which comes from these things are reserved for members of the dominant (i.e. Anglophone) culture or (and, the qualification here is important) for members of the subordinate group who choose to embrace the dominant culture (including its language). This suggests that, **within the UK union, the ongoing colonial oppression of Scots is ethnically driven**, much as it was in Ireland, and at root it is Anglophone and hence English elite driven. Whether the slogan is 'black is beautiful' or 'an Irish Ireland' the message from oppressed peoples is essentially the same; that is, the colonised wish to be free and bring an end to the 'scourge' of colonisation, which is clearly ethnically driven oppression.

Hechter researched the characteristics between England and the Celtic fringe countries of Ireland, Wales and Scotland and found that inequalities between England and the peripheral nations reflected such characteristics. There are also different and distinctive voting patterns and cultural characteristics that differentiate these nations. There were and remain ongoing attempts by the 'core' state to extirpate Celtic and Scots languages and customs. Meanwhile, indigenous elites sought to abandon and disregard the mores and languages and religion of their own Celtic nations and become Anglophone in order to progress themselves within the preferred domains of the core administrative Power entity. This seems broadly similar to what John Cleese described, in reference to some Scots, as 'obedient retainers seeking social status'[56].

Recent years have witnessed a resurgence of so-called 'separatist' sentiments among national minorities in many industrial and post-industrial societies, including not least the United Kingdom. In 1997, the Scottish and Welsh both set up their own parliamentary bodies, albeit devolved by Westminster, while the tragic events in Northern Ireland continued to be a reminder of so-called 'the Irish problem', which is really rather more of a 'British problem'. These socio-political developments call into question widely accepted social theories which assume that ethnic attachments in a society will wane as industrialization and political integration proceeds; however, ethnic demographic change must also be considered here and in particular the risk that a fringe nation is simply subsumed, as appears to still be happening to Scotland.

There is clearly a need, given the ongoing momentum towards 'separatism' and the colonial power base, to consider the social basis of ethnic identity, and changes in the strength of ethnic solidarity in the United Kingdom, particularly over the last two centuries. Hechter's work suggests that internal colonialism of the kind experienced in the British Isles has its analogues in the histories of other industrial societies. He examined what might be considered as the unexpected persistence of ethnicity within the politics of industrial societies in the British Isles. For example, why do many of the inhabitants of Wales, Scotland, and Ireland continue to maintain an ethnic identity quite different from England? Moreover, whilst in England there seems little evidence that national identities are constitutionally significant, in Scotland, Wales and Northern Ireland national identities remain highly significant when it comes to support for constitutional change (Bond and Rosie 2010).

Hechter explained the salience of ethnic identity by analysing the relationships between England, which he referred to as the national core, and its periphery, or the Celtic fringe, in the light of two alternative models of core-periphery relations in the industrial setting. These are a *diffusion* model, which predicts that intergroup contact leads to ethnic homogenization, and an *internal colonial* model, in which such contact heightens distinctive ethnic identification. Findings from this research lends support to the *internal colonial* model indicating that, although industrialization (and imposed linguistic imperialism policies) did contribute to a decline in interregional linguistic differences, it resulted neither in the cultural assimilation of Celtic lands, nor in the development of regional economic equality. Hechter concluded that ethnic solidarity will inevitably emerge among groups which are relegated to inferior positions in a cultural division of labour, which in the UK union context is and remains arguably the most likely socio-economic destination for many Scots, and particularly for Scots speakers. So long as Scots speakers are afforded a 'subaltern' status within an Anglophone meritocratic dominated UK 'union', Scots will tend to be regarded (by the Anglophone core) as an inferior ethnic community. **Thus, the Scottish independence movement, in Hechter's *internal colonial* model, predominantly reflects the**

ethnic solidarity of Scots speakers.

Hunter (1977) considered that Hechter's work represented an important contribution to the understanding of socioeconomic development and ethnicity. A common thread from this research is the Anglophone elite hierarchy retaining control over the industrialisation process in the Celtic lands. In the wider societal sense, the dominant position of Anglophone elites extends much further than merely industrialisation. It seeks to inhabit and control every aspect of public and social institutions, from government, state agencies, education, justice, police, military, religion and the third sector. In the Anglophone dominated internal colonialism reality, the Scots speaking Scot is generally rendered as and reduced to an inferior ethnic participant parroting an 'invalid' language and made devoid of much status or opportunity. In other words, the Anglophone elite dominated UK 'union' renders the working-class Scots speaking Scot much like Jimmy Reid's 'alienated' worker, and little better than Nietzsche's Untermensch ('inferior people'); such is the brutal ethnic oppression reality in most if not all colonies. This 'superior' ethnically driven ideology evidently has no qualms about displacing millions of Scots or supplanting them with an Anglophone meritocracy.

> *Thay SNP are ane o the least nationalist pairties campaigning for autonomy onywhar.*

Fortunately, or so it would appear, Scotland has not also suffered from partition, that oft used British imperial 'divide and rule' policy and practice intended to worsen matters even more for colonised peoples seeking self-government. Historically, of course, British or rather English colonial partition policy seldom works out well and generally has led to significant further long-term conflict (McKenna 2018), which was no doubt its intention given it was repeatedly played out so often in so many now former colonies, e.g. Cyprus,

Palestine, India, Ireland, numerous states in the Middle East, Africa, Latin America, Asia, etc. That ruthless and exploitative 'empire' has thankfully virtually ended though now it is the turn of the retained 'internal' colonies finally seeking decolonisation, and liberation.

Decolonisation

Technically, Scotland might have been independent in 1960 when the United Nations ratified the Decolonisation Resolution of which the UK is a signatory[57]. It was only because the UK brought to UN attention The Act of Union 1707 declaring *"United into One Kingdom by the Name of Great Britain"* that the UK was permitted to stay together. The Republic of Ireland perhaps offers Scotland a more relevant precedent, however, in that the United Nations considers Ireland to be a former colony, and this despite the fact Ireland was, as Scotland is now, supposedly, a 'partner' within a UK 'union'. Clearly, if the UN regards Ireland as a former colony then there should be little difficulty in defining Scotland similarly, irrespective of any supposed 'union'. Decolonisation more generally remains an important goal of the UN, and this could be used to Scotland's advantage, though it generally tends to be ignored.

Hallas (1969) likewise defined Ireland as a former colony, highlighting the nation's historic role as *"a source of cheap food and raw materials for England"* (Hallas 1969). Ireland, according to Hallas, was controlled by *"a relatively small group of English landowners"*, which should sound familiar to many Scots. The colonial overseers in Ireland brought about levels of *"poverty unknown in any other part of Europe"*, the displacement of over one million people, and the death of another one million people from starvation due to the famine of the late 1840's, this at a time when wheat was still being exported from

Irish ports. It was this genocide that led to the subsequent revolt against *"the English ruling classes and their Irish supporters"* and eventually to Irish independence. Scotland's loss of population due to displacement resulting from colonial rule, or rather misrule, is even greater than Ireland's. This was in large part because it persisted over a longer period, from the 1700's until well into the twentieth century.

Any number of nations might be expected to propose Scotland's inscription on the UN List of Colonies to be decolonised, not least Ireland, or perhaps Argentina given the latter's ongoing dispute with the UK regarding the Falkland Islands. Another UN member state's proposal for a new listing is all it takes, according to the UN's response to the author on this matter. Coincidentally, the UN has rejected as invalid the UK organised Falklands/Malvinas referendum on self-determination there on the basis that the latter only surveyed British settler voters and ignored the indigenous people (or rather their descendants) who were expelled some 150 years previously by the British settler occupation. That UN decision also rather implies that Scotland should not so readily ignore its own diaspora of people displaced and scattered to the four corners of the globe during the period of British colonial rule, or their descendants.

It remains somewhat surprising that the SNP Scottish Government and the majority of 'nationalist' MP's in Scotland has never formally activated alternative options aimed at securing independence, such as via a UN decolonisation listing for Scotland. Their dependence on another dubious Westminster sanctioned and influenced 'open' franchise referendum seems a high-risk, and perhaps unnecessary strategy. Scotland's democratically elected representatives and 'nationalist' Government could instead make a valid direct appeal to 'The UN Special Committee on the Situation with regard to the Implementation of the Declaration on the Granting of Independence to Colonial Countries and Peoples' (also known as the Special Committee on

Decolonisation or C-24), the United Nations entity exclusively devoted to the issue of Decolonisation' and to ending what the UN refers to as *"the scourge of colonization"*. This UN Committee exists for good reason, that is to end colonisation, and Scotland should seek to use its services for that purpose, i.e. for the purpose of decolonisation.

> *Mind ye, hid Scotlan takken ower England, an no the ither wey aboot, hauf the warld wid noo be spikin Scots, nae Englis!*

Unionists tend to misuse the term 'union' to imply that Scotland is in some form of 'partnership of equals' with England, and hence is not a colony. UK political parties have even gone to the extent of naming their 'regional' parties 'unionist', e.g.: Scottish Conservative and Unionist Party, and the Ulster Unionist Party. The Welsh Conservatives were initially formed as the Wales and Monmouthshire Conservative and Unionist Council in 1921, despite the fact that for much of their history they were dominated by the party in England, even to the extent of supplying Welsh Secretaries of State. This labelling seems more a matter of presentation than substance given that the term 'unionist' is clearly a preferable description to present a political party to voters across the Celtic Fringe than as the 'colonial' party. However, the meaning in practice seems little different, especially if one happens to be from a colony, internal or otherwise.

'Nationalism' is a term often linked to cessation and tends to be portrayed by 'unionists' as negative and even aggressive. However, British unionism is itself a trans-national nationalist political ideology, which is and remains one of its most aggressive forms, as history confirms. All trans-national political 'unions' (e.g. UK, Spain, Soviet Union, Yugoslavia etc.) depended on coercion by an imperial core entity to enforce its cultural and linguistic norms and enforced 'integration', combined with the imposition of a meritocratic elite primarily representative of the culture and language of the dominating core country controlling the 'union'. Such 'unions' are by their nature oppressive and aggressive and the UK 'union' seems little different, witness events in Northern Ireland, the recent treatment of Scotland with respect to Brexit, and the UK ignoring of successive SNP mandates for Scotland to hold a second referendum on independence.

Small nation 'nationalism', in contrast, merely relates to oppressed colonies seeking to end their oppression by foreign powers through self-determination and hence decolonisation. Self-determination enables a nation to free its people from the scourge of cultural and linguistic bondage and socio-economic control and oppression imposed by foreign elites, often aided by the usual 'little helpers' locally. Thus, self-determination nationalism is about decolonisation, which is the reverse of trans-national nationalism often referred to as 'unionism', the latter involving cultural and linguistic imperialism, occupation, and exploitation of other neighbouring countries and peoples.

> *"Och aye, you Scots are different". Deid richt. Thon's whit we're fechtin fir - oor nation, oor langage, oor cultur, oor wey o daein awthing, an oor verra bein.*

British 'unionism' might also be viewed as England's *Lebensraum*. England contains, after all, a relatively modest land mass which houses a large and increasing population, now ten times greater than Scotland's population. Scotland in contrast offers space, a lesser population, and plentiful resources, all especially attractive features to England's far larger and mobile managerial and professional elites, much as Wales still does to some extent, and Ireland used to.

Unionists often confuse the British 'union' with the British 'empire' and claim in a wider and more general sense that Scots somehow benefitted from the empire. However, it may readily be argued that both the empire and the union have impoverished Scotland and the vast majority of Scots, a great many of whom were forced to leave Scotland as a result. Scotland's Anglophone elite may have made considerable wealth and status out of the empire and its slavery and exploitation (as numerous grand monuments in Scottish kirk cemeteries, and monies bequeathed to Anglophone private schools in Scotland amply testify), much as they did out of a dubious 'union', however the majority and masses of Scots paid and still pay a high price for this. The Scottish people paid for this through their displacement (i.e. removal), poverty, unemployment, constant wars overseas, in lost opportunities and discrimination in their own land, as many Scots still experience today. Once a people and nation realise they are treated and exploited as a colony and therefore regarded as an inferior people and culture, they will reject it, as Ireland did, and many in Scotland are now coming to the same conclusion. **For Scotland, as for all former colonies which are now independent countries, independence is decolonisation.**

Devolution 'Bone'

Most Scots nowadays appreciate that devolution is not 'real' power, but Scots might also ponder what devolution is. 'Devolution' is something akin to a political bone thrown to restless colonies and regions by a controlling 'administrative Power'. Devolution also demonstrates and reflects the unequal sovereign status between the Celtic 'fringe' nations of Scotland, Wales and Northern Ireland, and Britain's 'core nation' of England; the latter 'core' nation simply assumes it is in sovereign control of Westminster which, numerically and politically, is a fact, and therefore it is in control of the UK as a whole. In other words, sovereign power over the UK and hence political control of the Celtic fringe 'devolved' nations rests with England, that is the brutal practical and political reality of the UK 'union'.

Oor unfreendly Tory maisters an aw thair unionist Anglophone thirlfowk wid blythely raither Scotlan wis nae mair, nae mair.

Devolution is therefore merely a political bone, with little meat on it, thrown to restless colonies or regions in order to deflect calls for cessation. Scotland has chewed on the devolution bone and found there is indeed little meat on it. After the 2014 referendum, and 'the Vow' to give more powers to Holyrood, Lord Smith's Commission for the UK Government[58] provided another bone with little or no real meat on it. Unionists know this and former Labour First Minister Lord McConnell was tasked to send Scots a further new bone to chew on, perhaps in the form of a second chamber at Holyrood. That was also found to have little meat on it, aside from some added social status for Scotland's Anglophone unionist elite. Many Scots are rightly dissatisfied with such periodic unionist crumbs falling from Westminster's table. More and more Scots want to taste the far better fare on the independence menu. Why chew on yesterday's sausage roll in a greasy devolution cafe when you can dine a la carte in the independence restaurant? That is at least one major difference between devolution and independence – a far superior menu of quality options.

The constitutional powerlessness of Scotland as a nation seems clear from recent events, as does the emptiness of any notion of Scottish sovereignty within the UK colonial straitjacket. Almost two-thirds of voters in Scotland opted to remain in the European Union (EU), and to remain as EU citizens, a democratic decision that has simply been ignored by Westminster. And the Scottish National Party (SNP) were elected in 2017 and 2019 on a mandate to deliver a second independence referendum, securing a Scottish majority at Westminster (in UK General Elections in 2015, 2017 and again in 2019) and at Holyrood to back this up. Yet the democratic wishes of the Scottish people have been ignored as Westminster refused to sanction another referendum, although whether Westminster has the power to prevent a referendum in Scotland still remains questionable.

Westminster simply chooses to ignore the democratic decisions of Scotland's people primarily because of the domination of the UK parliament by England's 533 MP's. Despite the creation of a Scottish Parliament (with limited powers) in 1999, the democratic deficit that that institution was supposed to end, remains. Clearly, a devolved parliament is just that, devolved. The Scottish Government also tested the relevance of the Sewel Convention (allegedly 'requiring' Scotland's permission on various matters) during the Supreme Court case on the triggering of Article 50 to withdraw from the EU. This ended with the Court asserting the right of Westminster (and hence its overwhelming majority of MP's representing England) to legislate on any matter in Scotland, devolved or not. Its inclusion in the Scotland Act gave the Sewel Convention 'recognition' but no actual legal effect.

We're fechtin fir oor nationheid, an tae bi unalike! Fir Scotlan's fowk tae bi juist alike anither kintra's fowk is fir thay fowk an oor nation an cultur an langage no tae exist at aw, thon's whit bein an Anglophone an colonisation's aw aboot - i.e. tae wrack an remuive oor cultur, oor langage, an oor nation an fowk tae, stick-an-stowe.

The UK Supreme Court's ruling asserted the sovereignty of Westminster which is effectively 82 per cent controlled by MP's representing England. The outcome of this is that the present Scottish Parliament is not a sovereign body. Such powers as it has, are simply powers devolved upon it from Westminster, the latter being the sovereign parliament for the whole UK yet controlled by the 'numerical preponderance' of England's MP's. Scotland's First Minister Nicola Sturgeon rightly described claims about Scotland being an equal partner in the UK as nothing more than empty rhetoric and that the supposed 'statutory embedding' of the Sewel Convention has been shown to be worthless.

So, a 'union of equals' the UK is clearly not. Recent events suggest that, rather than being a sovereign nation and people, Scotland is indeed in all practical terms treated akin to a colony in that decisions taken by the Scottish people are simply brushed aside by what is in effect an 'administering Power', which is Westminster and, in terms of overall voting power, Westminster is effectively England's MP's. There is therefore no 'union of equals' to speak of, (and no 'Scottish' veto over anything, it appears) which now seems a charade, a pretext, implying that the term 'unionist' is also a misnomer.

The rather obvious conclusion here is that, politically and in practice there is no 'union', Scotland and its erstwhile subject-people lack sovereignty, and are effectively rendered a colony.

Definition of Colonialism

More than 80 former colonies comprising some 750 million people have gained independence since the creation of the United Nations in 1945. At present, the UN 'lists' 17 Non-Self-Governing Territories (NSGTs) across the globe that remain to be decolonised, several of which are UK colonies. Thus, the process of decolonisation has come a long way but is not yet ended. Finishing the job involves a continuing dialogue among the 'administering Powers', the UN Special Committee on Decolonisation, and the peoples of the territories concerned, in accordance with the relevant UN resolutions on decolonisation. Reflecting its impatience with the administering Powers, the UN still refers to what it views as *the scourge of colonisation*, calling on member states, and notably the UK, to end this as soon as possible, and for them to be 'on the right side of history' in such matters.

It is important to recognise here that, to a significant extent independence and decolonisation are therefore one and the same thing. Of relevance here to Scotland's present situation is the fact that the UN considers Ireland to be a 'former colony'; this further indicates that Scotland is no different given that Ireland was likewise at one time deemed to be part of a supposed UK 'union', albeit the latter remains a constitutional arrangement dominated by England's MP's.

So, what are the specific features that define a colony? Historians distinguish between two overlapping forms of colonialism, namely: *settler colonialism* involving large-scale immigration, often motivated by religious, political, or economic reasons, and; *Exploitation colonialism* which may involve fewer colonists and focuses on access to resources.

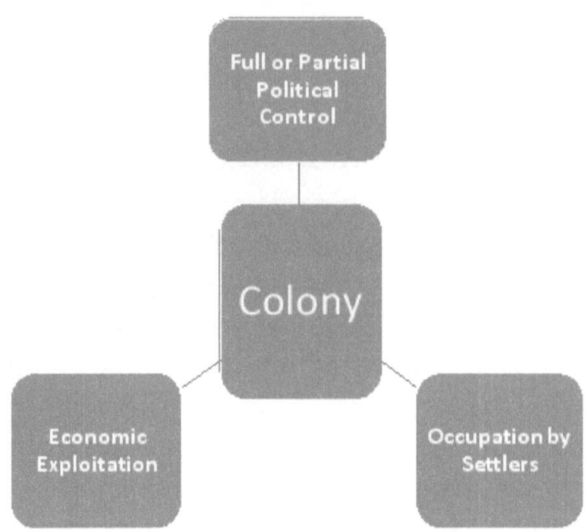

Key Elements of Colonialism

Common definitions of colonialism, which also relate to imperialism, include: the control or governing influence of a nation over a dependent country, territory, or people[59]; the practice by which a powerful country directly controls less powerful countries and uses their resources to increase its own power and wealth[60], and; the policy or practice of a wealthy or powerful nation maintaining or extending its control over other countries, especially in .... exploiting resources[61].

Colonialism therefore typically involves the following three key elements, each of which is analysed here in subsequent sections of the chapter in the specific context of Scotland (Baird 2017):

a)   the policy or practice of acquiring full or partial political control over another country:

b)   occupying it with settlers, and;

c)   exploiting it economically.

Political Control

It seems indisputable from recent events that Westminster (and hence England's 82 per cent majority of MP's there) controls Scotland politically and is therefore in effect Scotland's 'administering Power'. This 'political control' is evident whichever party happens to be in power in Westminster at any given time, as they can do as they wish with Scotland, despite having few (if any) MP's elected in Scotland. The Scottish Parliament and Scottish Government are merely devolved 'creatures' created by Westminster, with limited powers, which in any case can be overruled by the administering power, as the Supreme Court decision on Brexit confirmed.

Mike Small of Bella Caledonia, stated in relation to the Brexit chaos, that: *"Scotland emerge from this chaos as a subaltern people – derided in Westminster and denied a Section 30 Order, told that a mandate in Holyrood and a mandate at Westminster wouldn't count. Effectively we're being told that there is no democratic route to self-determination"* (Small 2019).

The term 'subaltern' is highly relevant here, as it generally means a lower ranking officer, or a lower status. More specifically, in post-colonial studies the term 'subaltern' designates the colonial populations who are socially, politically, and geographically outside the hierarchy of power of a colony, and outside of the empire's metropolitan homeland (Gandhi 1998). The Scottish people may vote however they wish, but their decisions in referenda and in national elections can be and indeed are ignored and overruled by the administering Power, as has been the case on numerous occasions. Any perceived sovereignty of the Scottish people does not exist within the current UK union 'arrangement'; Scottish sovereignty is simply not recognized by the administrative Power, the latter considering any sovereignty over Scotland's territory and people to reside only with Westminster, as reflected in the Supreme Court ruling. The administrative Power may claim Scotland has representation via a supposed 'union', however, in practice the administrative Power (and England's 533 MP's, 82 per cent of the Westminster Parliament) ultimately controls the politics of Scotland irrespective of democratic decisions made by Scots. Scotland is therefore in precisely the same position Ireland was prior to the latter's independence, when Ireland was likewise considered to be a part of a 'union', whilst since its independence (i.e. post-decolonisation) the UN considers Ireland to be a 'former colony'.

Scotland is therefore under the full or partial political control of an UK administering 'Power' (i.e. Westminster and hence England's MP's who form its majority), and thus meets the initial defining feature of a colony.

Settler Occupation

The earlier chapter on 'Demographics' outlined and explained the extent of population displacement and replacement in Scotland since the 1707 'union'. Historical census data confirms that the largest single ethnic migrant group coming to Scotland over the last one hundred years and more has been people from rest-UK, mostly England, and particularly representing the professions (science, engineering, education, managerial etc.). A colony's recruitment of many of its professionals and managers largely emanating from its administrative Power is clearly a typical norm of colonial administration and is aided here in that most of Scotland's professional and managerial vacancies are primarily advertised in the London metropolitan press and therefore are aimed at candidates within England's far larger population. The standard language recruitment criteria for job candidates to speak only English coupled with a zero requirement to speak (or understand) the Scots language reflects the Anglophone ethnic prioritisation of the 'administrative Power' and serves to confirm and reinforce the colonial (i.e. subaltern) status of and disregard for Scots speakers.

In recent years, inbound migration of people coming from rest-UK to Scotland appears to have accelerated; over the twenty-year period between 1995-2014, approximately one million people moved from England to Scotland, with peaks of over 70,000 a year. This implies that, over the past half a century, possibly as many as two million people may have moved from rest-UK to Scotland. For a nation with a population of little over 5 million people, such inflows are indeed very considerable. Over the same period there has been a somewhat lesser outflow of migrants from Scotland seeking opportunities elsewhere.

Clearly, the population of Scotland is both being boosted and replaced through 'occupation by settlers' from rest-UK, primarily England, a movement oriented towards the Anglophone professional classes, and which has been a long-term phenomenon lasting a century or more.

Scotland has experienced substantial, long term, focused, and rising occupation by settlers mainly from the UK 'administering Power' (England), coupled with significant displacement of its own people, and thus exhibits the second defining feature of a colony.

Fowk cannae ser twa maisters; ye aye luve ane an spite the ither.

Economic Exploitation

Aided by prevailing laws enacted by its 'administrative Power', Scotland has experienced centuries of highly concentrated land ownership, much of it speculative and wasteful, holding back economic development, and this continues today. Resultant inflated land values have constrained development and led to other economic limiting factors such as a shortage of affordable housing, now made worse by relatively low wages for many people who are unable to secure mortgages. This and the UK Government's policy to sell-off Scottish council housing stock massively increased the private rented sector resulting in increasing levels of poverty, including in-work poverty.

In terms of Scotland's natural resources, oil and gas represents a loss of enormous financial proportions since the 1970s, squandered by Scotland's larger 'administrative Power' in its failed attempts to overcome its own seemingly endless economic problems and ever rising national debt. The 'administrative Power' intentionally suppressed information for thirty years ('McCrone' Report, 1974[62]) concerning the true worth and potential impacts of Scotland's oil and gas reserves (Baird 2019). That report suggested that an independent Scotland holding such extensive oil and gas reserves would have a *"chronic surplus to a quite embarrassing degree and its currency would become the hardest in Europe"*. This exploitation continues today, e.g. with extensive gas reserves in Scottish territory effectively 'sold off' to international firms yet with little if any of the value or benefit gained from the resource flowing through to Scotland's people.

It was a fine report that McCrone, then a senior civil servant, produced in the 1970s and he could have leaked it at the time, like any Scottish patriot might. But had he done so he would perhaps not be withdrawing his UK civil service pension, and he would maybe not have been given a university chair, or been made a Companion of the Order of the Bath by the Queen, nor made a Fellow of the Royal Society of Edinburgh where many of the 'top' Anglophone unionists who administer Scotland's social institutions regularly meet to discuss matters of common interest. McCrone will always be remembered by the 'union' side for his loyalty to the UK administrative Power (hence his ample unionist rewards, baubles and status) and by the nationalist side for quite the opposite reasons insofar as Scotland is concerned.

Conspiring with the administrative Power's political leaders of the time to deceive a nation of its wealth was one thing. McCrone then went on to head up the Scottish Office Industry Dept under Margaret Thatcher's Tories and hence presided over the rapid de-industrialisation of Scotland and the destruction of much of what remained of the economy with its resulting mass unemployment. McCrone and other elite Scottish unionists are well worth their unionist rewards, though perhaps equally worthy also of Burn's description: *"We're bought and sold for English gold-Such a parcel of rogues in a nation!"*[63].

The more important question here remains, what would the impact of independence have been had it occurred in the 1970's and with Scottish oil & gas revenues aplenty? Clearly, Scotland would have benefitted from cheaper energy and electricity for the last 40+ years as well as from vast financial surpluses. There would have been no need for expensive nuclear power stations to be built in Scotland, the latter forming a key part of UK energy policy. Low cost electricity would have allowed Scotland to become one of the most competitive European countries for manufacturing goods and for attracting inward investment. Instead, the UK imposed energy privatisation inflicted on Scotland the highest electricity prices in Europe, which no industry can withstand, so most industries have since up and left Scotland. What has been and therefore remains the opportunity cost of remaining within the UK union? Scotland's energy policy and industrial development policies would clearly have been totally different under independence as would its national treasury.

Wi a furrin leid garred doon Scots bairns' thrapples throu-oot schuil, whit daes onybody expect? Thon aye maks Scots bairns awfu confuised an haein a lack o confeedence.

The British Tory deindustrialisation policies in the 1980s left Scotland an industrial wasteland with closures of steelworks, shipbuilding, coal mining and heavy engineering. And this occurred just prior to the global boom in steel and shipbuilding from the mid 1990's onwards, with Scotland missing out entirely. Scotland even today remains more than self-sufficient in oil and gas and could still develop an energy and industrial policy vastly different to that which exists within the UK. The West of Shetland fields alone contain enough gas to sustain the whole of Scotland for generations. Ineos invested £1bn in a new Forties-Grangemouth pipeline upgrade and refinery modernisation also for the next thirty years production. Aberdeen is developing a new £350m seaport to serve offshore activity. Atlantic frontier fields are now being developed. However, none of these oil & gas financial surpluses will accrue to Scotland, they are extracted from Scotland by the UK 'administrative Power'. Clearly, Scotland would be quite different with independence as to be unrecognisable to the colonial economic basket case it became within and due to the UK 'union' stranglehold over its key resources.

Many areas of Scotland suffering from de-industrialisation over the past thirty years have still not fully recovered and the impacts were wide ranging covering adverse health effects, unemployment, lower incomes, increased part-time working, increased welfare costs, poor housing and infrastructure, poverty and deprivation (The Coalfields Regeneration Trust 2019). Replacement jobs due to deindustrialisation, where they exist, tend to be low wage, with today's relatively low unemployment levels masked by masses of people on zero hours contracts and many others pushed into self-employment, with in-work poverty rising.

Other major resources incude aggregates, e.g. Glensanda, Europe's largest granite quarry with 800 million tonnes reserves lasting for another 100 years[64], and fisheries, including aquaculture, are important areas of economic exploitation where 'rents' have been intercepted by corporate entities due to inadequate regulations designed by Westminster primarily working in favour of vested interests. UK regulation of power supply has meanwhile tended to hinder development of renewable energy in Scotland whilst ensuring continued surpluses for private energy suppliers given strategic monopolistic positions in the country, resulting in higher energy prices for Scottish consumers.

Scotch whisky is a unique location-specific high-volume, high-value global export product, and the UK's major food and drink export, yet likewise any major benefits accruing from this sector to the Scottish economy and people remain limited. Increasingly automated, the industry's ownership has been allowed to move mostly outside Scotland, offering opportunities for transfer pricing which makes stated export values appear considerably less than what they might otherwise be. Export sales in 2018 were stated as worth £4.7 billion for 1.28 billion 70cl equivalent bottles which amounts to just £3.67 per 70cl bottle[65]. Yet even in duty free outlets the lowest price blended scotch price is seldom less than £10.00 per 70cl bottle equivalent, with most deluxe and malt brands tending to be well over £30.00 per 70cl bottle up to £100.00 per bottle and even higher[66]. The actual export value of whisky appears to be heavily understated by perhaps two-three times, possibly more. In addition, any taxation raised from UK whisky sales goes directly to the 'administrative Power'. Curiously, the Scotch Whisky Association key personnel appear to be drawn largely from the UK Foreign Office and other UK Ministries within the administrative

Power signifying the strategic importance of this sector, not least to the UK trade balance as well as to private interests controlling the business, most of which are based outside Scotland.

Intra-UK trade and the purchases England makes from Scotland are often cited as a reason to maintain the union. However, Scotland's annual exports (goods and services) to rest-UK of £45bn are dwarfed by Scotland's annual retail spend of £106bn, almost all of which comprises goods supplied through Regional Distribution Centres (RDC's) and from major retailers based in England, with most supply chain jobs located there rather than in Scotland. Scotland therefore imports (i.e. buys) from rest-UK firms at least twice as much as it sells in return. Whether this imbalanced 'arrangement' offers good value for the Scottish people remains uncertain, not least given the retail sector concentration whereby relatively few large UK retail firms control much of the Scottish market.

A study by Graham Ennis argued that the misuse of land in Scotland due to concentrated land ownership is 'criminal' (Wiszniewski 2018). Ennis's study on the misuse of land found that the potential of a Finland sized forest cover was entirely practical in Scotland, as the climate here grows trees about twice as fast. Basically, Scotland's potential forest products output could equal that of Finland (i.e. €23bn a year). This is somewhat greater than the mere £32 million 'the lairds' claim to generate for Scotland from their private shooting and fishing estates. By adding to this agroforestry, small farms and crofts etc., Ennis estimated it would be possible to accrue about €35bn of economic product from Rural Scotland annually. This would take about 25 years in all to develop, but in the very first year the impact would wipe out the £32 million from killing wildlife. Clearly Scotland's land could be far better used than simply as a dormant asset play for the global rich.

Since the 1980's, the privatisation (i.e. sell offs) and de-regulation of Scotland's major public utilities (energy, ports, airports, council housing stock and other assets) has resulted in numerous examples of market failure, including exploitation of consumers by private sector successor company monopolies. Inadequate regulation and increased UK-style industry self-regulation has led to excessive corporate profits with consumers left worse off due to higher prices. Low initial sale prices achieved for state sell-off's meant successor firms became asset rich overnight with the public (i.e. the Scottish people) not receiving due compensation. Frequent sell-on's of public utility assets since at higher and often inflated prices (e.g. to non-transparent offshore registered private equity 'funds') reflects their regulatory and monopoly power and high profits, rather than infrastructure quality, the latter suffering now from a historic lack of investment, partly due to highly leveraged/ indebted transactions. Scotland today has some of the highest energy prices in Europe effectively hindering commercial and industrial competitiveness and economic development whilst creating rising fuel poverty. Privatised utilities making limited investments in new infrastructure means Scotland's infrastructure is increasingly outdated, obsolete, inefficient, congested, unreliable, and costly to maintain and operate. All of this makes for an economy that is not globally competitive, as reflected in a deteriorating trade position and collapse of Foreign Direct Investment.

Corporate law reforms and deregulation policies introduced by the UK administrative 'Power' facilitated numerous takeovers of major Scottish businesses, particularly since the 1960's, many of which were subsequently closed down with resultant job and skills losses which further diminished exports. Many firms, including owners of privatised utilities operating in Scotland, are nowadays offshore registered in UK crown dependencies hence pay little or no tax. The City of London deregulation and 'light touch' emphasis championed by the UK administrative Power helped pave the way for the virtual collapse of what was once a highly differentiated and internationally respected Scottish financial sector after the deregulated UK banking system failed in 2008.

Falling exports suggests there has been inadequate trade facilitation and trade development initiatives undertaken by the UK administrative Power or its devolved agencies. Trade development has been further constrained by the privatisation of ports in Scotland, with new 'offshore' owners unwilling and not required to make investments in what are now high cost, obsolete (mostly Victorian) ports, wholly unattractive to international shipping services or the needs of modern ships and trade logistics systems. Enforced routing of most Scottish trade through distant ports in the south of England is subject to high and rising land transport costs and is adversely affected by increasing congestion and road/ rail capacity limitations throughout England. These supply chain constraints added to high factor costs especially in energy and transport has made manufacturing in Scotland uncompetitive.

Most of Scotland's imports (by value) now enter the UK through southern England ports and proceed through logistic centres in mid England prior to despatch to Scotland. This practice helps create transport and supply chain jobs mainly in England whilst the extra land transport costs adds to Scotland's logistic expense. Scottish international logistics initiatives have been few and far between and inadequately funded or supported by the State. The Rosyth-Zeebrugge ferry service which started in May 2002, offered a fast, daily connection to Flanders and easy access to most continental markets. However, increases in port charges at privately owned Rosyth and a lack of adequate terminal space there for freight, coupled with the absence of a proper 'Motorway of the Sea' (MoS) long term contractual arrangement between the State and operator (the UK Government opposed support for international maritime transport, despite the EU allowing such aid), led to the operator ending the service, notwithstanding the increasing traffic volumes carried and positive modal shift and environmental impacts.

Scotland badly needs investment in major new Scottish central belt ports to cater for more modern and larger ships now in service on the North Sea. Compared with port infrastructure developments in Denmark, Norway, Ireland, Finland, Estonia, Poland etc. Scotland looks more like a less developed nation, so it seems rather obvious why Scotland's trade performance remains lacklustre – i.e. Scotland is simply not competitive, due to outdated and expensive infrastructure and high energy costs. Scotland also lacks an adequately funded state National Investment Bank[67] to help support and facilitate export trade and to provide loan guarantees in industries such as shipbuilding.

Long-term and ongoing economic practices and policies imposed by the UK 'administrative Power' across all key economic sectors therefore serve to hinder Scotland's international competitiveness, resulting in the prevailing zero or near zero growth reality and declining export trade position. Scotland's economy is constantly struggling to avoid heading into recession, disadvantaged through being tied to the administrative Power's high inflation and an ever-weakening GB£ currency.

Scotland is subject to ongoing economic exploitation by the UK administering power, and therefore meets the third and final defining feature of a colony.

Independence is Decolonisation

There is clearly no UK 'union' insofar as Scotland is concerned. Any alleged 'union' in which 533 English MP's controlling 82 per cent of the votes in Westminster may do as they wish with Scotland, or a 'union' with no Scottish veto on anything, is clearly not a 'union' or partnership 'of equals'. Scotland is effectively a territory controlled by the UK 'administrative Power' (i.e. England) and hence to all intents and purposes is a colony. Scotland demonstrates all three essential features of and hence perfectly fits the definition of a colony, namely:

a)   Scotland is subject to full or partial political control by another country (i.e. England, which is effectively the UK's 'administrative Power');
b)   Scotland has been and continues to be occupied by significant numbers of 'settlers' from the UK 'administrative Power', and;
c)   Scotland is exploited economically by the UK 'administering Power'.

The Declaration on the Granting of Independence to all Colonial Countries and Peoples was adopted by the United Nations General Assembly in 1960 (resolution 1514: XV). International law is clear on this matter, in accordance with the General Assembly's mandate under Article 13, paragraph 1 (a), of the Charter of the United Nations (McWhinney 2008):

-        That the subjection of peoples to alien subjugation, domination and exploitation constitutes a denial of fundamental human rights (art. 1);
-    That all peoples have the right to self-determination, but that this necessarily includes the right to freely determine their political status and freely to pursue their economic, social and cultural development (art. 2);
- That all armed action or repressive measures of all kinds directed against dependent peoples shall cease (art. 4);
-    That immediate steps shall be taken, in United Nations Trust and Non-Self Governing Territories or all other territories which have not yet attained independence, to transfer all powers to the peoples of those territories (art. 5).

The Declaration's juridical status has since been elevated to the rank of imperative principles of international law (*jus cogens*), binding on the United Nations and entering into general international law.
Scottish independence is therefore also about decolonisation. Given this reality, there would seem good reason for

Scotland's 'nationalist' elected majorities and government which advocate independence to have Scotland 'listed' on the UN List of Colonies to be Decolonised in an effort to end what the UN itself describes as *the scourge of colonisation*. Scotland's longstanding and continuing colonial experience and suffering as an exploited economy and repressed people means that independence is a fundamental necessity to ensure the equitable and proper social and economic development of the nation and its people.

Only sovereignty can fully encourage and allow for the further development of Scotland and its people, whilst at the same time protecting a threatened culture and language (Hechter, 2017: p. xvii).

CHAPTER 7: NATIONALISM

Nationalism Objectives

Nationalism is a political ideology about promoting the interest of a nation or group of people, with the aim of gaining or maintaining the nation's sovereignty and hence self-governance over its homeland (Smith 2010). A basic principle of nationalism is that a nation and its people should be free to govern themselves, which is effectively self-determination. Related to nationalism is the issue of national identity which is based on shared social characteristics such as culture, language, and a common history (Triandafyllidou 1998). This form of nationalism is typically referred to as self-determination nationalism, or anti-colonialism nationalism (Velychenko 2012). This is the form of nationalism Scotland seeks through independence.

On the other hand, there is what is termed 'trans-national nationalism', where one nation, with a common ethnicity, culture and language, extends its sphere of influence and control over other, often neighbouring nations which have a different ethnicity, culture and language(s) (Hochman 2015). The latter form of nationalism will often be developed through force or threat of force, seldom by invitation. Trans-national nationalism may also involve racial or ethnic discrimination, where certain 'non-core' ethnic groups are marginalised and disenfranchised, for instance they may be excluded from taking up positions of authority.

There are clearly different objectives and different nationalisms depending on which form is being pursued and promulgated. On the one hand a given nation and people defined by ethnicity, culture and language may feel dissatisfied in the way they are governed and hence controlled by another nation and its people, the latter also defined by holding to a different ethnicity, culture and language. There are a great many examples, not least the Baltic States, various nations in the former Soviet Union and earlier Russian empire, and numerous former colonies globally, including the more than eighty nations that have secured independence since the creation of the UN.

> *Scotlan needs a gey 'lang spuin' tae deal wi Westminster, nivver mynd ony ither naition.*

One might therefore distinguish here between trans-national nationalism which is the occupation by one country of other countries and assuming control over them, and self-determination nationalism which relates primarily to the self-determination of a single nation and its people. The latter may also be referred to as decolonisation.

The objective of Scottish nationalism is clearly not about occupying neighbouring countries. Despite this, so-called Scottish 'nationalists' only need to mention 'England' to be accused of xenophobia and racism. However, the definition of xenophobia does not readily fit with the desire of the Scottish people for independence, which is merely about the self-determination and decolonisation of a people, i.e. the Scottish people. Xenophobia involves *"the irrational fear and distrust of that which is perceived to be foreign or strange"* (Bolaffi 2003, p. 332). Xenophobia therefore seems more the condition of the British/English rulers over Scotland when taking it upon themselves to oppose and block the self-determination of Scotland and its people, and to continue to support trans-national nationalism and with that the Anglophone colonisation and cultural imperialism imposed on Scotland. In the context of Scottish independence, British/English xenophobia is essentially a fear and distrust of Scottish culture and language and hence a fear and distrust of the Scottish people being dominant in their own land, i.e. within Scotland. Thus, the objective of Scottish self-determination nationalism is clearly quite different from British trans-national nationalism; the latter is concerned with continued oppression and colonisation of other 'peoples', whilst the former is about decolonisation and hence liberation of a 'people', i.e. the Scots.

National Identity

Previous research suggests a close alignment between national identities and political attitudes to the constitutional question in Scotland (Bond 2015) with primarily two competing identities in competition for votes, i.e. Scottish and British. Other influencing factors proposed here include subjective national belonging and sense of affinity with a British 'social union'. One problem here is that many Scots have, since the 1707 union, developed what has been termed a 'dual identity', *"a complex mix of Scottishness and Britishness"* (Devine 2013). It is argued that a binary referendum question (on idependence) does not *"capture the full complexities of duality"*. This research points to the 'Moreno Question' (named after Luis Moreno, a former PhD student at University of Edinburgh) who proposed the existence of no less than five identities in Scotland: only Scottish, not British; more Scottish than British; equally Scottish as British; more British than Scottish; and only British, not Scottish. Such outcomes inevitably reflect cultural and linguistic influences, as well as the impact of appropriated racial oppression which influence and determine national identity preferences. For example, the expanding rest-UK population resident in Scotland might be expected to have little affinity with Scotland culturally or linguistically, and hence may be least likely to identify as Scottish.

> *Dae ye no ken ony Scots wirds? Ye widna lairn ony in Scottish schuils whan ye wis a bairn, anely Englis wis garred doon yer thrapples thare.*

Those searching for an explanation to the question of national identity (or to independence) from the purely political perspective are destined to remain wide of the mark. As Bond (2000) noted, the question of national identity among the Scottish electorate *"is characterised by complexity that has been insufficiently explored or ignored completely"*. Research in Scotland has tended to ignore cultural-linguistic influences as well as Scotland's ever changing demographics and the impact these and other factors (e.g. ethnicity) have on national identity, as far as the Scottish electorate and hence Scottish independence is concerned.

In analyzing the question of national allegiance in Northern Ireland, Pettigrew (2016) refers to a 2015 Behaviour & Attitudes cross-border opinion poll which found 91 per cent of Irish-identifying participants stated their support for Irish unity in the long-term, whilst 94 per cent of British-identifying participants preferred to remain within the UK union for the foreseeable future. Unionist appetite for a united Ireland is thus stifled by the very nature of Northern Ireland unionism itself, which Pettigrew views as a form of British nationalism.

In this regard the binary usage of 'nationalist' and 'unionist' in Northern Ireland political discourse inadvertently disguises the fact that Northern Ireland unionism is an ideological nationalism of its own, as is likewise the case of unionism in Scotland. Political unionism (or rather trans-national nationalism) is not simply a mere pro-union point of view; it is, according to Pettigrew, a *'culturally-intertwined political identity'*. Trans-national nationalism (e.g. the UK 'union') involves the fusing together of diverse cultures to seek to manufacture a supposed 'union', albeit a 'union' controlled by, and reflecting the culture of, one dominating 'core' entity. Clearly not all cultures are quite so easily infused and such union entities remain essentially what they are, i.e. artificial political constructs.

Kuper and Symanski (2014) noted that *"places like Gibraltar and the Falkland Islands have more symbols of Britishness than many areas in the UK, where ostentatiously displaying union jacks might be seen as old-fashioned or embarrassing"*. This analogy could be applied just as well to the UK itself when comparing Northern Ireland unionists to inhabitants of the British 'mainland'. Polling in 2015 found that 55 per cent of northerners rejected Irish unification *even* if there was a financial incentive to support it. Notably, of those with a British identity who participated, an overwhelming majority rejected it (90 per cent). Any economic 'argument' for, or against constitutional change would therefore seem of far less significance than culture and language and, with that, national identity and associated emotional attachment and sense of belonging are clearly more influential factors in any voter decision.

Heid bummers an e'en schuil maisters invitet in tae rin Scotlan's institushuns dinnae hiv tae lairn oor leid aither, dae thay?

Whereas some may believe that 'Scottish' unionists were motivated more by self-interest, not sentimentality, in voting against independence in 2014, Northern Ireland unionists clearly exhibit an innate emotional attachment to Britain alone, and therefore they approach the constitutional question through a prism of identity rather than via any monetary lens. It is therefore the sense of identity that is the predominant factor here when it comes to the constitutional question. The position is perhaps far more similar in Scotland than many seem to think, where any economic case (for independence) is similarly unlikely to sway unionists to vote 'Yes' for exactly the same reasons that an economic case would not sway Scottish nationalists to vote 'No'. In Scotland, however, the prevailing political narrative still largely assumes the economic case for or against Scottish independence to be above that of identity, and the debate to be less 'ethnic' so to speak. This view ignores the critical role that culture and language play in decisions or emotions concerning identity, with demographic change further influencing outcomes as far as Scottish independence is concerned.

As in Scotland, language also forms a key influence in the cultural divide in Northern Ireland, where nationalists want the Irish language taught in schools and unionists want Ulster Scots to be taught. Whilst language is not the only indicator of cultural distinctiveness it is certainly one of the most basic and fundamental influences when it comes to national identity. Perhaps the most significant historical cultural difference, other than language, is religion, and this is more evident in Northern Ireland than in Scotland, although some distinction between Catholicism and Protestantism remains in Scotland also. In mainland Britain another fissure is between Anglicanism and Presbyterianism which are also different 'beasts' and underpin quite different social structures and national ideologies-ethos, and indeed are representative of further cultural difference between Scotland and England, as reflected in the Treaty of Union itself; the latter specifically guaranteed the continued role and hence national significance of the protestant Church of Scotland, as well as the Scottish legal system.

In any political battle over national identity, for many people language and hence culture as key influencers will always overcome mere economics. According to Medeiros (2017: p. 375) *"...it is an individual's linguistic perceptions that directly determine their national identity."* This emphasis on language is especially important within multinational 'countries' such as the UK in which a minority ethnic group such as the Scots will feel tension and a loss of distinctiveness in part through language oppression and other forms of discrimination. Medeiros established that perceptions of discrimination by minority group members may lead to negative feelings towards their (multinational) 'core' country. Globally, most groups in conflict are separated along linguistic lines and Scotland seems little different, even despite the British State's suppression and intended replacement of the Scots language.

Any 'people' seeking national self-determination will

therefore share a common identity which is linguistically and culturally determined, also reflecting the wider criteria and definition of 'a people' (United Nations ICJ 2017). This also implies, however, that those opposing self-determination of a minority people will tend to share another different identity that is also linguistically and culturally determined; in Scotland's case this is predominantly the Anglophone or 'British' identifying community. Scottish self-determination and independence is clearly, therefore, in large part a question of national identity, contested between those who have a sense of belonging to Scotland and who hold to a Scottish national identity (and hence Scottish ethnicity), and those who do not.

Civic Nationalism

A term generating significant interest in the Scottish independence debate is 'civic nationalism', which is based not on ethnicity, nor on culture, language and common history, but rather on supposed liberal values of shared and equal rights. However, crucially, civic nationalism is also dependent on an association of people who identify themselves as 'belonging to a nation' (Nash 2001, p. 391). Where civic nationalism seems to fail insofar as Scotland's pursuit of self-determination is concerned is that a significant proportion of resident 'No' voters evidently do not primarily identify themselves as 'belonging' to Scotland. This is largely due to cultural and linguistic influences and differences, and hence relates to national identity, given that 'No' voters by implication reject the offer of Scottish identity and therefore reject 'belonging' to Scotland, and indeed reject the very offer of Scottish citizenship when they vote to block and oppose Scottish independence. Logically, therefore, a focus on civic nationalism undermines the quest for self-determination and must stand the risk of failing within a nation in which a significant portion of the voting population demonstrate absolutely no desire for the identity of, or hold a deep sense of 'belonging' to, the nation and people seeking self-determination.

Civic nationalism may be described as 'liberal and inclusive' and ethnic nationalism as 'illiberal and exclusive', however such distinctions are not nearly so straightforward (Bond 2015). The perhaps excessive desire of the SNP Scottish Government to be seen to be ultra-inclusive and open (to other nationals) tends to ignore what voters are actually being asked to identify with in a referendum on Scottish independence, which is the creation of a 'new' national identity and the quest for self-determination of a distinct defined group of 'people', i.e. the Scots. This 'ask' represents a major challenge more especially for those voters who do not primarily identify as being a Scottish 'national', and particularly when they are not Scottish (i.e. by culture/heritage or linguistically) to begin with.

> *Wha bides in Bute Hoose nor Holyrood maiters naething, Scotlan's institushins are aye full o thon preeviliged, conservative an unionist, an maistly Anglophone heid bummers.*

Ethnicity, culture, heritage, language, shared history and a common suffering remain the core defining features of 'a people' and hence shape their (national) identity and sense of 'belonging', as well as their sense of injustice. In this regard 'civic nationalism', involving as it implies peoples representing multiple national identities, may represent a liberal ideal, however, civic nationalism cannot be relied upon to deliver self-determination of 'a people' or free them and their nation from colonisation and oppression. Indeed, the unique and irregular form of civic nationalism adopted in Scotland may merely serve to block and prevent self-determination and perpetuate colonisation, as was arguably the outcome in Scotland's referendum in 2014 due to an open voter franchise based on residence. As Bond (2015) notes: "*Many of those who contributed to the decision on Scotland's constitutional future in 2014 would not understand themselves as subjectively Scottish at all".* Moreover, a far greater sense of belonging would be expected among those Scots living outside of Scotland, especially by birthplace, also by ancestry (McCrone and Bechhofer 2008), yet who were excluded from voting.

Not surprisingly, empirical research has established that those who identify exclusively or primarily as Scottish have the greatest propensity to vote for Scottish independence than those who do not identify as Scottish (Bond 2015). This suggests that self-determination and independence of a distinct people and nation must first be fulfilled and secured before national voting rights and equal citizenship can be handed out 'willy-nilly' to peoples of other (national) identities who may, or may not, wish to apply for Scottish citizenship. Scotland appears to be endeavoring to do things the other way around (or 'airse fer elbae', in Scots) by embracing supposed civic nationalism 'ideals' and seeking to promote a form of 'social union' between diverse ethnic national groups prior to first securing the independence of its own 'people', whilst at the same time making the rather optimistic (and clearly incorrect) assumption that all residents will hold a 'sense of belonging' to Scotland and hence will wish to vote for a 'new' Scottish nation State and take up Scottish citizenship. Clearly, independence must be viewed as an essential prerequisite before any form of civic nationalism can occur, not least because a nation cannot legally offer its national citizenship to other 'nationals' prior to becoming an independent State in any event.

National identity is therefore a highly significant factor and indeed represents a critical issue in the quest for Scottish independence, yet it has arguably never been properly considered despite demonstrable empirical evidence of its importance. The British Attitudes Survey, for example, asked people what they thought made them 'truly British' as an identity. It was found that 'being British' for most respondents

(63 per cent) is dependent on two main factors: (1) being able to speak the English language and (2) being born in Britain (British Social Attitudes Survey 2013). These were regarded as 'ethnic' factors. Only 31 per cent of people stressed 'civic' factors as making people 'truly British' and primarily this involved holding British citizenship, and therefore reflecting a strong desire for respondents to hold British citizenship, as reflecting national identity.

If we factor the same question into the Scottish national 'situation' one might reasonably expect similar results. For example, if Scots were asked what it is to be 'truly Scottish', likewise most Scots might reasonably be expected to similarly respond that this involves speaking the Scots (or Gaelic) language and being born in Scotland. Moreover, as a formal Scottish national citizenship cannot exist or be offered until after Scotland is independent, this implies that 'ethnic' criteria (i.e. primarily language and country of birth) will be by far the most significant factors when it comes to determining identity and support (or not) for Scottish independence. This further demonstrates the importance of language and culture in determining identity and helps explain why the vast majority of pro-independence voters are Scots speakers who are born in Scotland and hold to a Scottish national identity, whereas many if not most anti-independence voters are Anglophone and hold to a British national identity, the latter rejecting outright any offer or prospect of Scottish citizenship. Clearly, the SNP Scottish Government's misguided and premature embrace of 'civic nationalism' ideals only serves to increase the anti-independence vote and effectively acts to thwart self-determination and decolonisation.

Self-Determination Nationalism

British 'Unionism' is clearly a nationalist political ideology and indeed one of the more aggressive forms given it is generally focused on the occupation and control by one dominant core country of other nations and cultural minorities comprising neighboring countries, which is effectively trans-national nationalism. Trans-national nationalism has a long and largely dubious history often leading to conflict (e.g. former Soviet Union, former Yugoslavia, Spain, UK etc.). Self-determination nationalism, on the other hand, is about a people reaching out for and accessing their own inalienable human right to self-determination, which are presently denied, as set out by the UN Charter[68]:

> *"The right to development is an inalienable human right by virtue of which every human person and all peoples are entitled to participate in, contribute to, and enjoy economic, social, cultural and political development, in which all human rights and fundamental freedoms can be fully realized. The human right to development also implies the full realization of the right of peoples to self-determination, which includes, subject to the relevant provisions of both International Covenants on Human Rights, the exercise of their inalienable right to full sovereignty over all their natural wealth and resources."*
> ((Articles 1.1 and 1.2, Declaration on the Right to Development)

As noted, British 'unionism' is clearly a trans-national nationalist political ideology in which one's attachment and sense of belonging to 'Britain', even as an artificial national construct, and as with any national attachment, is based on identity, emotion and nationalism, and rather less on matters of economics or any other general policy issue (Hassan 2013). In this respect it is unionists, or to be more precise, British nationalists, who remain in denial that their ideology is not nationalism, and indeed one of the more dangerous and aggressive forms. It is also unionists who tend to obsess about the perceived threat an independent Scotland presents to their

'British' identity, however artificial that notion or 'nation' may be, and hence 'threatens' their British nationalism (Maxwell 2014).

Key in this regard, particularly in the context of any referendum or national election, is the question of an individual's national identity and hence their emotional allegiance and sense of belonging to a nation or people. In any referendum on Scottish independence, voters are faced with the straight and unambiguous choice to demonstrate their national allegiance to either a British State or to a new Scottish State, and this is fundamentally a choice which reflects one's identity. This implies that **the allegiance of voters in Scotland to a British national identity and hence to supporting trans-national nationalism therefore represents the main barrier to Scottish independence.**

This further implies that a difficult challenge (for Scottish self-determination and hence for independence) exists so long as Scotland continues to insist on offering what remains a unique and irregular voter franchise at the highest national and constitutional level whereby more or less any 'resident' and of any nationality in Scotland is invited to pick and choose whether the nation and people of Scotland may exist as an independent state, or remain as an exploited colony. Like any Imperial Roman Emperor, those who have the least allegiance or identity or cultural and linguistic connection or sense of belonging to Scotland may be expected to give Scotland the thumbs down, as occurred in 2014. Here the unnecessary and prematurely initiated 'civic nationalism' approach of the SNP Scottish Government serves to undermine efforts toward self-determination and independence insofar as the Scottish people are concerned.

Self-determination nationalism is therefore specifically about a defined people seeking self-determination and decolonisation, it is never about peoples holding to other national identities who happen to live in the same place as the people seeking self-determination. As Scotland, politically at least, may readily be defined as a colony, this means the UN Declaration on the Granting of Independence to Colonial Countries and Peoples and subsequent resolutions applies as much to Scotland as to anywhere else. This provides the required legal linkage between self-determination and its goal of decolonisation, and a postulated new international law-based right of freedom also in economic self-determination (McWhinney 2008). It is also worth remembering that the Declaration's legislative objective, which has largely been fulfilled, was to legally terminate the former Colonial Empires. As far as the UK 'Celtic Fringe' internal colonies is concerned this is still work in progress and there is a need to press on to successful conclusion of the process, within which Scottish independence should be viewed a part.

Trans-national Nationalism

Trans-national nationalism invariably involves a State's aggressive and xenophobic oppression of minorities, taking control over other, often neighbouring, national territories, their social institutions, and their 'people' (Hochman 2015). Historically the British state has undertaken aggressive actions in many if not most of its former colonies, this is nothing new. Nowadays it is known what went on for decades in Northern Ireland with, for instance, the collusion between British authorities and unionist paramilitaries, some of which the British state helped to establish, finance and arm (Cadwallader, 2013). Similarly, events in Catalonia involve Spanish police beating up peaceful protestors and imprisoning Catalan political leaders (Bambery and Kerevan 2018; Herald Scotland Online 2018).

Any action taken to interfere in, block and deny the self-determination and independence of another people and their nation is self-evidently anti self-determination. Yet that is arguably the purpose of British trans-national nationalism within a Scottish context. This implies that those actively campaigning against or voting to block the Scottish nation and its people from enjoying their own citizenship and nationality and seeking their own self-determination may be construed as anti-Scottish. An illustration here is the British State removing the Scots' EU citizenship against their will through Brexit, which reflects a further aggressive British nationalist posture that willfully discriminates against an ethnic (i.e. Scottish) minority.

Many Scottish 'No' voters claim to hold 'both British and Scottish' identities yet such a stance merely reflects a degree of confusion about one's 'national' identity. Being 'British <u>and</u> Scottish' within the UK union cannot even be dual nationality because Scottish nationality does not exist without independence. Within the present UK 'union' only one nationality and citizenship exist and that is British nationality and British citizenship. This means, prior to independence at least, that Scots cannot hold both British <u>and</u> Scottish nationality, they can only access the former. In 2014, a majority of Scotland's voters chose to prefer British national identity over Scottish national identity, this being the essential outcome of the majority No vote. However, research has established that a majority of Scots voted in favour of independence and that the 'No' vote depended on voters from rest-UK, this again reflecting the importance of national identity.

Trans-national nationalism in the UK 'union' context involves a British Anglophone ideological and political culture being imposed on Scots. Culture is about 'the way we do things', aspects of which endure even in midst of political oppression, however subtle, or not. If Holyrood demonstrates anything it is that Scots do things, and want to do things, differently from their neighbours south of the border; their (i.e. England's) culture is their concern, or should be, although an Anglophone culture and language and political control has been and remains imposed on Scots, which reflects the purpose and consequence of trans-national nationalism. Whilst it is evident with devolved powers that Scots clearly seek to do things differently, there is no reason to suggest this would not also be the case with reserved powers assumed by Scotland after independence.

Anti-Colonial Nationalism

Unionism is clearly a trans-national nationalist political ideology and one of the more aggressive forms of nationalism not least because it depends on coercion to enforce cultural integration and assimilation (cultural and linguistic imperialism) and to effect control over other neighbouring peoples' and their territories. Scottish independence, in contrast, is about self-determination, liberation, freedom, and yes, decolonisation. Scottish independence has nothing to do with occupation of neighbouring countries, or to enforce Scottish cultural and linguistic imperialism on minorities, nor does it involve the exploitation and coercion of other peoples and their economic resources; these are all negative and provocative and aggressive aspects associated with trans-national nationalism (and hence unionism also) which understandably often lead to long-term unrest, distrust and even conflict.

Self-determination and decolonisation on the other hand, as the UN maintains, is aimed at peaceful resolution of conflict. This requires nations to respect each other rather than to oppress or to interfere and seek to influence the outcome of a 'peoples' right to self-determination process. Scotland and its people are merely seeking self-determination which is also viewed as anti-colonial nationalism (i.e. the pursuit of independence) and this is clearly very different from trans-national nationalism, the latter also referred to as unionism.

Moreover, self-determination and hence the independence of 'a people' and nation must be secured prior to efforts to implement so-called civic nationalism; the latter may serve to inhibit and thwart Scotland's independence if adopted prematurely, as was arguably the case in the 2014 referendum due to the highly irregular residence-based voter franchise. National voting rights should only come with citizenship and Scotland, or any other non-independent nation for that matter, cannot feasibly offer its citizenship to peoples from other countries and to those of other national identities until after it becomes independent. Self-determination for Scotland and the Scottish people is primarily about liberation from British trans-national nationalist oppression and hence it is about decolonisation and this objective should remain paramount for Scotland's people, and should not be subject to external interference, as stated in the UN Charter.

CHAPTER 8:
INSTITUTIONS

Social Institutions

Any people and nation will require a range of social institutions which allow society to function. One of the strongest features of culture is social organisation, i.e. the way in which a society is structured and organised. Social institutions are needed to allow a society to fulfill its objectives, be they economic, academic, religious etc., and to establish relationships.

While social institutions may form the 'backbone' of a society and how it functions, they also comprise the 'establishment' of the society. The 'establishment' is generally viewed as a dominant group or elite that holds power or authority in a nation and its organisations (Barcan 1993). The establishment will often be formed within a particular class or social group of people which is closed to those who are not a part of the class or group of people. The establishment may also select its own members and have elite structures which remain highly stable or entrenched across a range of institutions, including government. It can therefore be argued that power within society is exercised socially, though not necessarily equitably. Fairlie (1955) viewed the establishment as not the centres of official power, though they are part of it, but rather "..*the whole matrix of official and social relations within which power is exercised*".

Sociologists define social institutions as "..*a complex set of social norms organised around the preservation of a basic societal value*"[69]. Social values form an important part of the culture of a society and guide behaviour of decision-making elites. However, it is recognised, not least from the discussion of 'enculturation' (Bourdieu and Passeron 1990), that the social values, behavioural norms and indeed the culture and language of power wielding elites may differ from that of much of the rest of society, the latter often remaining excluded from membership of social institutions and hence from exercising power.

Jings, maist o Scotlan's Anglophone heid bummers cannae e'en spik Scots!

Nelson Mandela referred to the State's many 'social institutions' and the need for them to change in order to serve the people, rather than to oppress them (Mandela 1994). Mandela's focus was on bringing down the brutal apartheid system in South Africa, which was based on ethnic and, with that, cultural and linguistic oppression and discrimination and often violence sanctioned by state authorities. Scotland and the Scots may not appear to face quite such extremes or violence due to state-sponsored oppression and discrimination or apartheid and segregation, nowadays at least; nevertheless, reflecting Scotland's colonial status, a powerful and privileged Anglophone unionist elite continues to oversee Scotland with wide ranging, yet often hidden and/ or ignored negative consequences for many Scots. Moreover, the potential for further hardening of (ethnic) oppression will always exist in colonial-like social hierarchical structured environments.

Anglophone Establishment

A fundamental democratic paradox (in Scotland) is that, despite election of a supposedly 'nationalist' devolved government that advocates an independent Scottish State, the culture and language and identity of 'establishment Scotland', i.e. those essentially still running the country through its many social institutions, remains predominantly Anglophone, unionist, and privileged. Scotland's establishment elite do not therefore reflect very well the Scottish people and their democratic decisions, nor their culture, the Scots language, or to a degree even their national identity. This (unelected) Anglophone unionist elite hegemony results in a cultural and societal mismatch, representing a formidable democratic obstacle.

A central part of Scotland's Anglophone unionist elite establishment is the Scottish Government itself. The term 'Scottish Government' sounds impressive, arguably better than 'Scottish Executive' (the previous Labour/Libdem coalition couldn't quite bring themselves to call the devolved administration a 'Government') but in truth, what is the 'devolved' Scottish Government in its present form? The Scottish Government's top civil servants remain selected by Whitehall which is the head of the UK 'home' civil service[70], not by Scottish Ministers, or 'drawn' from Scots. The 'Scottish Government' is and remains the British State's devolved vehicle of government in Scotland which means it is effectively a part of the British State[71]. Scottish Government civil servants' allegiance therefore remains to the British State, not to any Scottish State; the latter doesn't (yet) exist. The current 'nationalist' SNP political leadership of the Scottish Government is the political 'enemy' of the British State and therefore the political enemy of those working for the British State, including those within and leading its devolved administrations. Even the Holyrood Parliament itself is managed by officials selected by and sent from Whitehall. Scottish 'nationalist' politicians actually run nothing in Scotland. Scotland's institutions remain 'managed' and 'controlled' by an Anglophone unionist meritocracy which has an allegiance to the British State, as has been the case since the inception of the UK union.

> *Tae dae onythin ye'd hae tae stairt wi remuiven aw thon unionist elite ower-peyed heidbummers wha aye owersee maist o Scotland's institutions an wha aye mak a dug's brakfast o aw muckle*

deceesions on behauf o Scots fowk.

An example of this external management and control and potential conflict can be seen in the role of the senior civil servant in Scotland, Lesley Evans. Under Evan's leadership the Scottish Government undertook an investigation into former First Minister Alex Salmond in relation to alleged complaints of sexual harassment. Salmond won a judicial review concerning this investigation in January 2019 after the Scottish Government admitted to serious failings during its internal enquiry. At Salmond's subsequent High Court trial in March 2020, his defence lawyer Gordon Jackson QC raised suggestions of a Scottish Government orchestration of complaints against Salmond; this alluded to a concerted effort and alleged conspiracy by senior government officials which, it may be surmised, was intended to damage the former First Minister and the independence cause. A text sent by lead civil servant Evans around the time of the judicial review was reported to have stated: "We may have lost the battle. But we will win the war"[72]. The 'war' alluded to here might relate to the quest for the British state to remain as it is, and to prevent Scottish independence, and to seek to discredit high ranking 'nationalists' such as the former First Minister. At the highest levels, therefore, even in Scotland, the 'devolved' Scottish Government Anglophone administrators remain anti-independence and a fundamental part of their role is to stop Scottish independence.

Television is another key area in which Scots language speakers in particular remain discriminated against. Scotland has several English language channels, as well as a Gaelic language channel for the 50,000 or so Gaelic speakers. But what Scots require for equality and fairness and cultural respect if nothing else is a Scots language channel. A Scots language channel could help rid many Scots of the Cultural

Cringe which the English language channels are arguably partly responsible for, aside from schools who by law only teach Scottish children the English language. There seems little problem in some schools nowadays teaching Gaelic and English and both to Higher and Degree levels, so there should be little problem with learning the Scots language as well as English. Institutionally, discriminating against a minority people and depriving them of learning their language should be regarded as xenophobic and ethnically motivated, as well as disrespecting human rights.

Thon unionist elite cultur wid juist conteena an aye haud oor naition an Scotlan's fowk doon, whither independent or no.

A nation's social institutions are ultimately about the people in control and hence those in power. It is senior civil servants who implement long-term political decisions in Scotland, and who spend the national public sector budget, not the politicians at Holyrood or Westminster who merely agree a budget which State institutions then spend as they see fit. It is normally at the implementation phase where matters invariably go wrong in Scotland, with plenty of examples such as: failed industrial policies, endless educational initiatives and reforms, overspends on public buildings (e.g. Holyrood building), Edinburgh trams, railways, NHS hospitals, schools, PFI schemes, ferries, and justice etc. The significant number of policy 'problem areas' piling up in Scotland might suggest that an Anglophone unionist establishment has been tasked to create such problems intentionally, and to make it look like a 'nationalist' government is incompetent.

If Scotland is ever to lift up all its people, who are Scotland's greatest asset, and especially the increasing number of people living in poverty and alienation, Scotland will need to deal ultimately with the institutionalised Anglophone unionist meritocratic elite who have aye controlled and arguably held back the Scottish people and nation, primarily in their own interest (and in their own cultural and linguistic image). The majority of Scotland's public sector unionist Anglophone elite are by their culture and nature anti-independence. Moreover, by virtue of this elite's ongoing propensity for failure as far as Scotland's people and nation is concerned, their strategic decision-making role and competence in relation to Scotland's under development needs to be remedied. Scotland has no future so long as an Anglophone unionist establishment elite in thrall to a British State continues to undermine Scotland and its people.

Tae be 'recast', Scots wid hiv tae cast oot the unionist elite yoke in aw its mankit naitur.

The *'Elitist Scotland?'* research report found discrimination in Scotland to be far more widespread than might be imagined (The Social Mobility and Child Poverty Commission 2015). Scots are clearly excluded from jobs (and academic places) even in Scotland's universities and in other social institutions. It is sometimes said that Scotland has the best educated people in Europe. This is a fallacy as only around a quarter of Scots (26 per cent in 2011) are educated to degree level[73], and arguably Scotland's elite universities main focus is on attracting high fee-paying students from outside Scotland. A growing percentage of Scots children, now 1 in 4 (26 per cent) today live in poverty, many with little prospect of entering higher education[74]. That perhaps over half of Scotland's senior professional posts are not held by Scots simply reflects the fact Scotland is still importing much of its elite meritocratic leadership thereby boosting the already mainly Anglophone unionist elite to the exclusion and disadvantage of Scots.

And what of military institutions? In an independent

Scotland, would Scots really be sending their navy off to 'guard' far off colonies around the world? The new offshore patrol vessel, 'HMS Forth', was due to take up the furthest flung post of the British navy: 'guarding' the Falkland Islands. And that involves the craft, only 300ft long, crossing 8,000 miles of ocean (Leask 2018). In an independent Scotland such a vessel and others would surely be looking after Scotland's waters instead of guarding a far-off island that really should no longer be a colony.

Scottish nationalists appear to suffer from exclusion and discrimination in British institutions, and especially organisations active in state defence and security activities. Certain public sector jobs require a pledged allegiance from employees to a British 'nation', and to British royalty etc. Those with known political support for creating a 'separate' Scottish State do not necessarily 'fit the bill', or so it would seem by the example of Chris McEleny (Hutcheon 2018) and will therefore be excluded from such posts. This reinforces the fact that much of institutional Scotland continues to be led by British Anglophone 'unionists' who oppose the creation of a Scottish State and who are unlikely to appoint Scottish nationalists, especially to senior posts.

This raises the equally valid question that, if the British State refuses to appoint Scottish nationalists to run its social institutions then, after independence, should Scotland continue to appoint an Anglophone unionist elite to run Scotland's institutions and who hold no allegiance to a Scottish State? Similarly, after independence would Scottish institutions really still be advertising their senior and highest remunerated job vacancies in the London metropolitan press aimed primarily at England's much larger population, as is normal practice in the 'union'?

Professor John Robertson's detailed published research and

analysis found UK media institutions (the 'MSM') were the primary 'weapon' of the British state during the independence referendum campaign in 2014. For every ten 'metaphoric media cannons' on the 'No' side, the 'Yes' side had none. Robertson described the 'Yes' side as more akin to a 'guerrilla' outfit consigned to campaigning via assorted websites 'across the hills and glens and isles' plus various assembled speakers and their 'dugs'[75] gathered in village halls on dark misty nights. Scots should not be surprised at the inherent institutional bias as the UK MSM licensed to operate in Scotland is owned by persons and businesses from outwith Scotland; i.e. it is not Scotland's media, it is primarily England's Anglophone MSM. This Anglophone MSM has only a UK and hence British agenda to pursue and by implication this means a predominantly anti-Scottish independence agenda. Scots should consider themselves rather like Estonia or Ukraine when these countries had only a Russian state MSM to keep them abreast of events. Robertson for his part was more or less hounded out of his university, another institution run by Anglophone unionists, much like the experience of the author of this book, and no doubt others in the 'Academics for Yes' group who found their careers cut short post the 2014 referendum; there is clearly no place in Scotland's social institutions for Scots who don't comply with the Anglophone unionist establishment and their British one-nation anti-independence agenda. Meantime senior unionist politicians with limited if any academic expertise find a warm welcome and remunerative employment in Scotland's seats of learning[76].

The author's own publications around the time of the 2014 independence referendum rather upset the 'academic' and former university principal with the name politicians oft quoted yet badly mispronounced (Professor Von Prodzinsky) as well as other similar anti-independence interests within Scotland's university hierarchy[77]. The author's article on the leadership of Scotland's universities published in Scottish Review (Baird 2013), which also referred to the late Alasdair Gray's 'settler-colonist' paper, has sadly disappeared from its website. On its publication the author was also told sternly by his own University Director of Personnel not to publish such articles again. The author did publish again, criticising the Scottish university sector regarding its research focus (Baird 2013A), and he now no longer works in that institution – make of that what you will. Academic freedom arguably does not exist in the context of institutionalised oppression, with Scottish academics supporting independence discriminated against by Anglophone-led unionist institutions in their own land.

Sociolinguistic Prejudice

The sociolinguistics of Scotland and prevailing linguistic variants are said to 'carry a burden of social stigma' for Scots speakers (Aitken 1976, 2015). The takeover in the 1960s and 1970s of major Scottish educational publishers (Oliver & Boyd and Thomas Nelson & Sons) led to the end of the printing of textbooks written from a Scottish perspective thus depriving Scottish schools of basic written content. There are many works on English linguistics however nothing comparable exists for the Scots language today. By the 1970's Scotland's educated middle class teaching community was itself thoroughly Anglicised in speech whereas most pupils were Scots speakers, resulting in something of a cultural mismatch as soon as they met up in school.

Within the UK Government run 'Scottish Education Department' historically there has been very little if any central or official encouragement for the Scots language. As recently as 1998 a report by the Scottish Consultative Council on the Curriculum (SCCC) calling for a revival of Scottish culture across the board in schools was suppressed by government officials (Buie 1998). The implication here was that any proposed initiative to include the Scots language in the Scottish school curriculum was clearly considered 'dangerous', primarily from a political perspective, given the close relationship between language and national identity (Aitken 1981) and especially amidst the continuing constitutional pressure for Scottish self-determination.

There was nevertheless some recognition in education circles that the Scots language was indeed dying; however, the historic decline had been gradual, at least until the 1970's. Even today, many distinctive Scottish expressions continue in daily use. But the most completely native Scots speakers are increasingly limited to the rural and urban working class, whilst the professional class including the teaching profession have become ever more Anglicised. The accent of the 'laird class' has no roots at all in Scotland, *"it being the same 'high-status' accent of English origin which is obligatory in 'county' circles in both England and Scotland"* (Aitken 1976, 2015: p. 5). It is primarily because this form of speech is associated with influence and prestige and hence carries something of a 'positive cachet', that it has also been allowed to dominate broadcasting media and is even considered elegant.

> *Raither, Scotlan's 'lest' Secretary o State wad bi gey braw, naw? Thon chiel wisnae e'en in Mrs. May's Cabinet, Scotlan's juist an efter-thocht tae oor colonial heidyins.*

Sociolinguistics in Scotland includes a degree of 'style-switching' to reflect the circumstance of any discourse, the more formal tending to induce Scots to adopt a supposedly more 'proper' English tone, if they are able to, reflecting what Aitken termed as the Scots *dialect switching virtuosi*. However, it remains astonishing that the Scottish language receives so little attention within Scotland's educational institutions at all levels, and the explanation for this can only be political given that the necessary formal requirement for Scots language teaching in schools (preferably via an Act of Parliament, as with Gaelic) requires political approval.

The absence of any formal teaching of Scots language in Scotland's schools and the prioritisation of English means it is inevitable that social evaluations and hence judgements of 'others' will tend to be based around their speech. From this, inferences will be obtained regarding social background and education. This may in turn lead to unjust or inaccurate perceptions based around any social pretensions or otherwise of a speaker. In general, though, the supposedly 'proper' English speaker will be perceived positively (e.g. fine, clear, attractive, perhaps even 'articulate') whereas when judged by any Anglophone 'professional' (as is invariably the case within Scotland's institutions) the Scots speaker may be regarded somewhat less positively (e.g. uncouth, slovenly, working class, uneducated etc.), irrespective of the fact the latter is the native Scots speaker and the former, an Anglophone, is not. Subjective and biased (i.e. prejudiced) judgements of this nature serve to maintain the social differentials which effectively disadvantage working class Scots speakers at all levels of society and is arguably a root cause of the so-called 'attainment gap' and the 'Cultural Cringe'.

Linguistic prejudice in Scotland, according to Aiken (1976, 2015) really begins in school where Scots speaking children will often first encounter a (Anglophone) teacher with a fundamentally different speaking style, and which depends on a stereotype of what 'good' speech should be, and which of course excludes the natural mother tongue speech of the child. The teacher's speech reflects the establishment's values of what supposedly 'good' speech should sound like. Anglophone teachers therefore seek to 'correct' natural Scots speakers principally by driving out the Scots language from young minds. This, it may be argued, is harmful to the natural development of the Scots child in that it creates division and divided loyalties about their native speech. On the one hand there is the powerful loyalties of family and friends and on the other the teacher's instruction about what is 'good' speech (i.e. English language) and hence by implication what is 'bad' or 'inferior' speech (i.e. the Scots language). This supposed 'educational process' serves to instill in the Scots speaking child a degree of uncertainty as well as a self-consciousness and confusion which can result in the pupil being tongue-tied in any form of language (Aitken 1976, 2015: p. 6).

Thay Anglophone's dinna e'en unnerstaund us Scots whan wi spik oneywey – acause thay dinna hiv tae bather tae lairn an spik Scots thairsels.

Inevitably, the institutional requirement or demand to adjust one's speech in order to induce favourable responses from, for instance, potential employers and institutions, will be affected to varying degrees depending on the individual concerned. Many Scots speakers will simply be unaware of this prevailing sociolinguistic imperative and may consequently be socio-economically disadvantaged throughout their lives. Pupils will be judged objectively in terms of educational standards (e.g. in exams, coursework etc.) with the result that many Scots speakers may similarly be discriminated against linguistically. This despite the fact the Scots speaker is perfectly able to communicate just as copiously, fluently and effectively in Scots. However, with institutions and authorities insisting on

English as the only formal means of communication the price is a loss of confidence and fluency among Scots speakers, the latter rather consigned to Fanon's (1967) feeling of 'inferiorisation'.

Linguistic imperialism, i.e. teaching <u>only</u> English, which by implication has the institutional aim to eradicate the Scots language, is thus portrayed as a hallmark of educated status in Scotland, which it is not. It merely imposes various kinds of correctness and does so through linguistic oppression and hence is socio-linguistic prejudice.

Social Exclusion

In post-colonial research the term 'subaltern' people, attributed to Gramsci, is used to identify *"the social groups excluded and displaced from the socio-economic institutions of society in order to deny their political voices"* (Green 2011). Scots, and more especially Scots speakers within the working class, should not therefore be surprised that they tend to be excluded from such institutions and are therefore treated for the most part as a 'subaltern' and hence 'inferior' people. A standard norm of cultural imperialism involves colonial society hierarchical structures where socio-political and economic elites are largely composed of people drawn from the colonial 'administrative Power' and/or reflective of the latter's culture, language, and 'values'.

Scotland's social institutions therefore continue to be led primarily by a unionist Anglophone elite and the election of 'nationalist' SNP administrations to the devolved Holyrood Parliament has not altered this. In USA President Donald Trump's parlance, we might refer to this as Scotland's unionist 'swamp' (or 'slump' in Scots) which those advocating Scottish independence might wish to drain at some point and would arguably need to drain should Scotland ever become independent. Post-independence, the unionist elites holding senior positions of control throughout Scotland's social institutions would have a choice either to shift their national allegiance to the new independent Scottish State or to leave their post, though an independent Scotland's new political leadership might also be expected to make that choice for them. It is unlikely that the present Anglophone unionist elites would be able to maintain loyalty to two independent countries and two different national governments just as surely as colonial British ruling officials were required to depart their posts in post-colonial India, Kenya and so forth. No one can serve two masters for *"they will be devoted to one and despise the other"* (Holy Bible, Matthew 6:24). As to the inevitable 'unionist' question of 'where would good candidates come from', perhaps Scotland might be in a position post-independence to appoint a few more Scots to senior positions in Scotland, much like any other normal country does?

Long established practice is still for senior UK 'Home' Civil Servants to be sent to Scotland by Whitehall to 'manage' Scotland on behalf of the UK. These officials continue to function within a UK political, ideological and policy (i.e. Tory) context. Holyrood's 'nationalist' MSP's and Ministers seem impotent to change this from within the present devolved arrangement. It seems entirely plausible that senior British officials are sent north by Whitehall to undermine 'nationalist' policies and standing in Scotland. For instance, public procurement managed by Scotland's social institutions is generally considered to be something of a continuing disaster (e.g. highly expensive PFI contracts for hospitals, poorly built schools, late and costly ferries, etc.), land reform has not yet been implemented, whilst elite universities, private schools, and various other social 'institutional' arrangements merely perpetuate an apartheid and oppressive self-regulated regime which discriminates against many Scots, and especially working class Scots speakers. Regulation of key 'national' utilities such as energy, seaports and airports continue to be 'managed' through UK reserved powers in line with Westminster's policy priorities, primarily maximising profits for privatised utilities at public expense, and which do not reflect Scotland's 'values' or its current political leadership and voters.

An Anglophone unionist 'establishment' running Scotland's social institutions might reasonably be expected to use any excuse it can find to oppose and block policies which would benefit many Scots who support independence. For instance there was a suggestion, according to the Scottish Government's official forecaster, that middle class professionals risk being deterred from chasing promotions and pay rises and could leave Scotland as a result of any rise in Scottish income tax (Grant 2018). The supposedly 'independent' Scottish Fiscal Commission (SFC) also suggested that higher rate taxpayers could be left with as little as 30p in the pound once new Budget changes hit household finances. The Scottish Fiscal Commission, like many other 'Scottish' institutions, has very few if any Scots in it[78], far less leading it.

Fowk cannae ser twa maisters.

Scots all too often hear the mantra, even from the SNP leadership, that 'we need to attract the best talent to Scotland' to manage and run our social institutions, as if there was no talent among Scots in Scotland. The real question here should be, **why does Scotland need to import talent at all, are there really no talented Scots available**? Is Scotland somehow unique among all nations in that it cannot lift its ain fowk up sufficiently to develop the talents their nation requires to lead its institutions? Are Scotland's social institutions not simply discriminating against Scots by always advertising and recruiting, as a matter of course, via the London press, to fill most of Scotland top positions with supposedly 'superior' candidates from other countries, and invariably from England/rest-UK? Is such institutionalised discrimination against Scots not ethnic and colonial in its orientation? Why does an Anglophone unionist elite running Scotland's social institutions appear to assume that Scots are incapable of taking leading roles in Scotland's social institutions? Is this simply because Scotland's institutionaled Anglophone unionist elite establishment believe this to be the case, that 'ordinary' Scots-speaking Scots are somehow subaltern, or inferior, or invalid even, much in the same way their Scots language is considered?

It is said that the Scottish elite who made money out of slavery were of the same culture as those who sold out the Scottish nation in 1707 and would still do so again today (Ross 2008). An Anglophone elite largely brought in to run Scotland will also tend to recruit the leaders of Scotland's social institutions in their own image; that image may be expected to be Anglophone, unionist, and privileged, as the *'Elitist Scotland?'* report found (The Social Mobility and Child Poverty Commission 2015). Inevitably the domination and import of an Anglophone unionist elite, mostly from Scotland's more densely populated neighbour England, bring with them a managerial class lacking in-depth knowledge of Scotland. There is seldom a requirement for high level job candidates to know much about Scotland, its people, or their culture, far less be able to speak or understand the 'local' (i.e. national) language. This implies that many of the professional and managerial class that do end up running Scotland's social institutions will not know very much about Scotland, or its people, far less their needs and priorities.

> *Aye, thay'll be bannit Scots speakin MSP's neist, juist lyke mony Scots are prevenit fae bein appyntit tae maist o thay heid bummer jobs in Scotlan's social institutions. Whit's wrang wi a braid Scots chiel!*

During the 2014 independence campaign it was suggested that even the BBC lacked *"in-depth knowledge"* about Scotland[79]. The BBC didn't need it, of course, as knowledge of Scotland, of the Scottish people, or their culture and languages, is not a requirement for the leaders of Scotland's social institutions. Those managing Scotland's institutions don't even need to care about Scotland far less have an allegiance to the country. And why should they? So long as Scotland is regarded more or less as a British region or colony it will remain treated as such, and the long-established recruitment of an Anglophone unionist meritocracy merely serves to illustrate this rather well.

Such external institutional (i.e. colonial) control is rather more common than many Scots might think, that is if they even consider the matter. Given that most if not all of Scotland's top jobs are advertised primarily in the London press this inevitably implies that many if not most of the applicants and subsequent appointees will not be from Scotland. Scotland's population census confirms that over the past century and more Scotland has been importing much of its professional and managerial class from rest-UK, most of whom it might be anticipated will have little if any 'in-depth knowledge' about Scotland. There is the rather infamous example of a former Head of Creative Scotland who admitted to knowing very little about Scottish culture but who was 'keen to learn'[80]. In other words, the appointed leader of Scotland's main social institution 'responsible' for culture knew nothing about Scottish culture! This did not matter, one assumes, presumably because Scottish culture doesn't really matter in the wider British Anglophone unionist scheme of things.

Whan an Anglophone heid bummer daesnae unnerstaund the leid o a Scots chiel it disnae maiter in Scotlan, daes it?

Maybe Scotland should look to Finland, who gave us the 'baby box', for inspiration, and with the Finns casting off Russian imperialism (and language) as long ago as 1917. Today in Finland we would find there a 'Ministry of Education AND Culture' combined[81]. The Finn's, whilst introducing the teaching in schools of English as a globally useful administrative language, have not done so at the expense of their own indigenous language, as we see with the ongoing oppression of Scots language, which Scots children are taught neither to read or write, far less value. But clearly, culture is a lot more than simply the arts! The people themselves ARE the culture, the way they speak, the way they think, what they do, and how they do it. Culture, like language, is also about learning and hence knowledge.

Scotland remains for the moment, as it has been for some centuries, much like the three Baltic States prior to their independence when senior appointments to social institutions there might have been made directly from Moscow. Or perhaps one might try to imagine what Denmark would be like today if all the Danish top jobs were advertised primarily in Berlin, and with most of Denmark's social institutions headed up by a professional class drawn mainly from its far larger neighbouring country, Germany, instead of Danes, and speaking German, instead of Danish? Such an outcome would of course be politically unacceptable (if not unthinkable) to Danes just as it should be unacceptable to Scots. Yet, Denmark (and other territories) would have found themselves in exactly that position had German occupation in WWII persisted, which itself raises important questions about Scotland's 'status', and whether the supposed UK 'union' is perhaps, at best, merely an 'Anschluss'[82]?

Many Scots not only accept their ongoing institutionalised ethnic discrimination, they even expect and feel they deserve it, and some continue to invite it. Why is this, and why does this feeling of 'inferiorisation' persist amongst many Scots today? Perhaps the answer lies in Alasdair Gray's words: *"these colonists were invited here and employed by Scots without confidence in their own land and people"* (Gray 2012).

Institutionalised Discrimination

The prejudicial treatment of the Scottish people by a mainly Anglophone elite may be described as institutionalized discrimination. The inevitable outcome of this ongoing discrimination is that Scotland's elite running the nation's social institutions will continue to be predominantly unionist, Anglophone and privileged. As well as lacking in-depth knowledge about Scotland, its people or its culture and languages, this elite might also be expected to exhibit little, if any support for Scottish independence and hence for the creation of a new Scottish State.

Such an elite might also be expected to have little desire to alter their own national identity (i.e. British) to 'Scottish' and will likely reject any such offer, much as they did in 2014. Inevitably, an important consideration here must be that Scotland's Anglophone unionist elite may seek to use their senior positions controlling and managing Scotland's social institutions in efforts to block and prevent or to hinder independence in one way or another.

Scotland's nineteen universities form an interesting position in this regard. Influenced by UK policy priorities and reductions in public funding, they have been reconstructed *"as businesses designed to operate in and through markets"* (Valentine 2019, p. 3). This new corporate hegemony model has allowed mostly non-academic university managements to exploit traditional perspectives of academic autonomy in order to build their own inwardly privatised regimes. The focus has shifted toward generating external revenue, rather than anything else universities might once have been regarded for, such as raising up a nations people through education and knowledge and contributing to national development.

For whit raison shoud Scots tryst thay're institushins tae ither fowk
an heid bummers wha canna e'en speik oor leid, an forby want tae

*willintly doon-haud (i.e. suppress, via colonization) oor ain leid an
cultur an oor bairns an aw Scots fowk? Ir wi aw stupit in Scotlan?
Lats hae nae mair o thon blethers!*

Scotland's elite universities remain primarily focused on recruiting most of their students from outside Scotland, leaving fewer places available for Scottish students. The elite universities are motivated to do this because fees set for students from outside Scotland are considerably higher than for home-based Scottish students; moreover, there is no regulatory requirement in Scotland for them not to do this. Elite universities focused on global student 'markets' also impose high entry requirements on Scottish students, in turn leaving more higher fee places for lucrative fee students from outside Scotland. This should also be regarded as discrimination against Scots, though few of Scotland's political leaders seem to notice, or bother; indeed, Scottish politicians including the SNP leadership argue for ever more international higher fee students to be brought into Scotland from other countries to counteract what they claim to be a supposed 'skills gap' in Scotland. High-demand and hence higher-fee degree courses (e.g. medicine, law etc.) at elite universities thus tend to accept relatively few Scots and those few Scots who are accepted will generally mainly be drawn from private (independent) schools and hence from more privileged backgrounds, which represents another long-established feature of discrimination and segregation.

Such institutionalised practices imply that Scottish policymakers and universities are themselves the architects of Scotland's shortage of doctors and other skills and the propensity to import these skills is primarily related to the fact that Scots are excluded from accessing elite university courses in Scotland. A report by the Academy of Medical Royal Colleges and Faculties in Scotland (AMRCFS) confirmed such exclusion, proposing that medical schools in Scotland need to increase their overall intakes to ensure a much greater share of places go to Scottish students (McArdle 2019).

At postgraduate and doctoral levels, institutional discrimination against Scottish students and academics today seems even more prevalent. For example, perhaps even less than 10 per cent of PhD/doctoral students at Scotland's elite universities are Scots, based on published graduation lists and analysis of university department websites. As most of Scotland's future academics and professors will generally require a PhD qualification this means that few of Scotland's future academics will be Scottish, even less than today, where at elite universities Scottish academics are already in a minority. In most other countries this sort of institutionalized discrimination against the indigenous population would be regarded as politically unacceptable, if not illegal. Many other countries have a requirement for a set percentage of students and staff emanating from within the local indigenous population, but there is no such requirement in Scotland where institutions remain controlled by a mainly Anglophone unionist elite and whose only focus is on increasing revenue from global student 'markets', and rather less on developing and nurturing the host nation's people.

Data suggests that today only around one third of undergraduate students at Scotland's four ancient universities are Scottish. Students from private schools also appear to be given preferential treatment by Scotland's elite universities. In 2015, offer rates from Scottish universities were highest for students from non-EU countries, at 63 per cent, followed by fee paying applicants from England, Wales, and Northern Ireland with between 56 per cent and 58 per cent (Audit Scotland 2016). Offer rates were lowest for Scottish applicants and applicants from other EU countries, reflecting the fixed number of publicly funded places available for these students. Audit Scotland (2016) stated that: *"The offer rate for Scottish... applicants has fallen over the 2010-2015 period while offer rates for most other applicant groups have increased"*. Whereas the number of applications from Scottish students increased by 23 per cent the number of offers only increased by 9 per cent. According to Audit Scotland: *"This means it has become more difficult for Scottish applicants to be offered a place at a Scottish university"*, whilst meantime the doors remain held wide open to higher fee students from other countries who are taking ever more places, especially on premium courses such as medicine and law. In the ten years to 2014 the biggest percentage increases have been in students from other parts of the EU (97 per cent increase) and fee-paying students from outside the EU (58 per cent increase). And yet Scots wonder why Scotland has a shortage of Scottish doctors and other skills! The answer to this is that Scotland's elite universities have themselves largely closed the door on Scottish students whilst focusing on attracting higher fee overseas students and students from rest-UK.

> *Tak awa a fowk's langage, ye tak awa thair identity, an thair sel respect; imperial job duin!*

Consequently, very few of Scotland's academic experts regularly wheeled into Holyrood committees or BBC TV and radio studios nowadays to give their views and advice are Scottish, which also implies that these supposed 'experts' will often tend to know rather less about Scotland or its people, never mind its culture and languages. Scottish Higher Education has effectively been hijacked mainly by an Anglophone elite, although the sector is also now an attractive option for international academics, not least because many of those from overseas undertaking PhD studies in Scotland will often be offered a first research or lecturing post in Scotland after graduation here. As very few Scots are funded to undertake PhD work this means there is limited scope indeed for expanding the already diminished Scottish academic community. Such matters seem symptomatic of Scotland's universities which appear to be run as self-regulating international businesses and corporate fiefdoms masquerading as charities, with an ever-increasing emphasis on attracting higher fee students as well as academics from outside Scotland, and hence with a limited and diminishing focus on Scots.

Reflecting what is a class conscious UK (and Scottish) society, the rationale for creating several new universities during the 1990's was arguably so they might absorb the expanding working class Scots speaking intakes (also given largescale unemployment then due to de-industrialisation, and as ever a weak UK economy more generally) who aspired to higher education and which then allowed the ancient 'elite' universities to concentrate on their core businesses, which is not Scots but rather UK private school 'A' level students plus higher-fee overseas students. The outcome remains the perpetuation of social segregation and a class and caste system oriented not towards Scots, but towards Anglophone and now international 'customers' and elites with money to spend and seeking 'higher status' universities in which to spend it.

Scotland's Enlightenment thinkers appear to be the toast of universities the world over, however, the increasing lack of Scottish academics running or working in Scotland's universities today should be a major concern. Just two of nineteen Scottish universities have a Scottish principal and the senior management make-up of Scotland's universities is generally not dissimilar. In an analysis of over 50 departments across several mainly elite 'Scottish' institutions, the author found that out of several thousand staff, less than 25 per cent of academics were Scottish, and indeed many departments had less than 10 per cent Scots in them[83]; this implies that, in some cases[84] 90 per cent or more of the academic staff are drawn from outside Scotland.

Table 6.1 presents data for 15 departments and schools within three of Scotland's ancient universities – Edinburgh, St. Andrews and Aberdeen. This indicates that, out of a total of some 1,120 academics working in the departments/ schools analysed, only 11 per cent (120) are Scottish. The institutionalised discrimination strategies of Scotland's universities has therefore led to the Scottish academic being something of an endangered species, a modest and declining minority in their own home nation's universities.

In any other country such an outcome would be considered a national scandal. The abnormal academic staff make-up of Scotland's universities reflects uncontrolled colonisation as well as institutionalised discrimination of Scots. Recruitment of academics to Scotland's universities primarily from outside Scotland has been the norm for decades, rather than the exception as in many other countries.

Table 6.1: Estimated Share of Scottish Academics in Three Scottish Ancient Universities (selected depts, March 2020)					
Institution	Department	Scots	Others	Total	Share Scots
Edinburgh	Management Science & Business Economics	2	27	29	7%
	Accounting & Finance	6	46	52	13%
	School of Economics	3	33	36	9%
	School of History, Classics & Archaeology	12	115	127	10%
	School of Social & Political Science	28	295	323	9%
St. Andrews	School of Art History	3	28	31	11%
	School of Classics	0	28	28	0%
	School of Economics & Finance	5	44	49	11%
	School of Management	6	48	54	13%
	School of Philosophy	4	39	43	10%
Aberdeen	Business School	13	68	81	19%

	School of Social Science	5	36	41	14%
	School of Biological Sciences	11	85	96	13%
	School of Engineering	6	64	70	9%
	School of Geosciences	6	54	60	11%
	Total	110	1010	1120	11%

Sources: Data derived from University websites, academic staff only.

Importantly, and for many years, very few Scots have been given the opportunity to undertake PhD research; this virtually guarantees that most of Scotland's future academics and professors, who generally require a PhD, will also not be Scottish. The ongoing PhD student cohort is dominated by externally sourced, higher fee-paying students coming from outside Scotland, which means that Scotland's future academic make-up is already largely determined. This ensures that, in Scotland, very few professors or academics, never mind university principals or vice principals now or in future, will be Scottish. Scots are therefore effectively and in large part excluded from Scotland's elite academic institutions through established policies and practices; in any other country such an outcome would be unthinkable, yet here in Scotland few even notice or seem to bother, while politicians in their utter ignorance advocate policies supporting this discrimination continues and indeed strengthens in future.

The typical institutional and political response to this ongoing discrimination against Scots is that 'we must attract the best talent from elsewhere'. Yet such a crude and baseless argument falls flat on several counts. Firstly, it is rather a big assumption that Scottish universities are indeed attracting 'the best talent' as clearly this has not done much if anything to benefit the Scottish economy, which remains in a long-term zero-growth position and with numerous socio-economic weaknesses. What is the point of having supposedly 'world class' universities and as often claimed 'the best' academics from elsewhere when the Scottish economy remains in the perpetual doldrums? Second, must we always assume that Scots are not talented? Is this not ethnic discrimination and prejudice? To say the Scots are not good enough to fill the top positions in their own nation? That Scots do not make good intellectuals? Of course, Scots are good enough, the problem is clearly that many more Scots need to be given the opportunity to progress and advance in whatever discipline, yet their path into Scotland's elite universities and other institutions is invariably and unfairly blocked, by an Anglophone elite. And this does not seem an accident either, for how could it be?

> *Scots bairns lairn anely Englis an schuils aye mak shuir nae Scots bairns lairn their ain mither tung; thay Scots are aye cultural doon-hauden.*

Such outcomes suggest a lack of interest in Scots is perhaps because so few of the decision makers within Scotland's social institutions today are Scottish. Why should they care about the Scots when they don't need to? Scotland's Enlightenment days are long gone, though this it seems is primarily because Scotland no longer nurtures and develops its own people to be leaders, far less 'thinkers'. Scotland today invites most of its Anglophone leaders and thinkers in from elsewhere to lead and think for Scotland on behalf of Scots who, one assumes, are considered, by the elite and by some Scots, unable to lead and think for themselves, far less for their nation.

The actions of Scotland's social institutions invariably serve to inhibit the independence 'movement'. The Scottish

Government agency Historic Environment Scotland (HES), run like most other Scottish social institutions by a unionist Anglophone elite[85], was merely doing what all unionist elites do - undermining the notion of independence – when it sought to ban an All Under One Banner (AUOB) pro-independence meeting in Holyrood Park[86]. By such methods the unionist Anglophone elite seek to keep Scotland's people in their place, even by preventing them meeting in one of their own finest natural environments. Such decisions simply put one in mind of the notion that the black community might once have sought to organise a public meeting in a park in Pretoria, only for the apartheid regime to block that too though its 'banning laws'[87]. Actions like this reflect the cultural capital of an Anglophone elite and its colonial power structure which differs from and seeks to oppress Scots speakers, and especially those seeking self-determination.

The devolved 'Scottish Government' and the Holyrood parliament is likewise 'managed' by Anglophone unionist Whitehall appointees, i.e. the same people who evicted the 'indycamp people' in 2018[88]. The latter sought to establish a presence nearby the Holyrood parliament until independence is achieved. The SNP Scottish Government 'Cabinet' give the impression they run things in Scotland; they don't, and Scots will never 'run' their own country until they start appointing people to lead Scotland's social institutions whose allegiance is to Scotland and only to Scotland and that can only come through independence. The 'activities' of an Anglophone unionist elite running Scotland's governing institutions also seem evident from the Alex Salmond court case in March 2020, which former ambassador Craig Murray had earlier described as a model 'Fit Up' (Murray 2019), the implication being that senior Whitehall appointed officials within the Scottish Government and various state agencies were tasked to turn the 'British screw' on the former First Minister once he was no longer an elected politician. Ambassador Murray followed this up with an even more devastating article in March 2020 in which he levelled serious accusations towards 'establishment Scotland' and MI5 of conspiracy and corruption aimed at damaging the independence Cause.

'Scottish' Education

There is a general perception that Scotland has always run its own education system and that education has always been devolved. In fact, The Education (Scotland) Act of 1872 did the opposite by transferring the running of Scottish schools from being the responsibility of the Church of Scotland to a Whitehall department[89]. This was originally rather insultingly named the 'Scotch Education Department' and began life as a committee of the Privy Council of the United Kingdom, with offices in London. In 1885 the department became a responsibility of the new ministerial post of Secretary for Scotland, under whom the Scottish Office was set up in Dover House, Whitehall. Thus, education was organised in Scotland up to the 1870s and it was only after this, around 150 years ago, that it became centralised and controlled from London. In 1918 the department was moved to Edinburgh and the name changed to the Scottish Education Department.

Scots bairns aye juist hiv Englis garred doon thair thrapples in schuil.

One might anticipate that the Department controlling 'Scottish education' was mainly run by privately educated 'types', as the only people holding degrees at one time, who ran most other departments too, and Anglophone of course, which is also the case today to a large extent. That would be one reason why working class Scottish boys in state schools, even not so very long ago, were still forced to play rugby, a military and English class oriented game totally alien to most of them, not least the author. Meanwhile football (known as 'the beautiful game') was frowned upon by educational elites due no doubt to its working class image. Scottish pupils were also taught how 'great' Britain and its empire was, even when most of it had since become decolonised and independent. And, of course, children in Scotland were prevented from learning anything at all about the Scots language, their own mother tongue, and apparently 'not a valid language' according to British educationalists, and in many instances children would be punished if they dared speak it. 'Scottish education' was, and arguably remains to a large extent, a colonial priority controlled and administered by an Anglophone unionist privileged elite.

> *Cliver fowk in hie airts micht haiver a' thay want. Trowth be telt, Scots fowk are willintly haud doun, bi thon state offeecials, schuils, meeja, BBC, toun cooncils an sleek-gabbit elected politeecians wha aw connogue tae kep Scots fowk an bairns frae lairnin their ain leid.*

We may use the term 'devolved' but simply because the British State opens an office for education in Edinburgh does not necessarily mean that very much is in fact 'devolved'. Scots might look to Holyrood for evidence of that, and the Whitehall appointees and other Anglophone unionist elites who still rule the roost within Scotland's many social institutions. In education, the effectiveness of policy management and delivery also depends on what is meant by an allegedly 'egalitarian and inclusive approach'. Perhaps this appears to be the case where the more privileged in society go to school and then university, and in the institutions they are thereafter appointed to manage?

Another important aspect of what passes for 'Scottish education' relates to an ever-diminishing number of teachers in Scotland who are Scottish and hence are Scots language speakers. Whilst within Scotland's elite universities, Scottish academics and Scottish researchers are and remain an ever-diminishing minority. By no stretch of the imagination can Scotland even today under a supposedly 'nationalist' administration be described as 'an egalitarian or inclusive society', more especially where Scots speakers are concerned.

Lifting the Scots

So, what are the solutions to this longstanding institutionalised discrimination and oppression of Scots within an Anglophone dominated 'union'? To begin with it should seem obvious that Scots need to make the ability to speak (and to write) the Scots language (as well as English) a condition of employment at the highest levels in Scotland's institutions. That would bring Scotland into line with the Danes, Norwegians, Finns, and Dutch and many other nations too. Scotland therefore requires a Scots Language (Scotland) Act to deal with that anomaly. This would also help raise up the Scots who are currently discriminated against in their own land. How can Scots expect the leaders of Scotland's social institutions to function effectively if they cannot first understand the people they are supposed to serve? In Denmark, Norway, Sweden, Flanders, France, Italy etc. professionals generally must be able to speak the national language as well as English, and Scotland should be no different.

*Strowth, if Scots fund oot we haed wir ain leid, we'd shuirly want
wir ain naition bak anaw, dam swith tae.*

In the meantime, academic colonisation continues in Scotland[90], effectively closing the door on Scots and severely limiting the number of future Scottish academics and intellectuals being developed and nurtured. This in turn shifts much of the research emphasis away from Scotland as academics and researchers coming from other countries tend to undertake research focused mostly on their own home nation, not on host nation Scotland. Scotland and the Scots are therefore the big losers from the largescale sustained import of academic 'talent' from elsewhere as opposed to developing Scottish talent with a focus on research and teaching and with an emphasis on developing Scotland and its people and their role and input in the wider world.

Real progress will therefore first require a 'Scots Language (Scotland) Act'. It is now some fifteen years since the Gaelic Language (Scotland) Act 2005, and even with a 'nationalist' government in 'power' during much of that time, there remains no real progress for the Scots language to be formally taught in schools or universities. Scotland has a teaching profession and many related social institutions, yet they remain ill-equipped to teach Scotland's young people about their own country's culture, language, literature and history or their identity. This reality, which is arguably worse than stated, would be a national scandal and disgrace in any other nation. **Serious strategies are needed to 'lift the Scots' out of their colonial wretchedness; an essential building block of this will be to elevate and resurrect the Scots language.**

Health Impacts

Lectures by Sir Harry Burns, the former Chief Medical Officer of Scotland, discussed the reputation of Scotland as being the 'sick man of Europe' (Burns 2009). Burns also discussed the desperate health of men in Glasgow – due to substance abuse, violence and mental health issues, and explained that the statistics are very similar to those of aborigine peoples who have become dislocated from their culture. This is essentially what the destruction of the industrial and manufacturing economy did to the people of Scotland and what the neoliberal policies continue to do today. But this is also related to the ongoing loss of the Scottish peoples' culture, Scots language discrimination, and the enculturation process which serves to block the institutional advancement of far too many Scots, in addition to the artificial and enforced disruption of their natural way of thinking and development.

Sae, a unionist 'Establishment' elite conspeeracy, thon's whit it is!
We're a colonie so whit shuid onybody expeck.

A dual language requirement is a common feature in many countries and this would seem reasonable for Scotland. By continuing to suppress Scotland's main indigenous language, Scotland's Anglophone elite suppresses the Scottish culture and holds back the nation, leaving Scots subject to continued control and colonization by an Anglophone elite, and open to ongoing discrimination and exploitation.

Unchecked discrimination against any indigenous language (and the people who speak it) is akin to the slow death of a nation as well its culture. As Dr. David Purves noted, *"Scotland's loss of political and economic independence provided the conditions to misrepresent Scots language as no more than an incorrect or corrupt dialect, rather than the distinct language of a whole people with a special character of its own"*[91].

The BBC and other Anglophone institutions still parrot this gross untruth. The Scots language needs more than so-called 'respect' and annual Rabbie Burns events, or an online dictionary. Like Gaelic it needs an Act of Parliament, and it needs teachers in every school where children can be taught and inspired to speak Scots naturally. And, as with Gaelic this also requires a Scots Language TV initiative and school Highers, and a Scots Language Degree. Only then will Scotland and the Scots become a confident (bi-lingual) self-respecting nation. And as in any self-respecting nation, what Scotland also needs to do is make it a condition of recruitment more especially for any managerial (i.e. 'heid bummer') public posts in Scotland, that successful applicants should be able to speak and understand Scots, as well English.

> *Aa fowk appointet tae public posts in Scotlan shud hae an unnerstannen o' at least yin o' Scotlan's twa indigenous languages, as weel as Englis.*

Scotland must deal once and for all with the 'Cultural Cringe', which is a national disgrace, and its wholly negative and dysfunctional health impacts on the Scottish people. Research findings suggest that Appropriated Racial Oppression (internalised racism) can result in significant levels of anxiety and depression and this adversely impacts mental health (Taylor 1990). Oppression and discrimination, whether cultural, linguistic or in other forms, are not therefore limited to socio-economic impacts, but affect mental health and well-being.

'Subaltern' People

Scotland has been referred to as 'subaltern' and hence as a 'sub-nation' (Lehner 2007). The term 'sub' implies such as: under, below, beneath, imperfectly, nearly, secondary, subordinate, at a lower rank, or secondary level. In football terms 'sub-nation' Scotland might be viewed as sitting as a 'sub' on the geopolitical bench, waiting its turn, which never comes of course, while its 'betters' perform on the world stage, supposedly representing us, as 'their' 'inferior', as 'they' did with Brexit and in 'their' propensity to frequently engage in foreign wars and international conflicts. An Anglophone unionist elite hegemony controlling Scotland's institutions renders Scots and Scots speakers in particular as 'subaltern' .

Scottish Government Ministers know this feeling rather well as they are generally relegated to attending 'fringe meetings' at major international events (e.g. EU Fisheries negotiations, UN Climate Change – COP etc.) whilst UK Ministers 'bat' for the top team. This superior and 'exceptional' British Anglophone attitude is reflected in the fact that Scotland's highest-level jobs in its many social institutions and firms are still advertised primarily in the London press and hence are aimed at England's much larger labour market, yet Scotland's cleaning, manual, and 'lower level' jobs are only advertised locally in Scotland; for the latter only Scots speakers or perhaps EU migrants need apply.

The UK 'union' therefore exists only in theory, not in practice. Scotland is an occupied and exploited territory and colony with its social institutions to a large extent run by an Anglophone unionist elite hegemony who oppose and will work to prevent and thwart Scottish self-determination and independence.

Continued Anglophone unionist elite management and control over Scotland's many social institutions and hence domination of its people reflects the colonial reality of Scotland's 'subaltern' and 'doun-hauden' status which serves to inhibit the natural development of Scotland and its people.

CHAPTER 9: CONSTITUTION

Treaty of Union

Scotland's joint UK parliament with England (i.e. Westminster) was created and constituted by international treaty and subsequent Act in 1706-7 and passed into law by virtue of a simple majority of Scotland's MP's. One would therefore tend to think that this joint treaty-based arrangement may be undone in similar manner and that Scotland does not require 'permission' from its joint 'partner' (England) to withdraw from the UK parliamentary union. Withdrawal is, or should be, solely a matter for Scotland's people and their elected representatives, just as England's withdrawal from the UK union would be a matter for England's people and representatives. Scotland should not be able to hold England within any union just as England should not hold Scotland, or so one would think.

Westminster is not simply England's Parliament; it is both Scotland and England's joint Parliament as constituted in 1707 by international treaty and acts of the Scottish and English Parliaments (Riley 1978). The two sovereign nations of Scotland and England continue to exist and are merely sharing sovereignty and, by mutual agreement of each country's people and representatives, are sharing a joint (UK) Parliament and joint governing administration. The UK parliamentary union ends when that mutual agreement or mutual consent to it ends.

Ye wad hae thocht Scotlan wis a wee pouerless colonie whit disnae maiter a daw; aw thon naw votin 'unionists' sae makkit.

It may be argued that a referendum to determine Scotland's constitutional right to withdraw from the UK joint parliamentary union is not and never has been an essential legal requirement or prerequisite for Scottish independence. Indeed, any 'advisory' referendum may not be constitutionally necessary, nor advisable, in the sense that any such independence referendum result, as things stand, is assumed to then also require the agreement (or not) of 533 MP's from England who make up the vast majority (82 per cent) of MP's within the joint parliament. The UK parliament may wield joint sovereignty over the UK (together with Scotland's MP's), but on the matter of Scotland's right to withdraw from and hence to end the UK union and dissolve its joint parliament, sovereignty must rest solely with Scotland's representatives (i.e. its MP's) as it did in the foundation of the joint parliament by treaty and Act.

Separately, the supposed 'union' of England with Wales, if it could even be called that, was considered a 16th-century 'punishment' after the Glyndr rising (Williams 1991). Likewise, in the case of Scotland many Scottish nationalists might have little hesitation in agreeing that Scotland's alleged 'membership' (sic) of the UK 'union' similarly represents little more than a lengthy 'punishment' of sorts. This also fits well the UN description of colonisation as 'a scourge', which is likewise defined as an instrument of punishment. The dramatic loss of much of Scotland's population (with England's population remaining more or less intact) since and during the period of the union, and the continued oppression of Scots and the many constraints imposed on the development of Scotland, further suggests 'scourge' or 'punishment' to be appropriate terms. Such outcomes notwithstanding, the existence of an international treaty-based constitutional agreement suggests that, legally and constitutionally, Scotland is not a colony, despite being treated as such politically. The main geopolitical difference between Scotland and Wales, moreover, is that Scotland is and remains a signatory state party to the international treaty which created the United Kingdom parliament, whereas Wales is not. Wales was earlier subsumed by the Kingdom of England when it was annexed by The Laws of Wales Act in 1535, which merely extended English law over Wales[92]. Constitutionally, Scotland is and remains a signatory party to a union with England through the joint creation of the United Kingdom in 1707, with a treaty and Act to prove it.

Unilateral Withdrawal

The UKSC[93] and the ECJ[94] has concluded (in relation to Brexit) that ultimate decisions about political union membership by treaty are: (1) unilateral for the country concerned, and; (2) a matter for the elected representatives of the relevant country. Hence a majority of Scotland's national elected representatives, who hold Scotland's sovereignty on behalf of the Scottish people, should be able to decide to withdraw Scotland from any union, or indeed to maintain or join any union.

What the European Court of Justice (ECJ) and Scotland's Court of Session decisions (Grant 2018A) tell us about treaties and unions is that, when a member state has notified any 'union' administration body of its intention to withdraw from said Union, then that member state is at liberty to withdraw. Scotland may not be an 'independent state' (Hay 2001), however, Scotland nevertheless remains a signatory party to the Treaty of Union creating Scotland's joint parliament, the latter styled as 'United Kingdom of Great Britain', in much the same way as the UK was a signatory party to the European Union treaties. The Treaty of Union represents, in effect, the founding constitution of the UK union. It is therefore incorrect to assume that Scotland (or England for that matter) does not exist in any meaningful (i.e. constitutional or legal) sense. The nations and kingdoms of Scotland and England, which still exist, created by international treaty and acts a joint legislature together in order to pass and implement laws. Scotland's and England's parliaments may have both been dissolved, but this does not mean that Scotland and England, as legal and constitutional entities, were dissolved.

Westminster has acknowledged the 'Claim of Right' that Scottish sovereignty rests with Scotland's people. On 4th July 2018 Westminster acknowledged *"the sovereign right of the Scottish people to determine the form of government best suited to their needs"*, which followed the Scottish Parliament making the same commitment on 26th January 2012 (House of Commons Library 2018). It is therefore a not unreasonable contention of Scottish nationalists that there is both a political and a justiciable claim concerning the 'sovereignty of the Scottish people', and that Scotland is entitled to withdraw from its own treaty-based union arrangement as it so desires.

Lawfully Testing Withdrawal

Thus, Scotland exists as a nation, and Scotland's sovereign people exist. The real question here in terms of Scotland's constitutional and legal rights seems fairly straightforward, which is: can the Treaty of Union be unilaterally revoked by any one of its two signatory party kingdoms/nations, in the same way it was established, i.e. by a majority of Scotland's or England's democratically elected representatives? In this regard it would seem important to note that: *"As a matter of law, a referendum is not a required part of the process of becoming independent"* (McCorkindale and McHarg 2020).

Scotlan haes a gey muckle 'unionist' slump tae sook oot.

Scots might first wish to consider what the implications may be, in the event of a 'No' answer to this question from any court, and therefore a decision that a majority of Scotland's elected representatives cannot lawfully withdraw Scotland from the UK union. This would effectively mean that Scotland could be 'held' within the UK union against its will, in perpetuity, by the representatives of other UK nations. What would seem difficult to justify from that particular decision legally, would be the argument that only a majority of the UK Parliament's MP's representing constituencies within other nations (i.e. England, Wales, and Northern Ireland) could revoke the Treaty of Union on behalf of one of its constituents, and indeed a signatory party nation to the union (i.e. Scotland). Such an outcome would appear to rather ignore the matter of the sovereignty of Scotland and its people, and the Claim of Right, the latter previously acknowledged and accepted by Westminster MP's. It would also seem to ignore the fact of Scotland being a signatory party to the Treaty.

Other nations together acting as the 'UK' and seeking to stop Scotland's withdrawal simply by force of numbers (of MP's) might therefore seem unlikely, more especially given that the UK parliament is not itself a signatory party to the treaty. The joint UK parliament cannot itself therefore determine or rule against and hence prevent the withdrawal of any signatory party to the treaty (of union). However, if Scotland were judged as being incapable of withdrawing itself, despite being a signatory party, from its own jointly created union, this therefore implies that Scotland is deemed to be, to all intents and purposes, merely a territory or a colony of the UK, and hence not a sovereign signatory party to any joint union of nations. Clearly, any such assessment depicting Scotland as retaining a 'subordinate' position within the UK constitutional arrangement would seem to ignore the way in which the UK union was constituted, via international treaty, by Scotland. Such an assessment would hardly reflect the existence of the treaty and, indeed, why would Scotland's then representatives go to the extent of making Scotland a signatory party to an international treaty thereby creating a joint parliamentary union of nations if the 'reality' were that Scotland was merely deemed subject to a takeover, subsumed by a union it helped constitute? Whilst politically Scotland may be treated (by the UK parliament and UK administration) as a held territory or colony, constitutionally and legally, by virtue of the treaty, and the accepted fact of Scottish sovereignty, Scotland would seem anything but.

This is surely what the ECJ means when it stated that revoking and ending a treaty is a decision primarily for the treaty signatory party concerned. Any treaty signatory party is, indisputably, one of the principal and superior parties to that treaty; it is not a subordinate, it is a principal and hence sits above the entity created by 'its' treaty. A signatory party to a treaty cannot be told what to do by another entity that the signatory party may have helped to create and establish in order to represent its interests jointly with any other signatory party. The UK union parliament and its administration, in this sense, is merely the appointed *agent* of the 'superior' signatory parties which are the nations and kingdoms of Scotland and England; the UK parliament is arguably not the principal in this matter. The principals are the signatory parties to the treaty, in this instance a sovereign nation and its people, which is Scotland. The signatory party may share its sovereignty as it wishes, in any union of nations, for so long as it may desire; however, a sovereign signatory party may equally withdraw its sovereignty from and its consent to participation in any union as it wishes. A signatory party nation cannot therefore be forced to remain within the confines of a treaty-based institution it itself has created and may end as it sees fit. Scotland and England therefore remain as sovereign nations presently sharing their sovereignty together in a voluntary treaty-based joint union arrangement, a union that may be ended by either signatory party nation at any time.

> *Sae lang as fowk fi sooth (wha dinna hae Scots langage at aw onywey) get tae heid up maist o' oor public institushuns, there'll be nae progress.*

The sovereignty of Scotland at any given time is held by Scotland's national representatives, as elected by the people. The SNP, after the 2019 UK General Election, hold a majority of Scotland's MP's, 47 seats out of 59 (80 per cent). Therefore, it may be argued that this majority of national representatives has the legal and constitutional right to withdraw Scotland from its joint UK parliament. It matters less the grounds for withdrawal; however, more than adequate grounds exist given the colonial oppression and exploitation Scotland and its people have endured over the period of the union, and arguably still endure in various forms. And now, through Brexit, the Scots are deprived of their EU citizenship against their will, due to the UK union administration working against Scotland's interests and democratically stated preference.

Breaches of the Treaty of Union continue to occur. A further example of this is the proposed Northern Ireland 'backstop' or special customs arrangement as part of the UK's proposed Brexit 'deal' which contravenes the Treaty of Union, the latter stating:

> *ART VI, ToU, "Regulations of Trade, Duties, &c. That all parts of the United Kingdom for ever from and after the Union shall have the same Allowances Encouragements and*

> *Drawbacks and be under the same prohibitions restrictions
> and regulations of Trade and liable to the same Customs
> and Duties on Import and Export And that the Allowances
> Encouragements and Drawbacks prohibitions restrictions
> and regulations of Trade and the Customs and Duties on
> Import and Export settled in England when the Union
> commences shall from and after the Union take place
> throughout the whole United Kingdom " (Union with
> Scotland Act 1706)*[95]

Article VI of the UK union treaty will therefore be
breached if Northern Ireland is permitted a different customs
arrangement with the EU to that of Scotland. This is not
just about domestic trade within the UK. The treaty requires
that the Customs interface between all parts of the UK and
third countries should remain the same, and that is what the
Treaty of Union provides for. Any UK Brexit 'deal' containing
a different customs arrangement for Northern Ireland
fundamentally alters this. This implies that Northern Ireland
has a different Customs arrangement with other countries
relative to the rest of the UK and that the Treaty of Union
would be violated.

> *Lat's no bi sae hielan aboot thon: thay unionist elites ken fine weel
> that ance Scots bairns an fowk are taucht their ain leid thay'll
> shuirly want thair ain naition bak.*

The world will be watching Scotland assert its sovereignty,
peacefully, democratically, legally, and justifiably in terms
of Brexit, and in its just Cause of self-determination, also
taking into account the right of any signatory party state to
unilaterally withdraw from its own treaty-based arrangement.
A second referendum is clearly an option that is being denied
by Westminster in any event, the latter simply assuming it

has the power to prevent Scotland from holding a referendum. Scotland may decide to hold a referendum; however, a referendum is not a prerequisite, nor is it a legal requirement for Scottish independence.

This further suggests that Scotland may not have many other choices in the matter other than to use to best effect its democratically elected majority of nationalist representatives to extricate Scotland's withdrawal from the treaty-based union, and much in the same way that it was created.

Scotland's 'Right to Choose'

On 19th December 2019, only a few days after the UK General Election in which the SNP won 47 (80 per cent) of Scotland's 59 seats, the SNP Scottish Government published a paper outlining the 'case for giving the people of Scotland the right to choose their constitutional future' (Scottish Government 2019). The Scottish Government asserted the right of Scotland's devolved parliament at Holyrood to decide when a new referendum should be held and called on the UK Government to transfer such power to Holyrood, in order that a referendum could be held before the end of 2020.

Legally and constitutionally the SNP 'nationalist' majority could have announced Scotland's withdrawal from the UK union, but they decided instead to 'plead' with the UK Government to allow for another independence referendum.

The Scottish Government's paper correctly asserted that Scotland is not a region in a unitary state but rather a country 'in a voluntary union of nations' and that Scotland can only remain a part of the UK though the consent of the Scottish people. The Scottish Government asserted it had a mandate to hold another referendum through winning successive elections in Scotland and where its manifesto commitment was to hold a further referendum on independence. The EU referendum had created the condition of a 'material change' in Scotland's constitutional arrangement within the UK with a majority of Scots voting to remain in the EU.

Yon daeless Cultur Meenister's hid ten year tae gie us a Scots Langage Act, oor human richt an aw, an haes duin hee haw aboot hit. Thon Meenister kens an thochts naethin aboot Scottish cultur.

The paper set out draft legislation outlining several proposed amendments to the Scotland Act 1998 which would give the people of Scotland 'the right to decide their constitutional future'. This would include the power to hold a referendum and, in the event of a 'Yes' vote, to ensure that Scotland should become an Independent State 'as quickly, fairly and effectively as possible'. It was acknowledged that Westminster would be required to legislate for these amendments to the Scotland Act and, in the event of a decision in favour of Scottish independence, the removal of Westminster's ability to legislate for Scotland would also require legislation.

The initial reaction to this proposal from the new UK Government under Prime Minister Boris Johnson with its enlarged 80-seat Westminster majority was to immediately reject these calls for a further independence referendum. It also seemed unlikely that the Scottish Government's request for amendments to the Scotland Act would be considered by the UK Government.

Critics of the Scottish Government's paper (Murray 2019) suggested it first asserts and then rather ignores Scottish sovereignty by suggesting that a referendum 'must have' the agreement of the UK Government; if Scots are a sovereign people then surely what they do is up to the Scots? Moreover, given that independence is a matter of international law rather than domestic law, Ambassador Murray makes the further valid point that the right of Scots to declare independence cannot be restricted by UK domestic law or in the form of limitations placed by the UK parliament on any devolved Scottish parliament. Indeed, under the UN Charter there is an obligation on all States to respect the sovereign rights of all peoples and their territorial integrity (art. 7).

It might reasonably be concluded, here, that the Scottish Government's 'right to choose' paper was prepared by UK civil servants whose allegiance is not to an independent Scotland, but rather to its administrative Power who recruited them. The somewhat 'pleading' tone reflects a lack of belief in, or respect for, the right and power of Scottish national sovereignty. To the many peoples around the world who have sought and achieved decolonisation and independence, and hence liberation, it would merely seem a paper full of contradictions and subterfuge, more intended to undermine the cause of independence than to win it. One cannot and should not plead with an oppressor. Scotland's elected 'nationalist' majorities need to stand up and assert what is rightfully theirs – Scottish independence.

Referendum Pitfalls

A referendum is merely a mechanism to gauge opinion and is not in itself law. Moreover, a referendum is non-binding, as was the case with Brexit. Those advocating a second independence referendum, not least the 'devolved' Scottish Government which remains a part of the British State, do not appear to have quite thought things through in any event, that is assuming they desire independence. Another referendum would imply that Westminster's almost 600 MP's from other countries would still be expected to determine what an independent Scotland looks like in any subsequent 'Independent Scotland Act'. That is assuming these effectively 'foreign' MP's accepted any Yes vote in Scotland which, given the Brexit experience and Westminster's prolonged refusal to implement that referendum result, is by no means guaranteed. The constitutional and legal reality here is arguably more important than contemporary notions or definitions of what is or is not democracy vis-à-vis a referendum. Some claim that a referendum is a kind of 'gold standard', which is itself highly questionable. Moreover, the formation of the UK union was hardly a democratic matter given it was based on a fair degree of corruption and the self-interest of elites at the time. Constitutionally and legally, Scotland is not a mere region or a colony of the UK, regardless of the fact than in practice Scotland is treated as such politically. Scotland IS the UK State, and the UK parliamentary arrangement and its administrative machinery is just as much Scotland's as it is England's. Scotland established a joint parliament with England by international treaty and by majority decision of Scotland's MP's and the UK union or any union for that matter and its joint parliament must be able to be undone legally in the same manner.

This is surely the constitutional and legal reality of the treaty and act of union. To assume otherwise would be to call into question the way the union and its joint UK parliament itself was formed. The treaty and act confirm Scotland's constitutional status as a signatory party sovereign nation together with England in the joint UK union and parliament. There can be no disputing this, or that a simple majority of Scotland's or indeed England's MP's may undo what was done in the same manner.

However, some appear to believe that the UK union was quite different. They may think that England merely annexed and occupied Scotland (as was the case with Wales) and then somewhat deceitfully called it a 'union'. That may well have been England's intent. However, constitutionally, this does not reflect the reality of the treaty of union; it may reflect the political reality afterwards, but not the legal and constitutional reality, which are quite different matters, as recent court opinions given in respect of Brexit have served to demonstrate.

Arguably Scotland does not therefore require another dubious and irregular wide-open (i.e. voting based primarily on residence) franchise referendum, and with its initiation, oversight and eventual ratification and any subsequent enactment decided upon by 600 MP's from other countries who hold no sovereignty over Scotland, nor authority in respect of Scotland's withdrawal. A simple majority of Scotland's MP's should be adequate to constitutionally and legally dissolve the UK union insofar as Scotland is concerned, any time they wish, and reflecting the way the union was created.

If Scotland's constitutional position were ultimately dependent on the decision of almost 600 MP's from other (i.e. foreign?) countries (predominantly England), and hence not dependent solely on Scotland's representatives, it is unlikely that Scotland would ever be independent again. Scots believe, and Westminster has accepted, that Scottish sovereignty ultimately rests with the Scottish people and therefore with Scotland's elected representatives at any given point in time, and nobody else. The UK joint parliament therefore rules over Scotland only so long as Scotland's sovereign people and their elected representatives' consent to that rule.

As far as 'democracy' is concerned, a referendum is not necessarily a democratic option, as was discovered in 2014, and in 2016 with Brexit. Nor, it appears, is a referendum a legal requirement for independence. Neither is a referendum legally and constitutionally necessary for any signatory party to unilaterally withdraw from a treaty.

There are several reasons, aside from postal vote irregularities, why the 2014 Scottish independence referendum was not democratic. In line with UN concerns and guidelines[96] this relates to the self-determination process itself and especially the need to avoid any undue influence and intervention from external forces, including:

1. Virtually the entire British (i.e. English) media used all its means and resources to oppose Scottish independence;

2. The British civil service and hence the British Government used all its means and resources to oppose Scottish independence; and,

3. An extraordinary referendum voting franchise (based on residence) was unique and is unlawful in respect of national voting in most other countries where voting rights are based on parental descent and national citizenship, and for national self-determination are based on accepted definitions of what constitutes 'a people', which should avoid any influence by other 'peoples' and nations.

Constitutional and Legal Position

It is clearly important to distinguish between the political, constitutional and legal aspects of Scottish independence. What is surely of fundamental importance in the context of Scottish self-government (i.e. independence) is the constitutional and the legal positions, and this can be dealt with via a majority decision of Scotland's nationally elected representatives. Those objecting to such matters would have recourse to the courts should they wish, or via subsequent national elections to campaign for change. The question remains, however, as to why the SNP's Scotland majorities of supposedly 'nationalist' MP's have not sought to use the arguably more straightforward constitutional and legal route to withdraw Scotland from the UK union?

Westminster politicians, including former Prime Ministers and cabinet ministers, have previously acknowledged that if the Scottish Nationalists ever won a majority of seats in Scotland then they could negotiate Scotland's withdrawal from the UK. Mrs Thatcher accepted this as did John Major. According to the former Tory Party Chairman Norman Tebbit, *"(John) Major has made it clear that a majority of SNP MP's after an election would serve as a mandate to begin negotiations for separation. There are no plans to hold a referendum"* (Robertson 1997). Clearly, even Tory Government's considered that there was no need for a referendum and a majority of Scotland's SNP MP's would have a mandate to *"begin negotiations for separation"*. Similarly, the former Home Secretary Leon Brittan maintained that Scotland could be independent if the nationalists won a majority of seats in Scotland, albeit his caveat, for no apparent reason, was this should be at two successive general elections, suggesting this was a view *"almost universally shared among English Tory backbenchers"* (Woodifield 1988). Scotland's nationalists have won such a majority now at three successive UK general elections, yet thus far Scotland still remains stuck within the UK union, with Scotland's SNP majorities unwilling to assert sovereignty and extract Scotland from the union. As recently as 2010, Tories in Scotland were arguing that (Swanson 2010): *"If people in Scotland were bursting to be free would they not be taking this opportunity to vote SNP? Should the SNP not be campaigning to win a majority of Scotland's 59 seats.*" The clear implication here, again, is that if the SNP ever won a majority of seats in Scotland, they would have a democratic mandate for independence. The SNP have been winning a majority of seats in Scotland at every UK General Election now for several years yet still they take their oath, and their seats, and their salaries at Westminster.

The goalposts therefore appear to have been moved somewhat; now that Scotland is regularly returning nationalists majorities, Westminster and indeed Holyrood both appear to maintain 'the line' that a referendum is somehow necessary for independence, and that a majority of Scotland's MP's cannot now withdraw Scotland from the UK union. Despite this political prevarication, it remains that a referendum is clearly not a legal requirement, according to McCorkindale and McHarg (2020), who wrote that: "*As a matter of law, a referendum is not a required part of the process of becoming independent*". Indeed, as far as the politics of a referendum is concerned, McCorkindale and McHarg further argue that: "*..the Scottish Government's mandate to hold a referendum – though politically important – seems legally irrelevant.*" This suggests that what really matters here is what is legal, which can often get clouded by the politics or indeed notions of what is and is not considered to be 'democratic', or described as some form of undefined 'gold standard'. The latter are merely excuses for not taking the legal route to independence.

> *Maist foregane doon-hauden kintra's (i.e. ex colonies) noo lairn thair bairns twa langages an aften mair - e.g. Singapore haes Mandarin, Tamil an Malay, as weel as 'administrative English'. Scotlan'll aye hae anely Englis till Scots fowk gae thair ain wey agin.*

Many Scots are now asking if independence is really the SNP's raison d'être? Are they really 'up for it'? With the sort of national majorities the SNP holds, i.e. over 80 per cent of the seats in Scotland, nationalists in any other colony would have taken their country back long before now. And most former colonies now recognised states didn't even have any constitutional treaty and Act with which to legally justify their exit and liberation, far less Westminster's begrudged acknowledgement of Scotland's sovereignty.

And on the false referendum road all Scots hear from Westminster is 'now is not the time', whilst from Holyrood the message is 'wait for indyref2' or, given the residence-based voter franchise, more likely 'Quebec 2', if it happens, but that Scotland needs this elusive 'gold standard' exit from the UK 'that nobody can question'. Yet, even if an independence referendum were 'granted' by the UK, and even if there were a majority Yes vote, what does anyone really think that 600 Westminster MP's from other countries would write into any subsequent 'Independence Scotland Act', should Westminster ever decide to even draft one? Must the 'sovereign' Scottish people really depend on the elected representatives of foreign countries to enact and grant Scottish independence and for the elected representatives from these foreign countries to determine what an independent Scotland might look like? That seems rather a series of fanciful notions, more especially when considering who Scots are dealing with here – Perfidious Albion itself[97]. Meanwhile, as Scots MP's prevaricate and ponder in various courts about the sovereignty of Westminster's MP's, Brexit beckons, and ever more 'No' voters keep piling into Scotland from south of the border ready to vote to block Scottish independence should another referendum occur.

It may be instructive, if necessary, to seek the opinion of the courts on the constitutional and legal reality of the Treaty of Union vis-à-vis Scotland's ability to unilaterally withdraw from it. One cannot imagine a court deciding, for example, that Scotland is unable to unilaterally withdraw (from the UK union) as this would imply Scotland was subject to a takeover by England in 1707; that does not seem to reflect the content or the purpose of the Treaty of Union, and it would fundamentally destroy the very idea that Scotland was ever a partner in any union. Such a decision would effectively confirm that Scotland was to all intents and purposes a colonial territory (which alas Scots must accept to be the political reality) subject to the whims of MP's and elites from other countries.

On the other hand, were a court to agree on Scotland's legal right to withdraw (from the UK union), then the majority of Scotland's elected representatives may therefore give notice (to the joint UK parliament) to withdraw Scotland from that parliamentary union, as it was created and, as is their constitutional right, if not their moral obligation as 'nationalists'. Politically, Scotland's sovereignty rests with Scotland's elected national representatives who are put there by the people. Scotland might even thereafter arrange for its own independence ratification referendum, if this is deemed to be necessary. Scotland then would have no need to wait for 'permission' from representatives of other countries (rest-UK) in order to hold a further referendum, or for them to accept (or reject) the outcome of a referendum.

> *Scotlan's a muckle mankit wastit Brigadoon, sleepin fir chree hunner year an aye dozin awa, an thay SNP daein naethin aboot hit.*

The Articles of Union state that the Union is 'forever'. However, in legal terms 'forever' is about as certain as 'normally', and much like any 'Vow'. 'Forever' is also a term used in marriage vows and in fairy tales where the prince and princess live happily ever after and as we know things do not always happen like that in the 'real world'. 'Forever', in other words means for the 'foreseeable future' or until such time as one party wishes to end an arrangement. Some 81 per cent of Scotland's present MP's support independence, compared with just 61 per cent who voted to pass the Act of Union on 16th January 1707; the treaty was ratified by a majority of 110 votes to 69. Scotland has an even greater elected majority now in favour of independence and they should get on and deliver that.

Scottish Sovereignty

UDI in the UK context does not appear to readily apply in Scotland's case as it would to a nation, region or colony that has no treaty based constitutional arrangement, or sovereignty, and which was simply taken over and ruled by another nation. By Treaty and Act, Scotland is one of the two sovereign nations that constituted the joint UK union and which still constitute it. Indeed, who, or rather what, would Scotland be declaring independence from? UDI would seem to imply that Scotland were declaring its independence from its own jointly created (UK) union parliament, which Scotland formally constituted and still constitutes by international treaty and act. The 'legal authority' necessary not only to withdraw from, but to dissolve, Scotland's joint UK parliament must rest in the way it (i.e. the UK) was and remains constituted by Scotland, that is, through the consent of a majority of Scotland's national representatives who hold Scotland's sovereignty as given them by Scotland's people.

Constitutionally, irrespective of the UK union arrangement, Scotland remains to all intents and purposes a sovereign country and people that may re-assert independence at any time. Scotland is a country that has merely consented to enter a joint parliamentary administrative arrangement (styled as 'UK'). A majority of Scotland's 'nationalist' representatives could do this anytime, not least given that they have little purpose or effect otherwise.

The UK union constitution (i.e. Treaty and Act of Union) does not state specifically how the union should be ended, though this does not mean it should not be ended. Treaties are merely words on paper which by themselves have little or no determinative impact. A treaty can never be cast in stone for eternity for the simple reason that its relevance and import is inevitably bound by time and circumstance. Any treaty will only ever be upheld insofar as it serves 'the national interest'. There is here the age-old argument of 'alliance-determinism' which assumes both effective international law and honorable alliance partners; however, *"experts in international affairs would count those as among the most naïve hypotheses imaginable"* (Hamilton and Herwig, 2004: p. 231).

What can be said with some confidence is that the British State is seldom honorable, and also that treaties are ended. It is clearly time to end the Treaty of Union. Moreover, the British State is essentially 'at war' with Scots who seek independence. Scots can forget honour or integrity in return for threatening the United Kingdom with dissolution and should rather more expect lying and deceit in all its forms to be directed towards them, as was the case during the 2014 referendum. The despicable institutional conspiracy to put former First Minister Alex Salmond in jail and discredit the independence Cause is but one further example (Murray 2020).

The UK union can only exist so long as a majority of Scotland's representatives agree to participate in it. That is Scotland's only real veto over what has always been a rather one-sided administrative and political arrangement, given the 10:1 numerical preponderance of English MP's over Scotland's MP's, albeit it remains a political union of equals in other key respects, and not least in the power of each signatory party to the treaty to end it. To believe otherwise would be to deny the existence of any union at all, which would be to deny the existence of the Treaty and Act of Union and the constitutional basis and reality of the UK union itself.

In terms of process, the ending of Scotland's union with England need not be onerous. The majority of Scotland's national representatives would be expected to inform the joint union parliament of their intention to withdraw Scotland from the union, much as the UK has done with its EU withdrawal. This would then mean that full Scottish sovereignty would revert to a Scottish parliament. That sovereign Scottish parliament would then formally enact the withdrawal of Scotland from the UK union.

Of course, unionists in Scotland who remain opposed to Scottish independence may subsequently campaign for the renegotiation of any UK union agreement and Scotland's re-entry into it, if they wished to do so. And, if these pro-union supporters ever won a parliamentary majority in favour of such a policy then there is nothing to stop them taking such a policy forward. That is democracy!

Scottish sovereignty and the Treaty of Union is indisputable, as is, according to the UN Charter, the Scottish peoples 'right to self-determination….(which) necessarily includes the right to freely determine their political status and freely to pursue their economic, social and cultural development' (art. 2).

CHAPTER 10: ETHNICITY

Ethnic Discrimination

The British MSM and other institutional opponents of Scottish independence avidly look for any examples, however dubious, of alleged anti-English behaviour amongst Scots who support Scottish independence. To many unionists it almost seems as if Scottish independence is itself somehow anti-English. Examples are thankfully few and far between and any such claims are usually groundless. What is seldom, if ever, considered though, in the debate on Scottish independence, are the many examples of anti-Scottish behaviour from those opposed to Scottish self-determination and independence. The latter may be far more prevalent than many commentators appear to think.

Conventional approaches towards research of racism in the UK, and even in Scotland, focus mainly on colour racism and discrimination against minorities (Davidson et. al. 2018). What is often ignored here is that, in the UK sense, Scots themselves are an ethnic minority. Moreover, in a Scottish context, Scots speakers are also a minority people, largely due to displacement, selective in-migration, and cultural imperialism policies – each of which are arguably anti-Scottish. Such aspects of the Scots being an oppressed minority ethnic group both within the UK and in Scotland are seldom if ever considered.

The only sure thing we know about Scottish independence is that it would create a new Scottish State and with that it would also create a new Scottish nationality and Scottish citizenship. Those opposed to and hence voting against independence therefore seek to block and prevent a Scottish State from existing and by implication they also seek to reject and block Scottish citizenship and Scottish nationality. This in itself may be viewed as a fundamentally anti-Scottish act.

Unionists also tend to oppose any referendum being held on Scottish independence and hence they are therefore anti self-determination.

> *Whit daes fowk nae unerstaund aboot 'hoo noo broon coo'? Englis is Englis, Scots is Scots.*

Any such anti-Scottish acts and perspectives are by implication ethnically motivated. To block and actively prevent a 'peoples' right to enjoy their own nationality and citizenship is self-evidently to oppose that 'peoples' national existence and therefore is anti that nation and its people. This raises the prospect that the 'No' vote in 2014 was itself essentially anti-Scottish ethnic discrimination aimed at preventing and blocking the right of Scots to create and to enjoy and participate in their own Scottish nationality, Scottish citizenship, and self-government. A relevant question here may be, what kind of people vote against their own right to self-determination?

Ethnic and racial discrimination may take different forms. This includes the public ridiculing of Scottish people simply for speaking in the Scots language, which perhaps also reflects the inability of others (e.g. Anglophones) to understand (or respect) the Scots language; the case of the SNP MP David Linden is informative here, where English MP's at Westminster claimed not to understand him (Settle 2018). The theory of 'internalized racism' may further help explain anti-Scottish tendencies evident even amongst some Scots themselves and this is discussed later in the chapter. In this connection, Purves (1997, p. 2) noted in regard to Scottish children being made to feel ashamed of their own language in school: *"The psychological damage caused by this self-hatred is incalculable…"*.

> *Englis fowk shuid hae thay're ain pairlament onywey an thay widna be bathered aboot no kennin oor Scots langage.*

Long studied from both the points of view of the oppressed and oppressors (e.g. Freire 1970; Fanon 2004; Deutsch 2006), usage of the term *oppression* has shifted from meaning the exercising of tyranny by a ruling group to signifying the injustice some suffer due to the everyday practices and norms of a society. Those in the ruling or dominant group, an Anglophone unionist elite in Scotland's case, effectively limit the personal and intellectual freedoms of those in subordinate groups, leading to feelings of self-deprecation and fear (Prilleltensky & Gonick, 1996). Over time, oppression becomes a far more widespread, systemic injustice that creates systematic disparities affecting the well-being and development of individuals and groups.

Ethnic discrimination is thus a form of oppression which is widely embedded in any ethnically stratified society. Those in power (e.g. White people, or people of colour, or those speaking a specific language) perpetuate a system of oppression based on race/ethnicity against other people of whatever 'difference' may exist. This form of ethnic oppression consists of unequal distribution of systemic power in the areas of (Bivens, 1995):

(a) Decision making – there is a system in place that rewards those in the oppressed group who support the oppressor group and punishes those who do not;

(b) Resources – money and employment are in the gift of the oppressor group and the oppressed group have difficulty accessing resources for their community or to control resources for their community;

(c) Standards - what the oppressor group view as socially appropriate or normal behaviour is assumed to be the standard the oppressed group must conform to; and

(d) Naming the problem – problems of racism and ethnicity are assumed to be caused by the oppressed group themselves, e.g. working-class Scots speakers are assumed (by the Anglophone elite) to be less articulate, more violent, drunken, dysfunctional, lacking in achievement and attainment than the oppressor group with consequently state-sanctioned violence, penalties and general institutionalised forms of discrimination targeted towards the oppressed group.

This unequal distribution of systemic power contributes to both external and internal consequences for oppressor and oppressed. Racism and hence ethnic discrimination are essentially to do with power. Carter (2007) defined race as *"a sociopolitical designation in which individuals are assigned to a particular racial group based on presumed biological or visible characteristics such as skin color, physical features, and... language"* (p.15). It is therefore primarily aspects of language and ethnic identity that distinguishes Scots speakers from Anglophones, the latter comprising Scotland's dominant unionist 'governing class'[98].

Rangel (2014) looked at the internal dynamics experienced by people as a product of racism or ethnic discrimination and its psychological consequences and proposed three general ways whereby racism impacts the mental health of ethnic minorities:

(a) The internalization of racial stereotypes and negative images of individuals' racial group that harms their self-worth;

(b) Institutional racism, thus inhibiting the socio-economic development of the oppressed group; and

(c) That racism and ethnic discrimination themselves are stressful events for the oppressed group.

These serious negative impacts directly lead to psychological distress affecting the mental health of oppressed groups (U.S. Department of Health and Human Services 2001). In Scotland, and the UK more generally, there is a lengthy history relating to the negative racial stereotypes of Scots language speakers, often promoted by the British MSM, and also reflected in teaching practice in schools where those speaking the Scots language, even from a very young age, were punished and/or ridiculed for doing so. This results in Scots speakers being less confident or motivated to speak in class, or later in life in meetings and discussions that will often therefore tend to be dominated or controlled by apparently 'more confident' and supposedly more 'articulate' Anglophones.

Internalized Racism

Embedded within the racial/ethnic discrimination research is an indirect measure of the concept of 'internalized racism'. This term represents the internalization of negative stereotypes of one's own racial group mainly found in the first stage of racial identity development, which is referred to as Preencounter/Conformity, and where conformity involves matching of attitudes, beliefs and behaviours to group norms or politics.

The failure to agree on how to define and measure internalized oppression due to racism and ethnic discrimination has led to multiple definitions and interpretations of the construct. For example, Jones (2000: p. 1213) defined internalized racial oppression as the "*acceptance by members of stigmatized races of negative messages about their own abilities and intrinsic worth*", describing it as being characterized by individuals who are "*not believing in others who look like them, and not believing in themselves*". Similarly, Krieger (2000) defines internalized racial oppression as: "*members of subordinate groups — especially those experiencing greater social and material deprivation — internalize negative views of the dominant culture and accept their subordinate status and related unfair treatment as 'deserved' and hence nondiscriminatory*".

Thus, many Scots speakers will tend not to consider themselves to be ethnically oppressed despite the reality of their exclusion from key areas of Anglophone dominated institutions, elites and management, and/or from related policy formation, development and implementation, or even for that matter in terms of the allocation of, and access to resources and associated benefits. An example of the latter is the significant and ever widening gap in salary levels between the more privileged Anglophone elite and Scots speakers, the latter mainly working class (The Social Mobility and Child Poverty Commission 2015).

In offering a more comprehensive and holistic perspective, according to Rangel (2014), Internalized racism may be described and defined as:

> *".... the personal conscious or subconscious acceptance of the dominant society's racist views, stereotypes and biases of one's ethnic group. It gives rise to patterns of thinking, feeling and behaving that result in discriminating, minimizing, criticizing, finding fault, invalidating, and hating oneself while simultaneously valuing the dominant culture."*
>
> (Internalized racism is therefore) *"...the process by which an individual's racial self-image is based on direct and indirect negative stereotypical messages experienced throughout one's life that in turn influences the individual's self image and worth, thoughts, emotions, and behaviors."*

Tappan (2006) further suggests that the term 'appropriated racial oppression' itself implies that the phenomenon of internalized racism may be so deep and internal in those who are oppressed as to be rigid and unchanging once in place. Here the psychoanalytic implications of 'internalization' problematically leads to very rigid mindsets. According to Tappan, using the term 'appropriation' reflects 'a mastery of cultural tools' derived from one's environment that are by nature both oppressive and reflect the giving of privilege.

'Internalized Racism' – thenks tae bein doun-hauden ower chree hunner year an mair!

Thus, appropriated racial oppression is a form of mainly racial self-perception manifested in conscious and subconscious efforts to dissociate oneself from one's own ethnic group, and to seek identification with the oppressor or governing class. The Scots speaking Scot is therefore forced to adapt his or her language and to become more Anglophone in order to progress socially within the dominant Anglophone cultural and linguistic hierarchy. In this imposed cultural and linguistic environment, the natural yet deemed to be inferior (i.e. not 'valid') Scots language and culture is wilfully set aside and diminished, in order to avoid ethnic discrimination and to minimise prevailing socio-economic limitations to personal development and advancement. Appropriated racial oppression therefore consists of a complex interaction among multiple behaviours, emotions, and attitudes.

There are considered to be five dimensions of appropriated racial oppression (Lipsky 1987):

(1) appropriation of negative stereotypes;

(2) patterns of thinking that maintain the status quo;

(3) adaptation of 'superior' oppressor cultural standards;

(4) devaluation of one's own group; and

(5) emotional reactions.

Individuals subjected to ethnic discrimination learn and adapt to the negative stereotypes about their group. These (Scottish) individuals are socialized to believe in the superiority of another (i.e. Anglophone) group and the 'inferiority' of groups such as their own through messages from their family and friends, society, the media, education, and a variety of other influences. This learning process or *appropriation* may lead to denigration of racial self and feelings of inferiority about being an individual of a minority group, hence 'appropriated racial oppression'.

> *Whit A dae ken is thar's a 'Gaelic Language Act' noo, an thar's nae*
> *'Scots Language Act'. Thon's nae respectit o ma human richt tae*
> *lairn an ken ma ain mither tung, Scots.*

In the British Tory 'one nation' sense, Scots may already be correctly defined as a minority ethnic group. Given ongoing demographic change, with large and consistent population inflows mostly from England to Scotland, Scots could feasibly also become a minority group within Scotland itself. Census data from 2011 suggested that only 1.6m Scots speak the Scots language and this therefore confirms Scots speakers as representing a linguistic minority within Scotland; hence, most people living in Scotland today are Anglophone. This further implies that many Scots have abandoned the Scots language, their linguistic deceit facilitated by the British State's longstanding refusal to teach Scots in Scottish schools, as a response to and outcome of appropriated racial oppression. As Purves (1997, p. 2) notes:

"Since the Treaty of Union in 1707, generations of Scots have had to come to terms with a situation in which they were taught English at school, and where the way of speech natural to them was officially regarded as wrong by definition, or as a dialect unworthy of use as a serious medium of communication. The dilemma involved introduced a schizoid element into the national psyche. For with many people, the 'true self' associated with the complex of feelings and attitudes acquired at home in childhood had to be denied in the interests of material advancement, in favour of a false persona."

Related health impacts of this are immeasurable. Associated features of schizoid personality disorder include avoiding social situations, stilted speech, and feeling as though one is an 'observer' rather than a participant in life. Appropriated racial oppression may also manifest itself through such emotions as shame, embarrassment, depressive symptoms and low collective self-esteem (David, 2008; Speight, 2007; Watts-Jones, 2002). If an individual has adopted the belief that the oppressor group are superior and have begun to emulate the oppressor group based on this belief, he or she may begin to deny, normalize or tolerate discriminatory behaviours. This tolerance of current and historical ethnic discrimination may also be associated with beliefs and attitudes related to the belief in or perceptions of what appears 'a just world' (Lipsky 1987).

According to the literature, such negative stereotypes contribute significantly to appropriated racial oppression (Rangel 2014: p. 100). In this process a 'colonial mentality' involves denial and/or downplaying of the reality of discrimination or any past history of racism (e.g. wars, clearances and mass displacement, cultural and linguistic discrimination, institutionalised oppression etc. will be accepted, as somehow 'deserved'); this mindset may develop as a form of defence in dealing with a racist environment (Thompson and Neville 1999). The oppressed minority adapt to the imposed standards (*conformity*) in order to 'pass' as part of the majority group in their effort to avoid oppression, thereby maintaining and indeed strengthening the myth of a meritocracy (Stewart and Bennett 1991). Devaluation of or discrimination against one's own ethnic group is a further dimension of the 'condition', often involving a rebuke for those failing to adapt and continuing to display ethnically related negative stereotypes. Some Scots continue to devalue, for example, the Scots language and hence associate Scots language speakers and its close relationship to lower esteem within the oppressive 'order'. Shame, anger and embarrassment comprise the final dimension and are subconsciously reflected in behaviours and attitudes (David and Okazaki 2006). Internalised oppression therefore reflects a merging of both the individual's mental functioning <u>and</u> the sociocultural setting which combined help to construct appropriated racial oppression (Tappan 2006: p. 2115). In this we have effectively defined the Scottish 'Cultural Cringe' and by its scientific name, which is 'appropriated racial oppression'.

Anely Englis wis garred doon ma thrapple as wi aw Scots fowk, nae doot tae assimilate us aw tae be Anglophone an nae a Scot at aw.

Those exhibiting higher levels of appropriated racial oppression will readily accept a devaluation of one's own ethnic group, exhibit a low level of self-esteem, remain in denial of even blatant ethnic discrimination, and endorse low levels of belief in the existence of institutional racism. Researchers may use a scale to assess whether individuals have a high or a low level of appropriated racial oppression. Hence the reason many Scots vote against their own national independence, which remains a highly unusual phenomenon internationally, is likely to be a consequence of higher levels of appropriated racial oppression. It can therefore be hypothesised that Scots who oppose Scottish independence will tend to exhibit a higher level of appropriated racial oppression.

Meritocracy — which is the notion that opportunities and advancements are solely based on one's skill set and individual achievement — serves to perpetuate and strengthen appropriated racial oppression. Meritocracy obscures the ways in which institutional ethnic discrimination contributes to inequality among ethnic groups (Thompson & Neville, 1999). Any meritocracy will, generally, even subconsciously, seek to prioritise the progression of those who appear to reflect the image and advance the values of a meritocracy. In other words, an Anglophone and unionist elite meritocracy will seek to prioritise and protect itself, to the exclusion of those who do not quite 'fit' in with its image; hence nationalist Scots speakers might as well look elsewhere for social and economic or even educational opportunities for advancement, or give up trying. Scotland's penchant recruitment of a large and perhaps dominant element of its Anglophone meritocracy from a major neighbouring country perpetuates a linguistically determined social hierarchy which arguably feeds and strengthens internalised racism among Scots language speakers.

Internalised racism theory therefore helps to explain much of the hostility we see between pro-union Scots and pro-independence Scots. This involves pro-union Scots, themselves an oppressed racial group, supporting the oppression of another racial group (i.e. pro-independence Scots) by supporting, benefiting from, maintaining or participating in the set of attitudes, behaviours, social structures and ideologies that undergird the dominating Anglophone and unionist ethnic group's supremacy. This cross ethnic hostility remains one of the main problems for, and barriers to, Scots seeking independence.

The problem of internalised racism cannot be resolved personally or interpersonally because it is bound up with the dominant Anglophone ethnic structures, institutions and ideologies that continue to control people's lives in Scotland (Bivens 1995); ethnic discrimination and hence racism is, after all, to do with power. The solution to this conflict depends on removal of the 'power' imposed on Scots as represented by the dominant Anglophone ethnic group which underpins internalised racism amongst Scots, and which essentially divides the Scots into two broad groups; one for and the other opposed to independence. The UK 'union' and its imposed Anglophone linguistic power base and oppressive cultural hegemony has therefore ethnically divided Scots. Decolonisation and independence offers a realistic solution in concert with initiatives to formally teach the Scots language and to introduce the Scots language as a standard national language requirement in an effort to remove appropriated racial oppression, the latter at root Anglophone-based and a function of cultural and linguistic imperialism.

It may therefore be argued that the predominant ethnic or

racial 'issue' in Scotland is not colour race, but internalised racism based around language difference between on the one hand the Anglophone elite dominant culture, which is unionist oriented and, on the other hand the Scots language speaking culture which mostly relates to working class Scots supportive of independence. However, internalised racism is no less damaging to a society than colour-racism, far from it. For example, internalised racism primarily manifests itself in the form of fewer Scots, and more especially Scots speakers, being allowed to progress socio-economically within Scotland's Anglophone dominated social institutions; rather, Scots speakers will tend to be excluded, as we see with elite universities, elite schools and various other institutions, all Anglophone dominated. Internalised racism diminishes and pours scorn on the Scots language and hence Scottish culture, questioning its very 'validity'. Internalised racism creates, feeds and reinforces the Scottish 'Cultural Cringe' and diminishes the self-confidence, aspiration, health and well-being and development potential of the Scottish people, and this places a constraint on development of the Scottish nation also. Moreover, internalised racism arguably results in a significant proportion of the Scottish population rejecting the offer to hold 'Scottish' identity in any meaningful sense, with many Scots themselves rejecting their own access to and opportunity for Scottish citizenship, Scottish nationality and Scottish independence. Internalised racism explains why some Scots refuse to accept that their own people have the capability to manage and self-govern their own country and its affairs.

> *Langage is the foonds an grund o cultur, an cultur is wha we ir an hou we thocht, an thon's whit differentiates aw Scots an Scotland fi fowk fi ivery ither naition.*

Ethnicity and Language

Related to the issue of internalised racism, there appear to be numerous aspects of apartheid (i.e. institutionalised racial segregation) occuring in Scotland, though this is similarly not always quite so evident, far less discussed. South African and Palestinian apartheid was similarly characterised by settler colonialism and the displacement of the indigenous population[99] and, given the history, it is quite difficult to see outcomes in Scotland as being that much different.

British State broadcaster the BBC, which is said to employ some 2,000 journalists, suggested in reference to the desire for Scottish independence that *"the Scots are chippy"* people (Hutcheon 2019). 'Chippy' (adjective) implies that 'people are touchy and defensive, especially on account of having a grievance or a sense of inferiority'. This term itself represents both bias and ethnic discrimination, and from the state broadcaster no less. Within the present UK political arrangement, the Scots remain a people who are repeatedly told they are 'Too Wee, Too Poor and Too Stupid' to run their own affairs and that they are 'chippy' (i.e. inferior) and they indulge in a grievance culture. With such messages being broadcast daily into the populations front rooms it seems little wonder that many people north and south of the border accept these messages as facts. This is also a form of radicalisation that turns people who believe in independence into convenient targets for those holding extreme views, such as British nationalists. This kind of treatment seems to fit well with and serves to reinforce appropriated racial oppression insofar as Scots are concerned.

To a significant extent it is linguistic differences that explain why Scotland, Catalonia, Wales and Quebec etc. are unable thus far to be independent. In each of these nations the indigenous Scots, Catalan, Welsh and French-Quebec language speakers mostly vote for greater self-determination and for independence, whilst Anglophone and (in the case of

Catalonia, Spanish speakers) tend to vote 'No' to prevent and block self-determination of the respective peoples. Language is the basis of culture, influencing the way we think, how we act, and hence even how we vote. Language also helps form our identity, makes us who we are, and reminds us where we come from. Hence language assimilation and linguistic imperialism policies, combined with related institutionalised ethnic and linguistic discrimination and resultant appropriated racial oppression outcomes, explain why many Scots are 'minded' to vote against and deny their own nation's independence and, therefore, to a large extent, seek to block their own existence as a recognised nation and people.

Whilst the devolved 'Scottish Government' argues for the need merely to 'respect the Scots language', the present Scots language policy vacuum suggests precisely the opposite. The reality is that, in Scotland, government and its many Anglophone led social institutions do not respect the Scots language that many Scots speak day and daily; to respect one's own language one really needs to teach it and to learn it. A mostly Anglophone unionist elite running Scotland's social institutions will invariably make out that Scots are simply speaking 'bad English' and that Scots is not a 'valid' language. This is an ethnically discriminatory perspective that remains fixed within Scotland's Anglophone institutional hierarchies. The Anglophone unionist elites running Scotland's institutions have effectively banned the Scots language by refusing to teach it to the Scottish people. Moreover, the prevailing ethnic discrimination faced by many Scots speakers, mostly from the working class, endures because of this linguistic oppression foisted on Scotland by an Anglophone unionist elite. Within an Anglophone controlled and dominated society many Scots simply cannot be 'lifted' socio-economically as they otherwise would be. Anglophone elites dominate the cultural high ground in Scotland, they control the linguistic 'battleground' against who they view as their linguistic and cultural inferior – the Scots speaker.

Anglophone cultural and linguistic oppression is therefore all pervading throughout Scotland's social institutions. The resulting discrimination ultimately determines and limits the life chances of many Scots speakers who remain oppressed ('doun-hauden') in their own land, consigned to a life of poverty and inequality as a result. The Scottish Government has established a Poverty and Inequality Commission to help provide advice to Ministers on measures to address worsening marginalisation of large sections of the Scottish people[100]. It remains doubtful whether even that social institution will recognize the underlying cultural and linguistic and indeed colonial reasons as to why so many Scots remain marginalised and destined to live a life of poverty and inequality in their own land.

Given that language is a human right, Scots should expect to be able to learn to read and write in their own mother tongue much in the way other peoples' do elsewhere. More than this, any elites appointed to manage Scotland's institutions should really be expected themselves to have a good understanding of the Scots language. In most countries it is a legal requirement for those working in social institutions to have a reasonable or even perhaps fluent understanding of the 'national' language, as well as English in many cases. The present discriminatory English-dominated language 'system' in Scotland therefore restricts opportunities for ethnic Scots speakers, not least in the learning of their own language.

> *In ivery ither kintra its 'Vive la difference', yet oor heid bummers aye gar anither tung doon oor thrapples kiddin oan its oor ane. Cultural racism, thons whit it is, an it hauds Scots fowk doon in aw weys an mair.*

There are clearly going to be consequences when most of Scotland's top jobs in its social institutions and commerce are primarily advertised outside the country, in the London metropolitan press, or when Whitehall and many other British institutions appoint senior officials from outside Scotland (Tickell 2019). The inevitable outcome is an Anglophone unionist meritocratic elite running Scotland's institutions. This is no accident, being rather a pre-requisite of colonial control, reinforced and strengthened through what has become institutionalised Anglophone unionist opposition to Scottish self-determination and independence. Appropriated racial oppression implies that many Scots will accept such an outcome as 'deserving', which it is not.

Two of the key determinants of Scottish independence identified in this book are culture and language, both of which form the basis of identity. Linguistic and ethnic oppression of the Scots is clearly related to the 'Cultural Cringe', and to associated negative impacts on Scotland's people. These are psychological constraints and impediments experienced by many Scots, reinforced through endless Anglophone pro-British propaganda as well as other forms of cultural indoctrination. The Anglophone elite culture itself is naturally 'programmed' to vehemently oppose Scottish independence and to advance British exceptionalism and a sense of British superiority. Scots suffering from the 'Cultural Cringe' and/or appropriated racial oppression, will tend to accept and normalise the imposed 'superiority' of an Anglophone (or British) culture and language which naturally rejects Scottish independence, assuming largely on the basis of their own perceived ethnically reinforced 'inadequacies' that Scots are 'too wee, too poor, and too stupid' to run their own affairs (Campbell 2013).

With the Highland clearances, the banning of the kilt and Gaelic language etc., Scots tend to think of racial oppression as something historical, or perhaps something that is colour oriented (Ross 2008). Yet the cultural, linguistic and hence ethnic oppression of the Scots continues to this day. This oppression is reinforced primarily through the refusal of the state to teach Scottish children their own Scots language. Without the negative influences of linguistic oppression and appropriated racial oppression, the choice between either Scottish self-government or perpetual English Tory rule over Scotland might seem rather obvious and straightforward for most Scots, much as it would be for any other downtrodden people. That it is not so straightforward is in large part due to 'establishment Scotland' (Hassan 2019) and its Anglophone institutions, including the BBC and the rest of the British MSM and others, which project such negative ethnic stereotypes and focus on other false ethnically associated 'inferior' narratives as far as Scots speakers and Scotland is concerned.

> *Anither mebbe mair accurat wey tae conseeder thon 'creenge' wad bi 'internalized racism' an 'appropriated racial oppression'. Wad ye nae gree?*

We are where are today, in the Scottish and UK political context, not because of Scottish nationalism per se but because of centuries of imperialistic domination and oppression, in which Scotland and its people's distinct national needs have never been prioritised. Examples of the most successful nations today show that they focus primarily on their own people and their own peoples' priorities (e.g. Norway, Singapore, Oman, Dubai/UAE, Iceland etc.). Most successful nations are also rather modest in population and geographic terms and still well able to successfully work within a dynamic fast changing global economy. Each is happy to fly their own flags and do their own national 'thing', including teaching their own language as well as English, yet still working collaboratively and globally with other nations and within supra-national groupings where it matters. Nationalism in this sense can therefore be highly positive. This also relates to the happiest nations, the top four being Finland, Denmark, Norway and Iceland (United Nations Sustainable Development Solutions Network 2019), each modest sized independent (and Nordic) countries and all teaching their children in schools their own national language as well as English. Scotland and its people should not be deprived of accessing the same positive national and international development opportunities as these and many other successful independent nations.

It is therefore cultural and linguistic imperialism enforced through trans-national (UK) nationalism that is the main barrier holding down Scotland, the latter involving occupation and political control of Scotland and with this the cultural and linguistic (enculturation) and hence ethnic oppression of a minority people (the Scots) and their nation. This remains the rather obvious and enduring socio-political and constitutional difference between Scotland and numerous other comparable independent states such as Norway, Denmark, Ireland and Iceland, or for that matter the more than one hundred decolonised territories and peoples around the world that are now independent.

The choice between Scottish independence or perpetual Anglophone British Tory trans-national mis-rule of Scotland should seem rather obvious for Scots, much as it would be for any people who are mis-treated, exploited and ruled over as a colony. That this is not so obvious to many Scots is largely due to the ingrained 'internalised racism' that prevails, as exhibited within the personal conscious or subconscious acceptance by Scots of the dominant (Anglophone) society's ethnic views, stereotypes, prejudices and biases, which explains why some Scots continue to reject independence and hence oppose even their own liberation, decolonisation, and nationhood.

Hence the (two) main issues of racism affecting the mass of Scotland's people are arguably less to do with colour racism, and rather more concerned with colonialism which is itself racism, resulting in institutionalised ethnic prejudice and worse, and which also leads to widespread internalised racism.

CHAPTER 11: SELF-DETERMINATION

Right to Self-Determination

The right of a people to self-determination is a cardinal principle in modern international law, commonly known as a jus cogens rule[101]. This right is binding on the United Nations as an authoritative interpretation of the UN Charter's norms (McWhinney 2007, p. 8). It states that people, based on respect for the principle of equal rights and fair equality of opportunity, have the right to freely choose their sovereignty and international political status with no interference (United Nations 1945). In the matter of Scottish independence, it is perhaps worth repeating the last point: 'with no interference'.

The concept of self-determination was first expressed during the 1860s and spread rapidly thereafter (Fisch 2015, p. 118). During and after World War I, the principle was encouraged by both Vladimir Lenin and United States President Woodrow Wilson. Having announced his 'Fourteen Points' on 8 January 1918, on 11 February 1918 Wilson stated: "*National aspirations must be respected; people may now be dominated and governed only by their own consent. 'Self determination' is not a mere phrase; it is an imperative principle of action*" (Wilson 1918).

During World War II, the principle of self-determination was included in the Atlantic Charter, signed on 14 August 1941, by Franklin D. Roosevelt, President of the United States, and Winston Churchill, Prime Minister of the United Kingdom, who pledged The Eight Principal points of the Charter[102]. Self-determination was thereafter recognized as an international legal right after it was explicitly listed as a right in the UN Charter.

Article 1 of the Charter sets out the Purposes of the United Nations which highlights and makes specific reference to the importance of self-determination which aims[103]:

"To develop friendly relations among nations based on respect for the principle of equal rights and self-determination of peoples, and to take other appropriate measures to strengthen universal peace."

Here we see as one of the main aims of self-determination - to enhance the prospect of peace and harmony between nations and peoples. The implication of this is that defined peoples who remain oppressed and dominated under colonial or imperial rule and/or occupation may never be fully at peace with or accept their predicament, and neither should they be expected to do so. Such a people will always rightfully be looking to determine their own future as opposed to having another people, who are by implication of a different culture, language and national identity, determine their future for them, often through occupation and hence through colonisation, exploitation and oppression.

The concept of self-determination nevertheless has a degree of malleability about it given it may take different forms, including autonomy, federation or outright independence (Walter and Von Ungern-Stenberg 2014). Sometimes self-determination may be confused as to whether it is about a question of national sovereignty or has a focus on merely changing internal politics and general governance emphasising particular party policies (De Vries and Schomerus 2017). The meaning of self-determination in any given situation may also change over time, reflecting changing environmental circumstances, such as demographic change for example, and/or other external pressures including oppressive policies imposed on a group of people.

Weel First Meenister o Scotlan, here's a wee bittie wysins onywey. Ance upon a tyme, twa wee kinricks an kintra's jyned thegither in a union tae mak ane muckle kinrick an ane pairlament. Noo ane kintra wants tae feenish thon union acause its naething but a mankit cesspit an wis aye a fankle onywey.

Self-determination from a broader philosophical understanding emphasises the 'primacy of the individual will' (McLean and McMillan 2009) which implies that freedom and democracy are integral to an individual's right to determine one's future, as distinct from mere political decisions concerning specific policies. This reflects the more common interpretation of self-determination where groups of people with, for instance, strong social, cultural, heritage, and linguistic ties, and perhaps also their own distinct national identity (as in Scotland), have the right to form and determine the shape of their own government and nation within or outside the borders of the country in which they happen to find themselves (Fabry 2010).

Self-determination inevitably becomes more difficult in instances where the population has become more ethnically diverse through occupation and/or demographic change, and where a unified voice is less likely across ethnic lines (Green 2011a); this remains arguably one of the challenges facing self-determination of the Scottish people, with definition of the latter requiring careful, as opposed to the present cavalier consideration, given a matter of such importance.

Definition of 'A People'

The principle of self-determination does not state how the decision is to be made, nor what the outcome should be, whether it be independence, federation, protection, some form of autonomy or full assimilation. However, what is expected is that there should be due respect for the culture of the people concerned and for them to develop an appropriate form of self-government[104]. Neither does it state what the delimitation between peoples should be, nor indeed what constitutes a people. There remain conflicting definitions and legal criteria for determining which groups may legitimately claim the right to self-determination (Unterberger 2002).

Nevertheless, 'national' self-determination has been defined as *"creation of national governmental institutions by a group of people who view themselves as a distinct nation (for example, because they have a common language)"*[105]. In this regard, national self-determination is the opposite of, and is therefore wholly opposed to, the oppressions and domination brought about on a people through colonialism, imperialism or transnational nationalism. Scotland is arguably still very much subject to the latter forces hence its peoples' continued desire for self-determination and independence. Scotland is therefore clearly seeking 'national' self-determination and here we note the significance of 'a common language', which is the Scots language. And here we may also surmise why the Scots language remains 'doun-hauden'.

Scotland's yairns hiv tae be telt uisin wir ain Scots langage, no anither fowks tung.

Self-determination therefore involves the creation of national governmental institutions by a group of people who view themselves as a distinct nation (for example, because they have a common language, culture and history). By extension, the term self-determination has come to mean the free choice of one's own acts without external compulsion. In this regard the exclusion or avoidance of external influence has become a fundamental UN requirement during the process of self-determination of peoples; however, this aspect has clearly not been respected in the case of Scotland.

Specific criteria for the definition of a *"people having the right of self-determination"* was proposed during the 2010 Kosovo case decision of the International Court of Justice. These criteria, all of which appear to also well define a distinct 'Scottish people', include the following aspects (Uriel 2015):

1. traditions and culture
2. ethnicity

3. historical ties and heritage
4. language
5. religion
6. sense of identity or kinship
7. the will to constitute a people
8. common suffering.

Some authors propose territorial integrity as a moral and legal aspect of constitutional democracy and relate this to the so-called "*Remedial Rights Only Theory*", where a defined group of people has "*a general right to secede if and only if it has suffered certain injustices*", for which secession is the appropriate remedy of last resort (Gudeleviciute 2005). In addition, secession needs to be recognised if the state concerned grants, or if the constitution includes, a right to secede. Going further, Miller (2019) proposes three theories of secession:

- 'just-cause theory', which contends that secession is only warranted when the seceding group is the victim of serious long-term injustice at the hands of the state it wishes to leave;

- 'choice theory', which says that any territorial group which wants to leave a bigger group can choose to do so provided it does so democratically, and:

- 'nationalist theory', which finds that secession is justified when a nation, with specific cultural identifications and values which signify it as a nation, seeks to "break free".

Scotland might reasonably 'fit' on all three counts. However, the existence of treaty-based 'union' agreements between state parties, as exists between Scotland and England, are another aspect requiring careful consideration. This is more especially so where a written constitution does not exist, as in the UK. In the latter situation, the national entity/people seeking self-determination (i.e. Scotland/the Scots) is intending to withdraw from its own treaty-based arrangement, which is not the same thing as secession.

The existence of an international treaty-based joint 'state' arrangement (i.e. the UK is a treaty-based parliament and governing administration jointly created by both Scotland and England) reflects the constitutional reality that the Scots are already a sovereign people and nation and do not necessarily require to 'seek' self-determination per se from any other entity. Scotland is already a sovereign nation and people and hence constitutionally and legally may do as it pleases, within international law. This includes a sovereign Scotland withdrawing from any treaty-based alliance arrangement, notwithstanding its ongoing oppression, exploitation, occupation and political domination (i.e. colonisation) within that constitutional arrangement.

Langage is cultur efter aw, yet we sling a deifie tae wir ain langage,
an syne we sling a deifie tae oor ain cultur an aw.

Self-Determination is Decolonisation

The UN seek to bring an end to colonisation which it describes as 'a scourge' on a people, and which implies that colonialism is viewed as an 'instrument of punishment' that inevitably causes trouble and suffering, primarily for the colonised people and nation concerned. As noted previously, colonialism may be accomplished in a number of ways, not least through control of a nation's governance and social institutions, control and exploitation of its resources, the imposition of cultural and linguistic imperialism, and installing and maintaining a ruling cultural hegemony with its artificial social constructs and systems benefitting primarily the elite colonial ruling order.

In what has been a vast political reshaping of the world, more than 80 former colonies comprising some 750 million people have gained independence since the creation of the United Nations[106]. The big breakthrough occurred in 1955 when 16 new States were admitted, bringing UN membership at the time to 76 countries. Then in 1960 a further 19 new States were admitted (McWhinney 2008). In practically all these cases, independence has been achieved through the processes of self-determination, which implies that self-determination is also effectively decolonisation.

Currently the UN has Listed 17 Non-Self-Governing Territories (NSGTs) across the globe which remain to be decolonized. Thus, the process of Decolonisation is not complete. Finishing the task requires a continuing dialogue among the administering Powers, the Special Committee on Decolonisation, and the peoples of the respective territories, in accordance with the relevant UN resolutions on Decolonisation. The 'UN Committee of 24' (Special Committee on Decolonisation) and its Bureau are assisted in this task by the Decolonisation Unit of the Department of Political and Peacebuilding Affairs for substantive support and by the Department for General Assembly and Conference Management for secretariat services. The UN Department of Global Communications carries out a number of outreach activities in support of Decolonisation.

External Interference

British unionist MSP's and MP's do not like to see Westminster's hegemony being questioned as it is today by the increasing numbers of independence supporting 'nationalist' MSP's and MP's elected in Scotland. The focus and allegiance of unionists by implication is not to Scotland per se, as demonstrated in their patronising tone and essentially British nationalist and imperialist dedication to opposing Scottish self-determination, and hence to blocking Scottish citizenship, Scottish nationality and Scottish self-government. Moreover, British unionists active in numerous institutions from outside Scotland and who are not Scottish continue to frequently disrespect the UN requirement that other peoples (and countries) should refrain from interfering in the self-determination of another (i.e. the Scottish) people. Professor John Robertson's analysis, applying robust and applied methodologies, highlighted widespread British state BBC and media bias opposing Scottish self-determination during the 2014 independence campaign (Robertson 2014). The BBC journalist Alan Little's comments from inside the media merely served to confirm institutionalized external British and Anglophone bias against Scottish self-determination[107]. Further analysis of the *amazing litany of bias*' and the '*Propaganda Blitz*' on the part of the British MSM during the Scottish independence campaign was provided by Edwards and Cromwell (2018). This ongoing external 'interference' and intervention in Scotland's self-determination process contravenes the UN Declaration of Human Rights. In other words, no entity from outside Scotland should be permitted to interfere in the right to self-determination of Scotland's people or to try to influence the outcome.

The irregular and probably unique open residence-based voting franchise adopted in Scotland for a referendum further serves to invite added external interference in Scotland's quest for self-determination. The existing franchise permits and indeed invites those representing a range of other non-Scottish national identities to influence and indeed to prevent the self-determination of the Scottish people. According to the census, and taking into account ongoing demographic trends, there may be as many as a third of people resident in Scotland who do not consider their primary identity to be 'Scottish'. This group, mainly comprising people from other UK nations, mostly voted to reject the offer of Scottish nationality and Scottish citizenship, thus adversely influencing the self-determination of the Scottish people and indeed blocking

Scottish independence. Internationally there is widespread recognition and regulatory requirement that only a 'national' of the nation concerned qualifies to vote in its national elections and referendums. That seems clear and consistent. However, the Scottish national voter franchise is quite different, and highly irregular, based primarily on residence, and hence invites many people of other (i.e. non-Scottish) national identities to vote on Scottish self-determination, which constitutes external interference.

In a petition to the ECHR, Franks (2014) also questioned why Scots living overseas and the Scottish diaspora more generally had been excluded from voting in a referendum on independence, suggesting that: *"national self-determination is for the whole community of a people, it is never for part of it to reject another part, and that whole community includes family next of kin, and that always includes first generations of diaspora."* Franks suggested the irregular Scottish resident-based franchise amounts to 'birthplace racism', which discriminated against Scots born elsewhere, unnecessarily dividing families, and blocking their right to hold citizenship of what would be a re-constituted Scottish State. In this context, the right of a group of people (i.e. the Scots) to self-determination should be considered as paramount, as opposed to 'residents'; many of the latter holding to other national identities will understandably have and hold allegiance to their own respective national identities and citizenship and hence will not fit the criteria for defined Scottish 'people'. People cannot be forced to take on a national identity they do not have or do not wish to hold, and irregularly widening the national voter franchise to include such persons does not alter this fact.

The irregular national voting franchise applying in Scotland for the 2014 referendum, and repeated again as outlined in the Referendums (Scotland) Bill by the Scottish Parliament (Scottish Parliament 2019), therefore permits anyone who is merely included in the register of local government electors to vote in a national referendum in Scotland. It also permits a Commonwealth citizen, a citizen of the Republic of Ireland or a relevant citizen of the European Union to vote in a national referendum in Scotland. However, this is not reciprocated by the home nations of these residents to Scots living abroad: Scots are therefore refused the same national voter franchise in all these other countries. Scotland is therefore unique in this regard, in offering a 'national' vote to virtually any resident, no matter where they come from, or what their nationality and hence national identity and national allegiance may be. And, moreover, other nationals are being permitted to vote on (and hence to oppose) a matter of the highest possible national importance to the Scottish people, the matter of their own self-determination and national independence. This is absurd and inevitably seems merely a deceitful ploy by the British State aimed at blocking Scottish independence.

Scotland's highly irregular residence-based voter franchise is therefore fraught with uncertainty and added risk as far as identity and sense of belonging is concerned. As Bond (2015) noted in this regard: "*..the application of the marker of residence ..... is popularly considered to be a relatively weak marker that may be put forward as the basis for a Scottish identity. Claiming to 'belong' to Scotland based largely on residing in Scotland – even when that residence might be enduring and coupled with a firm commitment to remain in Scotland – is often seen as difficult both by migrants themselves and those who are born in Scotland*".

National Referendum Franchises in Other Countries

Globally, national voting rights are primarily dependent on parental descent and only apply to other 'nationals' from other nations after they apply for and are given citizenship of a country. Aside from Scotland, voting rights elsewhere are not ever merely dependent on residence, nor are they necessarily dependent on place of birth. It is informative here to look

at voting rights practices in other countries[108] which serves to confirm beyond doubt that the Scottish referendum voting franchise remains highly irregular and is never reciprocated; i.e. Scottish 'nationals' would not be offered the same national voting rights in any other country as are being offered to other nationals resident in Scotland.

In Ireland, only Irish citizens may vote in referendums there. Residents of the state who are Irish citizens or British citizens may vote in elections to the national parliament (this is reciprocal in UK). Residents who are citizens of any EU state may vote in European Parliament elections, while any resident, regardless of citizenship, may vote in local elections. Entitlement to vote is based on Irish citizenship. UK citizens lost the vote in European elections in Ireland after Brexit.

Voting Rights in Republic of Ireland					
Citizenship	Local Elections	European Elections	General (National) Elections	Presidential Elections	**Referendums**
Irish	√	√	√	√	√
British	√	√	√	X	**X**
Other EU	√	√	X	X	**X**
Non-EU	√	X	X	X	**X**

In Luxembourg, local voting rights were granted only in 2003, with no nationality restrictions, to all foreigners who have been resident in Luxembourg for at least 5 years. On 7 June 2015, a referendum was held on whether to grant the right to vote in national elections to foreigners resident in the country for more than 10 years. That proposal was overwhelmingly rejected, by 78 per cent to 22 per cent. Non-nationals cannot therefore vote in referendums or national elections in Luxembourg.

In Lithuania, non-national permanent residents were granted local voting rights in 2002. Non-nationals cannot however vote in national elections or in referendums in Lithuania.

In The Netherlands, 'non-citizens' were allowed to vote in local elections in 1985 though necessary reforms meant 'aliens' were not allowed to vote in local elections until 1986. Residents without Dutch nationality are not allowed to vote in national elections, only in municipal elections. Aliens holding a passport from another EU country are allowed to vote in European elections. Non-Dutch nationals are not allowed to vote in referendums.

In Norway, voting and eligibility rights were granted to Nordic Passport Union country citizens with a 3 years' residence condition for municipal and county elections only in 1978. These rights were extended to all foreign residents in 1983. However, only Norwegian nationals, including Norwegians living abroad, can vote in national elections and in referendums in Norway. [109]

In Denmark, the EU treaty ('Maastricht Treaty') gives every EU citizen the right to vote and stand as a candidate in local, municipal (if applicable) and European Parliamentary elections in the EU country where they are currently resident, under the same conditions as nationals of that country. However only Danish citizens may vote in Denmark's national general elections and in national referendums[110].

In Malaysia, Article 119 of the Constitution of Malaysia effective as of 2010 defines voting rights in the country as only for citizens of Malaysia. Citizens of other countries are not permitted to vote in Malaysia.

In Malta, since 1993, United Kingdom residents there enjoy the same voting and eligibility rights as Maltese citizens at the local and regional council elections only. However, only Maltese nationals may vote in national elections and referendums.

In Saint Kitts and Nevis, 'Allegiance to a foreign State' is a criterion for voting rights disqualification as is the case in most other countries.

In South Africa, only South African citizens may vote in elections, whether national or local. There are no voting rights for non-citizens. Foreigners cannot vote in national referendums.

In Switzerland, foreigners may not cast ballots at the national level. They may only be entitled to vote and, in some cases to run for office at the cantonal or community level. Foreigners cannot vote in national referendums in Switzerland.

> *Daes it maiter whaur yer born an bide? Naw, sae lang as ye hiv a Scottis mither an/or faither whit haes bided in Scotlan, yer a 'Scottish' naitional an ye shuid hiv a vote.*

In Chile, any national citizen over 18 can vote if they register, however people with visas, even permanent residency visas, cannot vote. Only Chilean nationals get the vote in national elections and referendums.

In the United States, no foreigner is allowed a vote at the national or state level. Foreigners cannot vote in national referendums.

International evidence therefore overwhelmingly confirms that the Scottish referendum process remains fundamentally flawed, highly irregular, and very poorly specified. The Scottish voter franchise is incoherent and unnecessarily open based simply on an individual having an address in Scotland, irrespective of their nationality or national identity. This renders the Scottish referendum franchise uniquely incompetent, albeit no doubt designed so by Scotland's 'administrative Power' and the responsible unionist social institutions, including the devolved Scottish Government, with the aim being, it appears, to ensure a 'No' vote is returned. Hence the aim of the irregular, open, residence-based voter franchise is essentially to block Scottish independence.

Scotland's confusion over this matter was further reinforced when the Scottish Minister ostensibly responsible for the 'constitution' in the Scottish Government, Michael Russell

MSP, in his response to the author on this subject, stated that: *"..Chile has a residence based franchise and Ireland is moving towards one"*.[111] This is not correct on either count, given the evidence above. This raises fundamental questions about the integrity and/or competence of the Minister and the Scottish Government given they *appear* to be so unaware of national voting right norms and rules internationally. The Minister further implied that Scotland's irregular residence-based voter franchise would be internationally common *"in a generation"* and that in this respect Scotland, somehow, *"are in the vanguard"*. Such a deeply flawed and naïve perspective reflects at best a high level of arrogance, as well as ignorance, and at worst simply a deception, given that it is very obvious that no other country appears to have any intention of changing to a residence-based voter franchise for its national elections or referendums. In this context Scotland's quest for self-determination has arguably been critically undermined by the SNP Scottish Government's own ill-informed, unique, and either dilettante or devious, residence-based franchise approach, as promoted by SNP Ministers themselves.

Furthermore, States owe it to each other as well as to their own nations, to have 'citizenship by descent rights compliant and unrefusable'. The Scottish residence-based franchise is effectively a 'closed border stance' to elements of Scotland's own community as the Scottish people, who share a common culture, language, history and suffering (the Scottish diaspora perhaps more especially), yet who are being excluded from the right to self-determination of their 'people'. Meantime the 'devolved' Scottish Government is allocating voting rights to peoples of various other national identities and national allegiances and national belonging; many of the latter clearly do not wish to be 'Scottish' and reject the opportunity to create a Scottish nationality and citizenship at the referendum ballot, thereby also blocking and interfering in the inalienable right of the Scottish people to self-determination.

Definitions of 'civic nationalism' promulgated by the SNP 'devolved' Scottish Government appear therefore to prioritise non-Scottish residents, ignoring the latter's far higher propensity to reject Scottish citizenship and nationality, which most did in 2014, primarily because 'it' (i.e. 'Scottish') is neither their own national identity nor is it a national identity they evidently wish to hold. A different (i.e. foreign) national identity cannot be forced on people who neither hold it nor want it. The concept of 'civic nationalism' assumes, and depends on, people 'desiring to hold the citizenship of their host nation and having a close sense of belonging' to that nation. However, a people and nation still at the pre-State (i.e. colonial) stage of seeking self-determination and self-governance, such as Scotland, are not in the position to offer national citizenship to anyone until after securing independence. This suggests that opening up Scotland's national voting franchise to non-Scottish 'nationals' is not only highly irregular, it is also premature, and fatally so; indeed, such a 'policy' only serves to prevent self-determination due to the significant numbers of non-Scottish nationals 'interfering' in a Scottish referendum on self-determination by effectively taking it upon themselves to vote to block independence.

Aye, e'en efter indy thon gey muckle unionist slump rinnin Scotlan wad aye hae tae bi dicht oot. Nae doot aboot thon.

It therefore still needs to be clearly defined, well in advance of any national referendum, what is meant by a 'Scottish national', not least because independence creates a need to know this; i.e. to establish who is or should automatically qualify to be a Scottish 'national' post-independence. Is a Scottish 'national' simply anyone from anywhere who happens to have an address in Scotland at the time of a national referendum on independence, as the referendum in 2014 and the latest Holyrood Bill set out in late 2019 implies? This is what an open voting franchise based on residence assumes – that virtually everyone resident, or able to provide an address, in Scotland is a Scottish 'national'. This is clearly wrong-headed and confused in several respects. Even the UK Brexit vote did not permit such a wide-open voter franchise.

The key issue here, referring to the UN again, is the need to avoid and hence prevent 'external interference' in the self-determination process of a defined 'people', yet the unique Scottish franchise merely serves to invite such interference thereby totally undermining the entire process, and in turn blocking self-determination.

The starting point in establishing national voting rights should be to first determine who in Scotland would automatically qualify to be a Scottish 'national' were Scotland already an independent country? Scotland therefore needs to begin from that base. Scotland is clearly not yet in any position to offer its citizenship to nationals from other countries simply because they happen to have an address in Scotland. Scotland must start at the beginning, and that means with ethnic Scots forming the basis of its national population, as is the case with any people seeking self-determination or independence. Who these Scottish 'nationals' are and how they are so defined is a relatively straightforward matter based on parental descent.

Further, any State's compliance with the European Convention on Human Rights (ECHR), obligatory for EU aspiration, would ensure that Scotland will have parental descent citizenship irrefusable. A franchise based on nationality and hence parental descent and not merely upon residence is clearly the global 'gold standard' and norm. Uniquely, Scotland has gone a highly irregular 'residence-based' route, which is clearly neither a good idea, nor is it necessary, and inevitably serves to inflate the 'No' vote simply because most of those whose identity is not Scottish will not wish to alter that identity. This also means that the vote is influenced by many different 'peoples', and perhaps in excess of one million voters representing a wide range of other nationalities and national identities, which again contravenes the UN rules on self-determination and Decolonisation[112].

It should further be noted here that Article 16 of ECHR permits states 'to restrict the political activity of foreigners'[113] in their country and this is precisely what all states do in practice. Scotland has rather done the opposite by inviting the 'political activity of foreigners' and indeed is going much further and giving 'foreigners' national voting rights to decide on whether Scotland should exist as an independent State, or remain as a colony. This is bizarre. Such an seemingly *altruistic* act, which some politicians seek to incorrectly define as 'civic nationalism', further ignores the superior right to vote of Scottish 'nationals' living overseas, the latter a right which no other country would ignore in the way Scotland has done.

The 'devolved' Scottish Government argues that it would somehow be 'wrong' for Scotland to deny the right of people who are national citizens of other countries who happen to be resident in Scotland a vote in a national independence referendum in Scotland. However, people from other countries already have and retain the right to vote for the self-determination of their own people in their own country of origin. Such a right is never reciprocal. It does not make any sense for people of different national identities to be given the right to vote on self-determination across multiple nations and multiple peoples. That is a rather confused perspective of what self-determination is about and who it is about, i.e. a distinct 'people' with a shared identity, culture, language, history, common suffering etc. The self-determination of the Scots is, or should be, a matter only for the 'Scottish' people, and no-one else.

British 'Exceptionalism'

While the large and expanding rest-UK Anglophone population resident in Scotland mostly oppose independence, research suggests the large English population living in Wales also tilted the vote there towards Brexit (Mangler 2019). Larger leave votes were recorded in areas of Wales with big English communities and a similar outcome occurred in Scotland. Research by Professor of Geography Danny Dorling found that 'Wales' voted to leave the EU only because of the high number of English retired people who have moved across the border. In other words, it was not the majority of Welsh people who voted for Brexit. According to Dorling: "*If you look at the more genuinely Welsh areas, especially the Welsh-speaking ones, they did not want to leave the EU"* and…."*Wales was made to look like a Brexit-supporting nation by its English settlers.*" A similar phenomenon appears to have played out in the 2014 Scottish independence referendum, with Scotland's significant English and hence Anglophone British-identifying communities overwhelmingly voting to block Scottish independence.

About 21 per cent (650,000) of people living in Wales were born in England, with nearly a quarter aged over 65. However, many English settlers in Wales will have families also living there who are likewise culturally, linguistically and in terms of identity, English, and they may be expected to vote a similar way. This would bring the total English extraction community in Wales to perhaps as much as one million people, or approximately close to half the total vote in Wales. The country voted for Brexit by a majority of just 82,000. Border towns and areas of central Wales with larger English communities, such as Wrexham and Powys, recorded a higher proportion of leave votes, whereas Welsh-speaking areas such as Gwynedd and Ceredigion had high remain votes. The English population in Wales may similarly be expected to have a high propensity to vote for parties opposed to Welsh independence given their national identity is not Welsh.

> *Maist Aye voters hiv a guid Scots tung in thair heids; maist Naw voters dinnae.*

Dorling relates this phenomenon to what he terms 'British exceptionalism'; beneath many voting decisions in any areas with significant English populations, he suggests, lies a centuries-old belief that British is somehow "*exceptional*". Here he argues that, unlike other former colonial powers, such as the Netherlands, Britain has never reviewed its colonial past. Instead, the UK, and specifically the more conservative South of England, preserve a deeply ingrained belief in British superiority up until the present day (Dorling and Tomlinson 2019). Dorling maintains that a major reason for this is the British education system on which he notes: "*We have a very high opinion about ourselves because of how we teach our history. We tell ourselves a story of empire which is very different from the story that is told elsewhere"*. Also important here, in the Scottish (or Welsh) context, is the language (i.e. Anglophone) in which we tell that history narrative given the close connection between language, thought, and identity; descriptions of the world as expressed in language provide symbolic models of the world which influence our beliefs (Spiers 2019).

There seems little reason to doubt, then, that the large and ever-growing English Anglophone community living in Scotland vote differently to that in Wales. Indeed, the evidence suggests that both the largest 'No' voting and 'Leave' voting constituencies in Scotland were in those areas in which significant English populations live. The English Anglophone communities will naturally be expected to wish to maintain their British/English identity and will mostly tend to 'vote Britain' and therefore seek to block Scottish independence rather than vote for what they might consider to be assisting their host nation, Scotland, to secede from what they view as an 'exceptional' British State.

> *A shuirly howp thon SNP Scottish Cultur Meenister an Language Meenister micht be listenin, an mebbe e'en thay're ower Anglophone heid ceevil servants fi 'elite' uni's anaw (e.g. Oxbridge, St. Andrews, 'Edinborough', etc). whair Scots langage is aye conseedert juist 'bad English'.*

Supporting this argument, the Scottish Referendum Survey found that a majority of Scots voted for independence and stated that: *"Scotland only remained in the Union because of the views of those who were born in other parts of Britain and further afield"* (McIntosh 2015). The latter survey established that **the majority of voters who backed the 'No' campaign did so primarily because they felt 'British'**, which clearly reflects identity, and hence Anglophone culture and language as key influencers. This suggests that those voters who do not identify as Scottish and/or who do not therefore consider themselves to be Scottish will tend to reject Scottish independence primarily because 'Scottish' is not their national or ethnic identity; 'Scottish' is neither who they are nor who they wish to be. Other related research findings confirmed that, even amongst younger age groups, over 80% of those with 'more British than Scottish' identities are opposed to Scottish independence (Eichhorn et al. 2014). Such rather predictable outcomes well reflect what the Scots author James Kelman says, that: *"our identity is to a large extent defined by who our relatives are"*[114].

The English form by far the largest single ethnic migrant group in Scotland, and in Wales. The English will understandably wish to retain and project their British/English and Anglophone identity and culture, in addition to the all too frequent tendency to express British exceptionalism, according to Dorling. This raises the question as to why 'peoples' from other nations and clearly holding to other national identities continue to be invited to influence, reject and hence to block the right of minority peoples (Scots and Welsh) to their own 'self-determination'. This seems rather an inevitable outcome, particularly for the English ethnic group, given its political and colonial dominance within the UK's distinct internal colonial context. Evidence from voter intention surveys and Dorling's research therefore suggests that those who are English in terms of culture, history, heritage and language and hence primarily hold to an English identity, may not very readily fit the UN definition or criteria of what constitutes a Scottish 'people' insofar as Scottish self-determination is concerned.

Defining Scottish 'Nationals'

A distinct 'peoples' national identity may be determined by a number of factors. From the 2010 Kosovo case decision of the International Court of Justice, definitions and 'Criteria for self-determination and defining 'peoples"[115] are already well established, as noted earlier in this chapter.

> *Mebbe thon Holyrood Meenisters shuid be cawed 'Meenisters for Anglophone Cultur & Langage' tae richtly reflectit whit thay dae? i.e. thay refuise tae taucht 'Scots' langage tae oor bairns an aw fowk wha bide in Scotlan.*

Many Scottish people, and especially so Scots language speakers, will readily identify with most if not all these criteria for self-determination and hence will 'fit' the definition of a Scottish 'people'. Those who do not hold to the same criteria may therefore be expected to view their identity and hence sense of belonging rather differently. Moreover, by implication, the latter group may be unlikely to be seeking or desiring Scottish national self-determination in any event.

It should therefore seem important, if not crucial, to avoid the possibility, or error, of peoples from other countries and who naturally are holding to other national identities, adversely influencing and hence preventing the right to self-determination of another people, in this case the Scots. Scotland's wide-open voter franchise based on residence criteria (and hence not based on nationality/ethnicity criteria) rather invites the 'wrong' outcome, resulting in a 'No' vote in 2014, and it may do so again. The UN Decolonisation Committee argues against any outside interference in a 'peoples' decision on the matter of 'their' self-determination and Decolonisation, which is a matter only for the defined people concerned. The usual approach taken in avoiding such an error is to define the voter franchise in line with globally recognised norms and practices, taking account of criteria to define 'a people' seeking self-determination.

So-called 'civic nationalists' who advocate the open franchise which is crudely based only on residence clearly miss the point here about what is and what is not Scottish self-determination; Scottish self-determination is about the self-determination of the Scottish people, i.e. those who identify themselves primarily as Scottish 'nationals', and who 'fit' the definition and criteria of 'a people'. What it is not about is the national self-determination of many other 'peoples' emanating from numerous other countries and holding to other non-Scottish national identities, and who simply happen to live in Scotland at a given point in time. 'Nationals' from other countries are perfectly entitled to participate in their own 'peoples' self-determination but should not be permitted to interfere in and/or block the self-determination of other 'peoples'.

Any individual may apply for citizenship of a country that offers it. However, voting and campaigning against the existence of a new national citizenship and a new State, and blocking a 'peoples' right to self-determination, opposing their very national identity, is a quite different matter. Those acting or voting to prevent a specific nationality and citizenship and nation from existing as a recognised independent State clearly means they do not have any desire to hold that nationality or citizenship or identity, and neither do they want the new citizenship to be offered to anyone else who may wish to apply for it. That is effectively what 'No' voters holding to other national identities did in 2014 and stand to do again if there is any second referendum. Such an outcome should of course be avoided, though it must be noted that the 'devolved' Scottish Government continues to invite such an outcome due to its highly irregular and non-reciprocal national voting franchise based on residence. This rather suggests that the 'devolved' Scottish Government, which remains part of the British State, is anti-independence.

Is a Referendum Necessary?

Scotland's First Minister, Nicola Sturgeon, was asked during a US lecture she delivered at Stanford University in 2017[116] why the Scottish independence referendum franchise was so open, or so it seemed, to the international community. Her initial answer was to the effect that Scotland's civil servants said it would be 'too complicated' to do otherwise, which is rather like a response straight out of 'Yes Minister'[117], plus the usual SNP mantra that 'everyone who lives and works in Scotland has a stake in the country'. Unfortunately, most of those voting 'No' and whose national identity is not Scottish, appeared to be taking the opportunity to rather put a stake into Scotland, effectively blocking self-determination and the independence of the Scottish people.

Dae Scots fowk hae tae hiv ony mair dubious referendums rin bi Scotlan's colonial maisters fae ootwith Scotlan?

The Brexit debate further tells Scots that Westminster could decide to ignore any referendum result if it wishes to do so. Even if Westminster did accept any Yes vote, it would still be enlightening to see the content of any subsequent 'Scottish Independence (Scotland) Act' proceeding through the House of Commons and House of Lords as 'crafted' by UK legislators who have little interest in, far less any right to wield sovereignty over Scotland, never mind to determine what an independent Scotland might look like. Westminster's legislators would surely carve Scotland up in any such Act, much like imperial powers have done many times over with 'troublesome' former colonies. This provides another reason for a majority of Scotland's MP's simply to withdraw Scotland from the UK union, as should be their legal right so to do. There seems little point in Scotland always voting for self-governing 'nationalist' majorities if Scotland is never 'allowed' to govern itself. The only thing Scotland can be sure of with its 'administrative Power' is deceit at every turn.

"Should Scotland be an independent country?" This is arguably the wrong question to ask in any referendum in any case. The Brexit referendum question differed markedly from the

Scottish independence question, the latter displaying a far greater level of uncertainty and a lack of respect for Scotland's actual constitutional status as a sovereign signatory party to a treaty-based union. Both UK and EU unions are treaty-based unions and therefore the questions should arguably be the same or similar. The Scottish independence question was quite different from the Brexit question in that it did not mention any union or treaty as such. Some voters might reasonably be left with the misunderstanding that there is no UK union formed by international treaty, and that Scotland is merely an annexed UK 'region' seeking to secede from its 'parent state', which is clearly not the case.

> *Thon mankit 'union' wis stairtit bi the mony MP's fae oor kintra o Scotlan sae it can be endit bi the mony MP's fae oor kintra an aw.*

A question similar to EU 'withdrawal' would therefore respect Scotland's rightful status, viz: *"Should Scotland remain a member of the United Kingdom Union or leave the United Kingdom Union?"*. Such a question demonstrates that sovereignty and power, and hence choice, rests with Scotland and its people and no-one else. Moreover, the initial independence referendum question implied Scots would be creating a new country with all the risk and uncertainty of that, which is not the case at all. The reality is that Scotland is an existing sovereign nation and people, and still a legal and active entity, via international treaty participating in a political union, from which Scots now seek to withdraw, and with Scotland already self-governing to some extent, with many institutions in place. Scots really do need to think and learn from Brexit, as well as from the unfortunate referendum experience in 2014, and perhaps change the question, as well as the voter franchise, assuming there is another referendum. There is also uncertainty about the legal need for a referendum given that: "*As a matter of law, a referendum is not a required part of the process of becoming independent*" (McCorkindale and McHarg 2020). So perhaps a referendum should be avoided?

If the SNP Scottish Government remain uncertain about the legal realities, they should endeavor to determine if a majority of Scotland's MP's may legally withdraw Scotland from the joint treaty-based union of parliaments in the same way it was constituted. A sovereign Scotland should have no need to plead for any other country's permission to hold a dubious open franchise referendum in Scotland (will they ever give it, again?), nor should Scotland need to ask other (UK) nations to ratify any Yes vote (there is no certainty that they would), far less relying on these countries to create an Act which would set out what an independent Scotland might look like. The simpler, more certain, legal and constitutional route must be to first establish the legal and constitutional reality: Scotland's democratically elected national representatives are either sovereign, or they are not.

The SNP MP Joanna Cherry has previously led court actions to determine the supremacy of Westminster MP's in regard to Brexit. She did this with revoking Art 50 and the ECJ subsequently noted that any party to a treaty may unilaterally revoke it. Is this not perhaps a clue as to what a sovereign Scotland should or could do vis-à-vis the Treaty of Union? Ms Cherry led a further case after Prime Minister Boris Johnson 'prorogued' parliament in September 2019, with the UK Supreme Court deciding that his action was unlawful. Similarly there is nothing to stop Scotland's 'nationalist' MP's and MSP's seeking a Scottish court ruling to determine if a majority of Scotland's elected national representatives may revoke the treaty of union, as it was constituted; that is, assuming Scotland's representatives remain uncertain of their sovereign power.

Oor praisent SNP Scotlan majoriti is aw whit's needit tae feenish thon dochtless ane-sidit 'union' boorach whit aye hauds Scotlan doon. Sae we micht as well dae it whiles we still hae the maist Scots MP's sittin in thon jynt 'union' pairlament! Sae dae it noo!

The Treaty and Sovereignty

Scotland is a sovereign nation and people only 'held' within the UK union by virtue of a single treaty, and rather an undemocratic and dubiously established treaty at that, passed at the time by a simple majority of Scotland's representatives. It is merely that solitary treaty which Scotland's people seek to revoke and which, in turn, would provide for Scottish self-government, independence and international statehood, once again. Rather than depend on a referendum (with a dubious 'weighted' voter franchise, and hence a questionable outcome), which is not a legal necessity for independence, the focus should be more concerned with Scotland's constitutional and legal withdrawal from the UK union, in revoking the Treaty of Union through a majority decision of Scotland's elected representatives.

The Supreme Court of Canada, in a landmark ruling re Secession of Quebec, was asked whether Quebec had a right to secede from Canada[118]. The court found that, due to Canada's constitution and federal structure, Quebec could not secede from Canada unilaterally; however, it decided that a clear vote on a clear question to secede in a referendum should lead to negotiations between Quebec and the rest of Canada for secession. The court found that international law does not specifically grant component parts of sovereign states the legal right to secede unilaterally from their parent state.

Scotland's sovereign status, and the legal fact of an international treaty-based constitutional alliance, however, confirms that the UK is not a federation like Canada, and this also confirms that the UK is not therefore Scotland's 'parent state', contrary to what some might think (e.g. McCorkindale and McHarg 2020). Clearly the UK cannot feasibly be Scotland's 'parent state' given that Scotland and England in alliance via the Treaty of Union jointly constituted and hence 'gave birth' to the UK state; in reality, the UK state is (sovereign) Scotland's and England's (wayward) child!

> *Thay SNP are gey 'democratic' an neoliberal tae, sae mebbe thay daes need tae be telt tae muive thay're airses? Or daes Scots fowk no maiter ony mair in thay're ain laund?*

The Supreme Court of Canada did nevertheless find that self-determination is about nations and, in instances of subjugation and oppression it is also about a specific defined people. The Court further stated that, under international law, colonies and oppressed states generally receive international backing for their sovereignty. Evidence presented here suggests that, despite the existence of a Treaty, Scotland is mis-treated (politically) as a colony and suffers subjugation and oppression, which arguably eases the burden of securing 'international backing'.

Clearly there are significant constitutional differences between Quebec (or Catalonia) and Scotland. This includes not least the fact that Scotland's people are sovereign, which is undeniable; and the fact that Scotland created and entered into the UK union alliance by treaty is also undeniable.

Ultimately a majority of Scotland's democratically elected national representatives can and must assert Scotland's sovereignty if they wish to make Scotland independent.

CHAPTER 12: DISCUSSION

Context and Methodology

The context within which Scottish independence is often discussed raises many questions. Arguably most of the harder questions are still to be answered and that is the knowledge gap this book has sought to address and answer. What are the real determinants of Scottish independence? Why do some 'Scots' vote against Scottish independence, and reject their own nationhood and national citizenship? Are all those permitted to vote in a referendum on Scottish independence, 'Scottish'? Do they need to be 'Scottish'? Should they be? What is 'Scottish'? Does identity matter, or does merely having an address in Scotland matter more? What demographic change is Scotland subject to and how does this influence the vote for and against independence? Is a referendum on independence even necessary?

In 2014 'No' voters opted for Scotland to be ruled over by what to many Scots seems an alien political ideology from another land – i.e. Tory England. They voted for England's 533 MP's (i.e. 82 per cent of UK parliamentary 'sovereignty) to do as they wish with Scotland. Is this really what most 'Scottish' people want? To be ruled over by another people, another culture and language, another identity and nation, and what seems an alien political ideology? Crucially, what is stopping more than 45 per cent of Scots from voting for independence?

> *Wi independence an Scottis naitionality thar's nae hauf wey hoose wi ane fit in an ane fit oot. Fowk cannae hae Scottis an Britis/Englis naitionality: hit's ane nor ither.*

What, in fact, is Scotland's constitutional and legal status? What does the Treaty of Union mean, if anything? Is Scotland not a signatory state party to the treaty which its national representatives signed? What does Scottish sovereignty mean? Does it even exist? And, if so, how can Scottish sovereignty be exercised? Or is the UK simply Scotland's 'parent state', rendering Scotland much like any former British colony, a 'helpless child' (tae dae whit hits telt!)?

The SNP's supposedly 'nationalist' political leadership depend on holding another dubious UK sanctioned open-franchise referendum in order to secure Scotland's independence. Is this a sensible strategy? Is there no other valid, constitutional, legal and democratic route to secure independence? The question of independence is about the right of the 'Scottish people' to self-determination, the key word here being 'self'. Must Scotland's vote on its peoples' self-determination include other 'peoples' holding to other national identities? What do other countries do?

To answer these and other relevant questions the methodological approach developed and applied here in the context of Scottish independence has involved 'grounding out' a theoretical framework from analysis of the data collected. The framework developed and overriding theme and sub-title of the book is collectively considered to be: *The Socio-Political Determinants of Scottish Independence*. Behavioural Determinism assumes our actions are reflex reactions developed in us by environmental conditioning. So, what is the environmental conditioning that determines the Yes/No vote choice? The main title of the book, 'Doun-Hauden', reflects the conclusion of the book; that the Scottish people have been and remain oppressed within the UK 'union', and that they and their nation are treated as a colony and will continue to suffer oppression until independence is secured.

The methodology provides a structured framework which can be applied to help investigate, analyse and better understand the phenomenon and dynamics of Scottish independence. The framework helps to elucidate the reality of Scotland's socio-political situation and constitutional status, or rather its predicament, and highlights the challenges that the Scottish people need to overcome, and how they may be overcome, if they are to secure Scotland's independence.

Key social institutions in Scotland loom large in this analysis; who controls these institutions controls the people and resources and uses institutional structures to oppress them. The constitutional status and position of Scotland, taking account of the Brexit related court case outcomes, serve to demonstrate the legal simplicity of a signatory state party withdrawing from a treaty-based union. So, what is stopping Scotland doing likewise? Is Scotland a sovereign people and nation, or not? Who represents that sovereignty? Is it Scotland's MP's, or is it MP's who represent other (foreign) countries and their peoples outside Scotland?

The question of self-determination and options in this regard are probed and analysed. Crucial in this context is the definition and criteria of what constitutes 'a people'. Here the role of the United Nations is considered, the latter highly relevant in the context of 'decolonisation' and independence which, it may be argued, are one and the same thing.

Ethnic discrimination may be involved in Scotland's anti-independence 'No' vote. Does this really surprise anyone? The blocking of Scottish independence and hence rejection of Scottish citizenship by non-Scots voters is arguably ethnically motivated, for they are blocking the self-determination of another people. Why do those holding to other national and ethnic identities act and intervene to influence and prevent the right of the Scottish people to Scottish national identity and citizenship? Why do these 'No' voters fear the Scottish people, and the creation of Scottish nationality and citizenship? The theory of appropriated racial oppression helps explain Scotland's constitutional dilemma whereby some Scots themselves vote against the existence of their own nationhood and hence reject their own national identity and citizenship. Why do these Scots hate their own nation and people so that they would actively thwart their own liberty, whilst accepting their continued colonial oppression as somehow deserving?

Analysis of the theoretical dimensions of culture and

language explain how national identity is determined and influenced. The influence of ongoing demographic change and with 'national' voting rights freely given to an ever-growing population of people now living in Scotland who do not primarily identify as Scots, merely serves to block and prevent Scottish independence. Uncontrolled demographic change and an open voter franchise based on residence also diminishes the prospect of a 'Yes' vote in future. Are Scots doing the right thing here? Not according to established national voting franchise practice in other countries. The devious hand of the British State seems to be guiding what is a highly irregular residence-based national voting franchise in Scotland.

The predicament the Scots and Scotland face is therefore multi-faceted. Culture and language are regarded as key factors and influences in determining national identity. The divide in the Yes/No independence debate seems at root linguistic; that is, it is primarily between Scots speakers who identify as Scottish and who mostly tend to vote 'Yes', and the ever-growing Anglophone population in Scotland who identify as British and who tend to vote 'No'. Hence, Scottish independence is primarily a question of culture and language, both of which serve to influence and determine (ethnic) identity. This means that independence has rather less to do with mere economics or general policy matters of governance than some seem to think.

Language is therefore the essential dividing line in the matter of Scottish independence, as it is in Quebec and Catalonia and elsewhere. The continued state-sponsored death (i.e. linguicide) of the Scots language and the historical displacement of millions of Scots combined with significant Anglophone in-migration has resulted in an ever-diminishing Scottish culture and language which is re-defining national identity in Scotland; such factors combine to diminish the prospect for Scottish independence.

The Socio-Political Determinants of Scottish Independence

Despite the existence of a Treaty of Union there is little evidence of any UK 'union' in practice. Rather, Scotland may more readily be defined politically and in all practical terms as a colony, and the 'union' as something of a masquerade and a political con trick played out on naïve Scots who, through language discrimination and other colonial oppressions, now exhibit a schizoid national psyche (Purves 1997) and developed an accepted sense of 'inferiorisation' (Fanon 1967).

> Fowk cannae ser twa maisters, thay aye luve ane an ill-will the ither.

Within this discussion the question arises as to what Scottish independence means and what its relationship with nationalism is? And, moreover, what it is not? Scottish independence is arguably less about nationalism per se; rather, it is primarily about self-determination. Self-determination is about liberation, freedom and, for oppressed and colonised peoples' independence is also about decolonisation. Conversely, the UK is an imperial construct and in terms of political ideology represents trans-national nationalism. Trans-national nationalism involves occupation and assuming political control over neighbouring countries, and domination of other peoples through imposing a new culture and language. The inevitable outcome of trans-national nationalism is oppression and exploitation through colonisation.

The socio-political determinants framework as developed therefore concerns critical aspects of societal power and control which in the main are inhibiting Scottish independence. The framework criteria, most of which Scotland and the Scots have limited power or control over, reflect a mostly colonial environment. So long as the socio-political determinants of independence are in the control of an Anglophone British unionist elite, Scottish independence will likely remain a formidable challenge. Nevertheless, it is hoped that Scots seeking national independence may be able to use the framework to their advantage, by focusing on each of the determinants and developing appropriate strategies. In this sense, it is argued that the framework may be used as a strategic analytical tool and thus as an aid to secure Scotland's independence. However, even if Scottish independence were to be achieved, Scots will still need to be aware of whom is running Scotland via its social institutions, and where their national allegiance really lies.

Culture

Scotland, historically, has suffered more than most from a heavy dose of British Anglophone cultural imperialism. This may also be referred to as cultural colonialism and involves an unequal relationship which favours the more powerful Anglophone 'civilisation' and its culture. Where power lies is the pertinent feature and power clearly does not lie in Scotland, far less with Scots speakers, the latter increasingly a minority in Scotland and generally excluded from key positions within Scotland's social institutions.

Scots appear to exhibit something of a *"packaged consciousness"* (Schiller 1989); in this the British MSM creates, processes, refines and presides over the circulation of images and information which determines beliefs, attitudes, and ultimately behaviour of Scots pertaining to British identity. Scots have been fed a concentrated British Anglophone 'package' for such a long time it is no surprise that many Scots hold to a British Anglophone 'national' identity and buy into the notion of British exceptionalism, and with that comes an implied Scottish 'inferiority'. An inevitable consequence of this cultural 'conditioning' process, for some, is a deeply entrenched feeling of Scottish inferiority (i.e. *Scottish Cultural Cringe*) and a 'schizoid national psyche' (Purves 1997).

Elites aye hidit thair guilt ahint poleetical seembols.

Many Scots remain blissfully unaware that they are a culturally deprived, diminished, de-humanised and alienated people in their own land – much like the experience of numerous other indigenous and aborigine peoples oppressed and colonised by imperial powers and hence downtrodden through the processes of trans-national nationalism. Here Gramsci's theory of 'cultural hegemony' reflects the ruling class order maintaining cultural control and usage of that control as the primary tool by which they (the ruling class) keeps itself in power. This is carried out through 'an illusion of culture' (Gaughan), and the idea or rather fantasy that there is one 'British' culture which is shared by one 'British' society within one 'British' nation; the foundation of this illusion is language, the English language. This cultural illusion, which is an artificial political, not a natural construct, extends to music and all the arts, though its basis is language, and specifically the English language, reflecting an Anglophone cultural hegemony. The British State has in effect built a 'racial separation wall' and a racial entity that can exclude others, such as Scots language speakers, under a mantra of the importance of the elevated Anglophone culture in which language plays a decisive role.

Those Scots of indigenous culture and identity for whom the Scots language remains predominant clearly form an overwhelming majority of the pro-independence voters in Scotland, much the same as indigenous language speakers in Catalonia and Quebec etc. seek secession. The anti-independence 'No' vote, on the other hand, which is greatly enhanced through the highly irregular residence-based franchise, may be predominantly Anglophone. The latter emphasizes and reflects a British Anglophone identity and hence tends to be made up rather differently and will be substantially boosted and indeed may perhaps comprise mainly people of non-Scottish indigenous culture and heritage, language, and identity.

Gramsci's thesis aptly reflects the ongoing cultural oppression of Scots and Scotland by a British Anglophone elite, viz:

> *'..the domination of a culturally diverse society, by the ruling class who manipulate the culture of that society—the beliefs, explanations, perceptions, values, and mores—so that their imposed, ruling-class worldview becomes the accepted cultural norm; the universally valid dominant ideology, which justifies the social, political, and economic status quo as natural and inevitable, perpetual and beneficial for everyone, rather than as artificial social constructs that benefit only the ruling class'.*

The cultural capital of Anglophone elites therefore differs from that of the indigenous Scots speaking working class in

Scotland; the latter have a culture imposed on them which is not their own and which makes them, and is intended to make them, feel inadequate and inferior, hence the 'Scottish Cultural Cringe'. Scotland and the Scots are thus inhibited by a form of cultural control and oppression, aimed at keeping the Scots 'doun-hauden' (oppressed) in their own land. This process is also referred to as 'enculturation' (Bourdieu and Passeron 1990) and is an inevitable and intended outcome of cultural and linguistic imperialism.

Given that every culture is first and foremost national, the aim of cultural imperialism is ultimately to remove and replace the national culture of colonised peoples. According to Fanon (1967: 45): *"cultural obliteration is made possible by the negation of national reality"*, implying that once national sovereignty is forfeited, the national culture is surely going to follow it. In terms of colonial domination, the Scots are 'doun-hauden' and culturally oppressed, giving rise to the Cultural Cringe and a negative feeling of inferiority amongst Scots, which is a falsehood imposed and embellished by a domineering Anglophone elite cultural hegemony. Scotland therefore needs to halt the 'symbolic violence' inflicted on its people by a British Anglophone cultural elite and allow Scottish culture and the Scots language, which collectively provide the basis of Scottish identity, to develop naturally and respectfully and without undue external influence and hindrance. **National sovereignty is the only guarantee of national culture.**

Language

The tenets of any society are founded on language. Language is the 'master tool' representing and making its own culture; language is therefore what makes culture possible, hence without a people's language the culture is lost for that people. It can therefore be argued that, without the Scots language there can be no Scottish culture, and that is where Scotland appears to be headed.

Languages are powerful political instruments, so powerful they may be viewed as a threat to national allegiance and identity. Language, culture and national identity intersect and form our belief in 'who we are'. When a people become incorporated into a more dominant imposed language and culture that has subsumed them, they have then lost their heritage, and their identity, and hence lost their way.

Because language is the fabric of culture, when a language dies, the demise of the culture that gave birth to it becomes imminent. Language wanes not because of physical extinction, but because of cultural subsumption. Yet, to the indigenous Scots speaker, English goes in one ear and out the other but will never touch the heart and soul of the people in the same way the Scots language does; to the Scots speaker the Scots language is natural, as a mother tongue should be, whilst any other imposed language always remains artificial.

The cause of language death is often attributed to the marginalization of indigenous communities and the subordination of their languages. This is the consequence of language subordination, where the speakers of a culturally dominant language in a particular area or nation marginalize the speakers of minority languages. The Scots language is a minority language in Britain and is now rapidly being made a minority language in Scotland; just 1.6 million Scots speakers remain, less than a third of the Scottish population. This is a consequence of the Scots language becoming marginalised in Scotland through Anglophone domination and the refusal of Scotland's institutions to teach the Scots language to Scottish children in Scotland's schools.

It is accepted almost universally that the English language is useful for communication, but language is far more than merely a means of communication; language is the principle means by which humans can claim diversity and define their identity. To preserve language is also an effort to preserve a people and their unique heritage and culture, as well as their very identity. Hence by ignoring and marginalizing the Scots language, a consequence of linguistic imperialism, which is clearly a policy objective of an Anglophone elite, this means Scots speakers are ever diminished and replacing their own Scottish culture, and with that Scottish identity.

Aboriginal and indigenous language communities have been similarly marginalized and this is nothing new. The *United Nations Declaration on the Rights of Indigenous Peoples Resolution* Article 14 holds that aboriginal languages should be treated as fundamental rights and that: "*A mother tongue is a human birthright.*" Hence the Scots language should be respected and protected but even more importantly it needs to be taught! If a language is not taught to new generations, it will be lost.

> *Remede? Plain as parritch, a 'Scots Langage (Scotlan) Act' e'en-haundit wi Gaelic anaw!. Nocht lest is wirth batherin aboot. Itherwise - tell it like it is - cultural discrimination an cultural racism bi oor unionist maisters will conteena.*

Depriving a child of their language at the 'sponge' time of life, the most precious learning years, means a bond is broken. Scots *bairns* go into Anglophone dominated classrooms and have their own language squeezed out of them, mostly by teachers who themselves have little or no knowledge of the Scots language. Anglophone elites are linguistically programmed to consider Scots speakers as less articulate than them, reflecting the prevailing view of social institutions that the Scots language is not a 'valid' language; this is linguistic and ethnic discrimination.

Scots speakers are discriminated against (from birth) in their own nation and are thereafter continually disadvantaged throughout life by the prevailing Anglophone language domination and prioritisation. Scots language discrimination and its effects in Scotland may be one of the root causes of the so-called 'attainment gap'; many Scots speakers are left behind, considered to be inferior and less articulate, discarded by an Anglophone elite, many of whom are not Scots yet who control Scotland, its social institutions and its people. This ongoing linguistic discrimination has *"introduced a schizoid element into the national psyche"* (Purves 1997) which inevitably has psychological repercussions.

Scots language speakers have a right to a 'Scots Language Act' to end linguistic oppression and discrimination and to reflect and respect the unique irreplaceable connection between their culture and language. The Sapir–Whorf hypothesis states that the way we think and view the world is determined by our language. Culture and language are undeniably intertwined. Cognitive research suggests that language profoundly influences the way people see the world. Yet, with just 1.6 million Scots speakers left in Scotland this is barely 30 per cent of the population. Coincidentally this is also the same number of 'Yes' voters in the 2014 referendum, which highlights the significance of language in relation to culture and identity.

Scots speakers are therefore disadvantaged throughout life by the prevailing colonial-like Anglophone cultural hegemony that remains dominant within key social institutions in Scotland. Anglophone elites tend to be ignorant of the Scots language and hence ignorant of Scottish culture. How can an Anglophone elite understand the people or their culture it purports to lead and serve without knowledge of their language?

> *Whaur is oor Scots langage in thon Scottish curriculum? Naewhaur.*
> *Englis is thair, an sae is Gaelic, tae Higher level an Degree level an*
> *aw. Scots langage isnae thair nor onywhair!*

Language is one of the key factors that serves most effectively to define and unite a nation. Language *gives* people their identity. Take away their language you take away their identity, which is the brutal objective of cultural imperialism.

Scots are not taught their own mother tongue in Scottish schools for a reason, a political reason.

People learn their place in the world by virtue of the language codes they employ. For centuries the Scots language has been 'scorned as the language of a backward people' (Bunting 2017), much in the way Gaelic was regarded until recently. British linguists and educators stressed the 'verbal-deficit' perspective (Bernstein 1971) which suggests that anyone who does not use standard English is verbally deficient, has less prospect of academic advancement, and does not even have a 'valid' language. Educationalists clearly still believe that Scots is not a 'valid' language, for if they believed otherwise, they would surely teach the language.

An Anglophone elite dominates Scotland's social structures including education at all levels. Social structures and institutions are language created hence an Anglophone narrative defines and determines Scotland's society and purpose. The stereotypical way Anglophone elites, broadcasters and educators depict the Scots language as the language of the gutter and of the lower classes amounts to ethnic discrimination. The Scottish working class are basically all that is left of *Auld Scotia* in linguistic terms and they are therefore the final guardians of Scottish culture. We might consider how a Scots language narrative, flowing naturally and unhindered, would help re-shape and strengthen the identity and culture of the Scottish people? One could surmise the 'Yes' vote in support of Scottish independence might be expected to rise if more Scots appreciated that they had their *ain braw langage*. Language is therefore a 'public phenomenon' but it is also a powerful political tool, as imperial language policies testify. It is therefore no accident, politically, that the Scots language is not taught to Scottish children in Scotland's schools; Scotland's Anglophone unionist elite make sure of that.

The political importance of language is well-established. Madeiros (2017) asserted that: *"it is linguistic perceptions that directly determine national attachment*". Or, to put it another way, national attachment and hence national identity are linguistically determined. Scots speakers will therefore tend to hold to a Scottish identity, whilst Anglophones less so, as seems apparent in the Scottish independence debate and in voting outcomes where the Yes/No divide is to a large extent a linguistic divide.

This is nothing new. Minority and 'national' or ethnic groups in conflict are invariably separated along linguistic lines and Scotland is no different in a British context. Quebec and Canada are frequently presented as a divide between a Francophone Quebec and an Anglophone Rest of Canada (RoC). Anglophone immigrants and their children continue to integrate into Quebec's Anglophone community; i.e. they do not integrate into the Francophone community. Conversely, Francophones unsurprisingly tend to have identification with Quebec and show a positive and significant relationship with support for secession. Identification primarily with Scotland is the same for Scots speakers who comprise the dominant group supporting independence, reflecting the fact that national identity is linguistically determined.

> *Mony o Scotlan's dominie's noo dinnae e'en hiv ony Scots langage thairsel. Hou can thay unnerstaund Scots speekin bairns, an hou wad thay lairn bairns oor Scots langage? Thay cannae.*

However, in Quebec the elite is predominantly Francophone, whilst Scotland's elite class is predominantly Anglophone. This is primarily because the Scots language is not made a linguistic requirement in Scotland, whereas the French language is compulsory in Quebec, as is English. If the Scots language were a linguistic requirement in Scotland it would therefore be anticipated that the elite in Scotland would consist more, or perhaps predominantly of Scots speakers, which is not the case today. Linguistic inequality thus favours the Anglophone elite so long as Scots language has no authority. The consequence of this is that the Scots-speaking community are largely excluded from taking many elite posts within Scotland's social institutions and are therefore 'doun-hauden' through institutionalised language discrimination and Anglophone elite domination. Moreover, Scotland's elite high-level jobs are advertised primarily in the London press and hence are mostly aimed at an elite Anglophone employment market outside Scotland which is ten times larger, and with no Scots language requirement for any post in Scotland.

A direct consequence of this linguistic-based ethnic exclusion is what has become known as the 'Scottish Cultural Cringe', a language based psychological impediment suffered by Scots (speakers) resulting in a lowering of confidence and self-esteem. Yet English is not the natural language of the Scots, it is a foreign language reflecting a foreign culture and identity. Only English language and culture have been and continue to be imposed on the Scots, primarily with the aim to diminish notions of Scottish national identity, and to elevate 'British' national identity, which is the purpose of cultural and linguistic imperialism. The more that Scots were to hear, and speak and understand and learn about the Scots language, the more that Scots would feel Scottish in terms of national identity, and the more likely they might then be to support Scottish nationhood and self-government; this explains why an Anglophone unionist elite deprives Scots of learning and fully accessing their language, their mother tongue.

> *Scots bairns hiv tae lairn thair ain langage. Wi anely Englis bein taucht, thon's whit gies Scots fowk cultural creenge an aye hauds thaim doon.*

Phillipson (1992) defined English linguistic imperialism as:

> *"..the dominance asserted and retained by the establishment and continuous reconstitution of structural and cultural inequalities between English and other languages."*

What English language imperialism means in Scotland is that Scots speakers remain societally and institutionally an unequal ethnic group and thus by implication are effectively regarded as a lower or inferior class of people compared to Anglophones. Phillipson's work concerned *"linguicism"*, which relates to the prejudice that leads to endangered languages becoming extinct or losing local eminence due to the rise and competing prominence of English. Linguistic Imperialism is a sub-type of Cultural Imperialism. Linguistic Imperialism permeates all other types of imperialism, including colonialism, primarily because language is the means used to mediate and express them. Conversely, granting linguistic rights to minorities reduces conflict potential instead of creating it. Yet Scots still do not enjoy any such human right, the right to their own *mither tung.*

Anglophone elites therefore remain prejudiced against other indigenous languages in the UK, and in Scotland this means they are especially opposed to the Scots language, which continues to be 'doun-hauden', as are the Scots who speak it. It is therefore ethnic prejudice that oppresses the Scots language. Linguistic imperialism by its very nature directly influences linguistic genocide; the latter relates to the extermination of a group's language, or linguicide, i.e. the death of a language. The process of linguistic genocide is generally deliberate hence the Anglophone unionist elites' aim has been and remains to eradicate the Scots language (i.e. by refusing to teach and give status to the language), to kill it off, and by doing so this is also an attempt to diminish and remove feelings of Scottish national identity too.

Moreover, heirarchisation of languages brings with it a rejection of authentic local values and their substitution of 'different' values reflecting the dominant language group. This serves to strengthen the elite language group's social stratification resulting in a segregated society reflecting class, status and power, all of which are distinguishable by language.

This in turn further limits potential for social mobility and serves to worsen the attainment gap for those Scots speakers subsequently placed lower down in the system due to language difference. Thus, Scots speakers remain 'doun-hauden', and the inequalities and attainment gap they are subjected to and which is created by an Anglophone elite structured society is perpetuated through linguistic prejudice: those who are not considered by the elite to speak even a 'valid' language may not therefore be expected to be considered (by the elite) to be a 'valid' people.

Language is clearly a key dimension in maintaining patterns of dominance in a society, along with class, gender and race, and through the heirarchising of groups. **The longstanding intentional oppression and marginalization of the Scots language by Anglophone elites clearly leads to inequalities as well as diminishing the number of Scots who might otherwise desire independence**. Further, according to Philipson and Skutnabb-Kangas (1994), it is important to note that: *"Linguistic underdevelopment parallels economic and political underdevelopment"*. This implies that it is not only the Scottish people who are doun-hauden in this regard through Anglophone linguistic domination, it is also the social, economic and political development of the Scottish nation itself which is hindered and constrained.

Demographics

Historically, the English comprise the largest ethnic migrant group in Scotland. For the last century and more, Scotland has imported much of its managerial and professional class from within England's far larger population. Population inflows from rest-UK to Scotland have reached an estimated one million people over the last 20 years alone. Meanwhile, over the last two centuries some 3-4 million Scots, mostly working class, were displaced from Scotland due to the chronic lack of socio-economic opportunities in their own land, coupled with State and other incentives to assist Scots to leave the country. Over the past 150 years Scotland has proportionately 'lost' more of its people than any other north-western European country.

Essentially, the national identity of Scotland's population has, and still is rapidly changing, now mostly through in-migration, and this is something over which Scotland currently has no control. Given that people from rest-UK resident in Scotland have the highest propensity to vote 'No' and hence to oppose independence, such substantial population shifts renders demographic change a key factor influencing and determining any prospect of independence.

Its nae wunner fowk fi ither kintras aften thocht Scots war juist liken tae thon Inglis whan oor fowk ir aa sooth-spaikit!

By the mid 1990's, politically Scotland had become a virtual 'Tory Free Zone'; however, since then changing demographics has breathed new life into the Tories fortunes north of the border. People coming from rest-UK to live in Scotland predominantly, and perhaps 'naturally', tend to vote against Scottish independence and opt for continuation of the UK 'union'. This ethnic group have around twice the propensity of Scots to oppose independence, primarily reflecting their dominant Anglophone culture, language and hence identity, which is British (or English, Welsh etc.), not Scottish. This implies that the cultural British Anglophone unionist and hence anti-independence vote in Scotland is constantly boosted through ongoing demographic change, over which Scotland has no control.

Census data confirms that Scotland historically and still today imports a significant element of its meritocracy and professional and managerial class from rest-UK, primarily England. Higher level posts in Scotland are as a matter of course advertised in the London metropolitan press and are thus targeted at the much larger labour market in rest-UK. Over the last twenty years since 1999 an average of around 50,000 people per annum have come from rest-UK to live in Scotland, according to the census. This implies that some one million people have moved to Scotland from rest-UK since devolution in 1999. The census also suggests that in excess of two million people will have moved from rest-UK to Scotland within the last half century. Such fundamental demographic change brings with it changes in culture, language, politics, values and indeed a change in the 'national' identity of the Scottish population. The census further indicates that this ongoing demographic change means there are now just 1.6 million Scots speakers left in Scotland, which implies that most of the remaining 4.0 million of the population will be Anglophone.

Scotland's in-migration therefore differs significantly from that occurring in many other countries in that it is predominantly people from what is arguably Scotland's 'administrative Power' (i.e. England) who comprise the largest single ethnic migrant group to Scotland, as has been the case for the past century and more, and traditionally oriented towards the professional and managerial classes.

To some people migration is basically about survival. However, this is not the rationale for migration insofar as inflows from England to Scotland are concerned. The import of a largely mobile managerial and professional class from a single country of origin cannot be described as migration for survival. Conversely, the outflow of millions of working-class Scots over the past two centuries and more may be described as migration for survival. Historically there are clearly significant differences between Scotland's out-migration and in-migration, and through this the major changes in the culture and language and hence in the identity of the population.

Neoliberal attitudes common to the SNP political leadership

maintains that all those living and working in Scotland are 'Scots'. National identity, however, cannot be forced upon people who do not desire it, as some two million voters demonstrated when they voted to block Scottish independence in 2014. Many 'No' voters will have opted to reject the offer of Scottish citizenship and Scottish national identity primarily because their identity is not 'Scottish'. Most residents in Scotland holding to other non-Scottish national identities tend to oppose Scottish independence.

Scotland's differentiated 'progressive' policies since devolution provide added incentives for people to come from rest-UK to live in Scotland, as well as an attractive natural environment and more affordable property prices than in many parts of England. Scotland is nevertheless one of few countries with no controls over its immigration, which effectively means Scotland's population may be fundamentally altered over time, as appears to have happened given the census data. The prevailing demographic change, with significant inflows mostly from rest-UK, appears to be facilitating an increase in the Anglophone pro-union, pro-British parties' vote and thereby an increase in the anti-independence 'No' vote. In-migration from rest-UK has also resulted in a strengthening of the Tory unionist and tactical unionist vote across numerous Scottish constituencies that today include a significant resident population made up of people from rest-UK. These are voters who do not primarily identify as 'Scottish' and who will therefore be expected to have the least desire to alter their national identity to 'Scottish'. This expanding 'expat' group of voters in Scotland therefore naturally tend to reject the offer of Scottish independence and Scottish citizenship and hold the highest propensity of any ethnic group to oppose Scottish independence.

Scotland has had no control over migration to or from Scotland for 300 years and more, since the UK union was formed. This means that Scotland's population can alter markedly, however Scots have no influence over this whilst remaining within the UK union. The British State is 'responsible' for immigration but has no specific policy for Scotland, at least not overtly. However, it might be expected that an anti-Scottish independence British State is more than happy to see a large and sustained influx of mostly 'No' voting Anglophone 'unionists' from rest-UK coming to live in Scotland. Whether or not there are covert approaches in play to facilitate such an influx, who knows, though some have suggested how this might be achieved (Scott 2019), and there are clearly no efforts to limit movement.

Given the available census data and ongoing as well as historic demographic change, it should not therefore be surprising that around half of voters in Scotland today reject Scottish citizenship, Scottish nationality, and Scottish independence. National identity reflects and is determined by culture and language. The clear evidence is that most Anglophones from rest-UK living in Scotland will tend to reject and vote to block Scottish independence. In this sense they are rejecting a Scottish identity and Scottish citizenship primarily because it is not what they identify as in terms of their own ethnicity. This implies that a large element of the anti-independence vote is ethnically driven.

It would seem inaccurate to portray Scotland as somehow a 'wealthy' society from its role in the UK union and former British empire, as historians tend to suggest. Scotland is not some homogenous classless industrial paradise, or remotely close to the Scandinavian 'model'. Wealth inequality in Scotland was and remains profound and is also in large part linguistically determined, reflecting the domination of an Anglophone elite. To reduce inequality and allow its people and nation to develop, Scotland needs to respect and facilitate the Scottish people in allowing them to more naturally progress socio-economically within their own nation. This is also necessary in order to close the attainment gap and address other institutional and structural inequalities. However, this cannot be achieved so long as Scotland continues to recruit, prioritise and elevate as a matter of course an Anglophone meritocratic elite, much of which is still sourced outside Scotland, and which is hierarchically positioned above Scots language speakers, reflecting an Anglophone hegemony within the British State. This results in institutionalised marginalisation, discrimination, prejudice, segregation and oppression of Scots speakers in particular, leading to differential and lesser opportunities that prevail for Scots in their own land, with many consequently 'doun-hauden'. This also suggests that Scotland and its people are not permitted to be as fully developed as they would otherwise be, especially socially and economically.

Independence is ultimately about a people having the power to deal with the fundamentals of their own country, and that includes its population. No other (independent) country would allow its population to be removed and/or boosted and replaced in such a way as to threaten the existence of its own people, or their national identity, far less their sovereignty. Unrestricted and colonial-driven demographic change serves to undermine a people and nation's sovereignty, and this will inevitably alter its culture, language and identity. In Scotland's case this can only serve to hinder any prospects for self-determination and independence or equality. All independent countries have an immigration policy for good reason and Scotland is clearly lacking in this regard.

To believe that mass displacement combined with selective replacement of Scotland's population was not somehow 'managed' or intended would seem quite naïve; countries do not simply misplace by accident 3-4 million of their people, i.e. half or more of the population of a country, and then proceed to partially replace them through steadily importing a meritocracy with a different culture, language and identity reflective of the cultural hegemony of the 'administrative Power'. This 'process' appears to still be in full flow much as it has been for at least the last century, and indeed now seems to be accelerating, and this perhaps reflects renewed efforts by the British State to block Scottish independence via a covert migration policy. National Governments naturally pay close attention to population change and there should be little doubt that the British State continues to monitor, 'control' and indeed manipulate Scotland's demographics, though not in the interests of Scots or Scotland, and certainly not in the interests of Scottish independence.

Colonialism

Aspects typical of oppression faced by colonies relate to external control over language, leadership, and land, each of which figure highly in the case of Scotland. What independent countries take for granted, colonies often do not have. Scotland is not globally competitive, for instance, and its economy has been stagnating for a long time. In the world of commerce, an independent country has an opportunity to do whatever it needs to do in order to develop a global competitive advantage, whereas a colony and its people are often held back (or 'doun-hauden') through exploitation, discrimination and external control by an 'administrative Power'; the latter has an imperial British agenda which will inevitably differ from any national agenda in an independent Scotland which would be more focused on developing Scotland and its people.

Internal colonialism theory contends that ethnic and cultural divisions within a state are not removed in the course of its development or industrialisation, they remain and indeed may fester (Hechter 2017). In Scotland, the institutionalization of a cultural division of labour is clearly evident. This division of labour is imposed by the ruling group and it associates deprivation not just with membership of an oppressed and exploited social class, but with membership of an oppressed and exploited ethnic group, i.e. Scots speaking Scots.

Here the top jobs, the high wages, and the social status which comes with these things are reserved for members of the dominant (i.e. Anglophone, unionist) elite culture or (and, the qualification here is important) for members of the subordinate group who choose to embrace the dominant culture (including language). Longstanding inequalities between England as core nation and the peripheral UK nations reflect such characteristics in the context of internal colonisation.

There is clearly a need, given the ongoing momentum towards independence from the colonial power base, which is Anglophone, to consider the social basis of ethnic identity. There have been fundamental changes in the strength of ethnic solidarity in the United Kingdom in the nineteenth and twentieth centuries, however, many of the inhabitants of Wales, Scotland, and Northern Ireland continue to maintain an ethnic identity quite different from England. In the UK context, as elsewhere, it is apparent that ethnic identity is predominantly linguistically determined.

> *Bairns wi braw Scots tung's wull aye hiv thair gabs steek in cless, whill thon richt Englis speakers gie it laldy.*

There is also a need to consider the discord between socio-economic development and ethnicity. A common thread is the Anglophone elite hierarchy retaining control over the industrialisation process in the Celtic lands. In the wider colonial society sense, the dominant position of Anglophone elites extends much further than merely industrialisation. It seeks to inhabit and control almost every aspect of public and social institutions, from government, state agencies, justice, education, healthcare, religion, transport, the third sector and more.

In the Anglophone dominated internal colonization reality

that immerses and controls Scotland, the Scots speaking Scot is generally rendered as, and reduced to, a minor inferior ethnic participant parroting a supposedly 'invalid' language and made devoid of much in the way of status or opportunity. In other words, the Anglophone cultural hegemony dominated UK 'union' which essentially treats Scotland as a colony, renders the working-class Scots speaking Scot much like Jimmy Reid's 'alienated' worker, and little better than Nietzsche's *Untermensch* ('inferior people'). **This brutally oppressive reality reflects and merits the strongest desires for independence (and hence decolonisation) amongst the Scots speaking oppressed group.**

Prior to its independence, Ireland was controlled by a small group of English landowners, a phenomenon which should sound familiar to many Scots. The colonial overseers in Ireland brought about levels of poverty unknown in any other part of Europe, the enforced migration of over one million people, and the death of another one million people from starvation due to the famine of the late 1840's; and this at a time when wheat was still being exported from Irish ports. Scotland's even greater population displacement over a longer period of more than two centuries should be viewed in a similar vein. Meanwhile, the colonial 'scourge' of Scotland is not yet ended.

> *Thon richt Englis speakers micht be expectet tae hiv better exaim merks tae, an get fester forder anaw, naw?*

The UN regards Ireland as a former colony (of Britain/ England) and Scotland should seem little different. Any number of nations including numerous former colonies now independent states might be expected to propose and second Scotland's inscription on the UN List of Colonies to be decolonised. Scotland could thus appeal to The UN Special Committee on the Situation with regard to the

Implementation of the Declaration on the Granting of Independence to Colonial Countries and Peoples (also known as the Special Committee on Decolonisation or C-24), the United Nations entity exclusively devoted to the issue of Decolonisation' to help bring an end to what the UN refers to as *"the scourge of colonization"*.

Devolution itself demonstrates and reflects the unequal status between the Celtic 'fringe' nations of Scotland, Wales and Northern Ireland and the 'core nation' of England. British 'unionism' is merely an Anglophone hegemonic trans-national nationalist political ideology, and one of the more aggressive forms of nationalism, as history confirms. British unionism might also be viewed in the context of England's perceived need for *Lebensraum*, its Celtic fringe offering space, resources and an altruistic, egalitarian, welcoming and trusting, if somewhat naïve peoples serving an over-populated, unscrupulous Anglophone elite and unsympathetic 'core'.

Mike Small of Bella Caledonia states in relation to Brexit events, that:

"Scotland emerge from this chaos as a subaltern people – derided in Westminster and denied a Section 30 Order, told that a mandate in Holyrood and a mandate at Westminster wouldn't count." (Small 2019)

In post-colonial studies, the term 'subaltern' denotes colonial populations that are socially, politically, and geographically outside the hierarchy of power of a colony, and outside of the empire's metropolitan homeland. Devolution is merely a political bone with little meat on it thrown to restless colonies to chew on. Westminster simply chooses to ignore the democratic decisions of Scotland's people, the latter having no status to speak of. Scotland thus demonstrates only too well the three essential features of a colony, viz (Baird 2016):

- Scotland is subject to full or partial political control by another country (i.e. England);

- Scotland has been and continues to be occupied by significant numbers of Anglophone 'settlers' from the 'administrative Power', and;

- Scotland is exploited economically by the administering Power (Kerevan 2019).

Scotland's longstanding colonial subjugation within the so-called British 'union' merely reflects what is an exploited land and people discriminated against and 'doun-hauden' by an Anglophone elite representing and projecting a ruling 'administrative Power'.

Independence and hence decolonisation are clearly a fundamental necessity for Scotland's social and economic development as only sovereignty can fully encourage development of Scotland and its people, whilst at the same time protecting a threatened culture and language, and nation.

Nationalism

Nationalism in its simplest sense implies that a nation's people should be free to govern themselves, which is effectively self-determination. On the other hand, trans-national nationalism is fundamentally different given it involves one country extending its sphere of influence and control over other, usually neighbouring countries. This is often undertaken aggressively and provokes conflict.

There are clearly different types of nationalisms each with different objectives. Trans-national nationalism requires the occupation by one country of other countries and assuming control over these territories and peoples. Self-determination nationalism, on the other hand, relates primarily to the self-determination and self-government of a single nation and its people; the latter does not involve occupation of neighbouring countries, or their economic exploitation, or enforced cultural and linguistic imperialism.

Scotland's yairns hiv tae bi telt uisin wir ain langage, no anither fowks tung.

British xenophobia as applying to Scotland implies fear and distrust by the British Anglophone community of Scottish culture, Scots language, Scottish identity and Scottish self-government (i.e. independence), all of which it seeks to suppress. This is the reaction of (British/English) trans-national nationalism and (Anglophone) cultural and linguistic imperialism which views Scotland as 'its' territory (or colony) and Scottish independence as 'separation' and thus as an 'enemy'.

'Civic nationalism', stressed by the SNP Scottish Government, is defined as an association of people from different nations and identities who identify themselves as belonging to a single nation. Civic nationalism may sound positive in theory, however, self-determination stands to be thwarted where voters do not in fact share the same aim or respect or desire for a given national identity as those seeking self-determination. Self-determination clearly stands the risk of failing within a nation/people in which, due to demographic change, a significant portion of the voting population have no desire to assume the identity of, or have a sense of 'belonging' to, the nation or 'people' seeking self-determination. Civic nationalism may therefore prevent and block self-determination, as occurred in Scotland in 2014 due to the unique and irregular open voter franchise based on residence; the latter ignored the essential defining criteria for 'a people' seeking self-determination which includes a shared identity, ethnicity, culture, language, history and common suffering.

The raison detre of Britain's Tories is a British 'one-nation' under the guise of a 'union'. This is clearly trans-national nationalism and therefore a nationalist political ideology despite being termed 'unionism'. Trans-national nationalism is inevitably a more aggressive form of nationalism given it generally involves a degree of occupation, exploitation, coercion and control by a dominant core country together with the imposition of its culture, language and meritocratic elite upon neighbouring nations. This involves oppressing cultural and linguistic minorities through cultural imperialism.

One's national allegiance to either a British State or to a new Scottish State is fundamentally a choice of one's preferred national identity; however, each involves a quite different form of nationalism. Political unionism in the UK, which is effectively trans-national nationalism, is not simply a mere pro-union point of view, it is a culturally intertwined nationalist political identity.

Voting to block and deny the self-determination of any people and nation is self-evidently anti self-determination and anti the 'people' concerned, and implies continued support for trans-national nationalism. 'No' voters often claim to be 'both British and Scottish' yet such a stance inevitably highlights a degree of confusion about one's actual 'national' identity. Insofar as Scotland is concerned, British trans-national nationalism essentially implies and enforces continued colonisation and hence oppression of Scotland and its people.

Scottish independence and self-determination clearly have nothing whatever to do with occupation of neighbouring countries. Neither does Scottish self-determination involve the enforcement of cultural and linguistic imperialism, or the economic exploitation and political oppression of other peoples. Trans-national nationalism, on the other hand, requires and demands all these oppressive acts in varying measures – occupation, economic exploitation, cultural and linguistic imperialism, and external political control.

The actions of Scotland's people in seeking self-determination are reflective of anti-colonial nationalism via the pursuit of independence, which is clearly very different from transnational nationalism. Scotland's quest for self-determination is therefore effectively anti-colonial nationalism. Transnational nationalism involving occupation, economic exploitation, cultural and linguistic imperialism and external political control is effectively colonialism, which the UN maintains is a 'scourge' and should be ended.

So-called civic nationalism may develop in Scotland post-independence. Civic nationalism involves a country offering its citizenship to 'peoples' from other nations (who desire it) and therefore to peoples holding to other national identities and national allegiances. However, Scotland is unable to offer its national citizenship to anyone, not even its own 'nationals', prior to its independence. Hence the voter franchise in any national independence referendum should be restricted only to the 'people' or 'nationals' concerned who are seeking self-determination and who share a common ethnicity, culture, heritage, history, language, identity, common suffering etc., as reflecting the established defined criteria for 'a people'.

Langage is cultur efter aw, yet we sling a deifie tae wir ain langage, an syne we sling a deifie tae oor ain cultur an naition an aw.

The unique, open, and highly irregular national voting franchise adopted by the Scottish Government based simply on residence and thus the giving of precious national votes to peoples of various national identities other than 'Scottish' may only serve to inhibit and thwart Scotland's independence, as was arguably the outcome in the 2014 referendum. Such 'external' interference in any 'peoples' 'self'-determination should be avoided, according to the UN, and this includes interference by peoples and institutions from other countries who hold different national identities and allegiances to that of the people seeking self-determination. As the residence-based franchise serves to boost the 'No' vote, it is likely this strategy has been determined by the British State, which is opposed to Scottish independence.

Institutions

Establishment elites hold and exercise power and run the nation's social institutions. The establishment is not the centre of official power, but rather "..*the whole matrix of official and social relations within which power is exercised*". Politicians may comprise the centre of official power, but this is not necessarily where power is exercised.

'Enculturation' refers to the imposition on a society of the social values, behavioural norms and the culture and language of power wielding elites. In Scotland the culture and language of Anglophone elites differs from that of much of the rest of society, and especially Scots speakers; hence more often the latter remain excluded from membership of social institutions and from exercising power and are thus rendered marginalised.

Nelson Mandela referred to the State's many 'social institutions' and the need for them to change in order to serve the people, rather than to oppress them. Often the latter seems easier for power wielding elites running a nation's social institutions, more especially when much of the elite reflects a different culture and language and has an allegiance not to that host nation or its indigenous people.

> *Scotlan's a gey muckle Anglophone unionist slump an maist Scots fowk noo kennit.*

The term 'subaltern' people, attributed to Gramsci, is used to identify the social groups that are excluded and displaced from the socio-economic institutions of society. Scots speakers within the working class should not therefore be surprised that they are largely excluded from running such institutions. Many Scots suffer from two main structural impediments and disadvantages within an Anglophone elite dominated society – namely, being working class and speaking the Scots language. Scotland's social institutions therefore continue to be run by a predominantly unionist Anglophone elite that is opposed to Scottish self-determination and independence. The Anglophone unionist 'establishment' running Scotland's social institutions might be expected to use various means to oppose and stall policies and initiatives which would improve the 'lot' of many 'ordinary' Scots, including for example the blocking of a Scots Language Act, and seeking to stop Scottish self-determination and independence.

Scotland's social institutions discriminate against Scots by advertising and recruiting, as a matter of course, primarily in the UK metropolitan press, to fill most of Scotland top positions with supposedly 'superior' candidates invariably from outside Scotland who speak a 'valid' language, though this is not the Scots language. Scotland's Anglophone unionist elite establishment appear to believe this practice is necessary, and hence assume that 'ordinary' Scots who speak the Scots language are somehow not 'valid', and hence are inferior, or 'subaltern' even. This seems not too dissimilar to the discrimination suffered by indigenous and aborigine peoples in many other parts of the world, particularly within former British empire colonies.

A further consequence of this practice is that much of Scotland's Anglophone managerial and professional class lack in-depth knowledge of Scotland, or of the Scots language and Scottish culture. They don't need it, of course, as knowledge of Scotland, and its people, culture and languages, is not a pre-requisite to be the leaders of Scotland's social institutions within a British State. Those managing Scotland's social institutions do not therefore need to know much about

Scotland, nor have any national allegiance to the country. Anglophone elite domination merely reflects and represents the external institutional (i.e. colonial) control of Scotland's social institutions and hence the external control of its people. Nevertheless, the idea that being Anglophone determines one's position in a (non-Anglophone) society clearly reflects ethnic discrimination and unjust and prejudicial treatment of the indigenous (Scottish) people.

Scotland's Anglophone unionist privileged elite might be expected to seek to use their senior positions controlling and managing Scotland's social institutions to block and prevent independence, this reflecting their primarily British identity and national allegiance and Anglophone cultural and linguistic orientation. Scotland's sports bodies, universities, civil service, justice, police, local and central government, the NHS, military and many others are all examples of social institutions run by an Anglophone elite.

In Scotland, the longstanding university focus is primarily about recruiting academics from outside Scotland which itself discriminates against Scots. For decades there has been a dearth of Scottish researchers sponsored to undertake PhD work in Scotland and an emphasis on attracting mainly foreign students to enrol for high fee courses including PhD study. A very limited number of Scots holding PhD's implies few lecturers and professors in Scotland will be Scottish. Significant numbers of students from outside Scotland holding PhD's, often gained in Scotland, fill this self-created 'void', aided by supportive visa offerings. Such discriminatory institutionalised policies serve to squeeze out aspiring Scots who, as a result, are lacking educational and intellectual opportunities in their own land.

According to Audit Scotland it has become more difficult for Scottish student applicants to be offered a place in a Scottish university. At the same time the doors remain held wide open to higher fee students from other countries who are taking ever more places, especially on premium fee courses such as medicine and law. Scotland has a shortage of medical doctors largely because its Anglophone-elite run universities refuse to enroll adequate numbers of Scottish students to study as doctors in their home nation.

The institutionalised global market-oriented strategies of Scotland's universities are therefore leading to the 'Scottish' academic being something of an endangered species. It also remains rather a big assumption that Scottish universities are indeed attracting 'the best talent' from outside Scotland as clearly this has not done much to benefit the Scottish economy, which remains in a long-term weak and largely under-developed condition, as has been the case throughout much of the period of the UK union. Moreover, academics from other countries often tend to focus on research matters relating to and hence benefitting their own home countries, less so their host nation (i.e. Scotland), which implies that perceived benefits to Scotland are often exaggerated.

Jings, maist Scots fowk dinna e'en spik thay're (i.e. Englis) langage. Maist o us raelly dinnae, dae we? We spik Scots sae we dae, an braw it soons tae.

Few of the academic or other experts and intellectuals daily wheeled into Holyrood committees or Scottish television and radio studios to give their views and advice on 'Scottish science' are Scottish. This serves to reinforce the rather less than subtle message that only an Anglophone elite holds sufficient intellectual knowledge and expertise to run Scotland's social institutions, and this implies that Scots speakers do not; in essence, there are or appear to be few Scots speaking intellectuals which in itself conveys a message of Scottish inferiority. Scotland exhibits here the perpetuation of social segregation and a class and caste system oriented towards Anglophone and increasingly also international elites. 'Attainment' for many Scots remains a forlorn ambition for the enlightened, yet more of an inconvenient nuisance to

Scotland's Anglophone unionist elite 'running' Scotland, and without much thought either way as to the end result of prevailing practice, which is the ethnic discrimination and marginalisation of Scots.

Managerial and professional jobs in social institutions in Denmark and Norway would never be primarily advertised in Berlin, whereas Scotland has aye advertised all its best and high remunerative jobs in its much larger neighbouring country's capital, London. Moreover, for anyone to take up a senior public post in Norway or Denmark or elsewhere one might normally be required to speak the indigenous language as well as perhaps English, whereas there is no such indigenous language requirement for recruitment in Scotland. No leaders or other professionals employed by social institutions in Scotland need to be able to speak the Scots language, or therefore be able to understand what Scots speakers might be saying to them; this even includes teachers responding to Scots speaking children in the classroom, forcing the Scots speaking child to 'adapt' their speech.

The cultural capital of an Anglophone elite and power structure therefore differs from Scots speakers. Scots might consider here that the ability to speak and understand the Scots language (as well as English) should be a condition of employment also at higher levels in Scotland's institutions.

In their efforts to eradicate Scotland's indigenous language, Scotland's Anglophone unionist elite controlled social institutions suppress Scottish culture and hold back development of the Scottish people and their nation. Linguistic imperialism leaves Scotland and the Scottish people open to continued colonization, discrimination, exploitation, marginalisation and oppression. Scots need to understand that, within the UK 'union', Scotland is and will remain an occupied territory and colony in the sense that its social institutions are run by an Anglophone unionist elite whose allegiance is not, and never will be, to Scotland. Within this colonial straitjacket, ordinary Scots speakers remain 'doun-hauden', regarded by the institutional Anglophone elite as inferior or 'subaltern', as is their nation, and hence they are generally excluded from positions of power, which is ethnic discrimination. **For Scotland and the Scottish people to be allowed to fully and naturally develop unhindered, the Anglophone unionist domination of Scotland's institutions, and hence 'the scourge of colonisation', must be ended; this can only be achieved through independence.**

Constitution

Scotland's joint UK parliament with England (i.e. Westminster) was created and hence constituted in 1707 by a simple majority of Scotland's MP's. The UK was constituted by international treaty, the Treaty of Union. The Scots are regarded as a sovereign people and nation which implies that Scottish sovereignty rests at any given time with them and hence with Scotland's national elected representatives.

It is clear from the ECJ Brexit decision that a signatory party to a treaty may unilaterally withdraw from its treaty-based agreements. Scotland is and remains a signatory party to the Treaty of Union that created Scotland's joint parliament with England, hence Scotland must be able to legally withdraw from this agreement.

The Treaty of Union represents, in effect, the founding constitution of the UK union. Neither Scotland nor England, as legal and constitutional entities, were dissolved, only their respective national parliaments were dissolved, and with both nations' distinct legal systems retained. Westminster and Holyrood have both acknowledged the Claim of Right that Scottish sovereignty rests with Scotland's people. This therefore raises the question: can the Treaty of Union be unilaterally revoked by any one of its two signatory party nations? Alternatively, as often seems implied by unionists, can Scotland be 'held' within the UK union against its will, and simply by a majority decision of England's MP's, the latter having 533 MP's or 82 per cent of the votes in Westminster compared with Scotland's 59 MP's (9 per cent)? Such an outcome would appear to disregard the sovereignty of the Scottish people, and their elected representatives, the Claim of Right, and the Treaty itself.

If Scotland were to be judged as being incapable of withdrawing itself from its own treaty-based union, despite being a signatory party to it, this therefore implies that Scotland is deemed to be merely a territory and a colony of England, given the latter's political domination over Scotland by virtue of its 533 MP's at Westminster. However, that would seem to ignore the reality of Scotland being a signatory party to a treaty-based union, and Scottish sovereignty.

> *If Scots canna e'en lairn wir ain bairns tae read an screed i thair ain langage, the ane thay uise at hame, in the playgrund, an doon the street, than we dinna deser naething, nivver mynd tae hiv oor ain kintra bak.*

Whilst politically Scotland may be treated by the UK/England as a colony, constitutionally and legally Scotland seems anything but. The ECJ stated that revoking and ending a treaty is a decision primarily for any treaty signatory party concerned. As Scotland is a signatory party to the Treaty of Union this would imply that Scotland may revoke that treaty. Indeed, Scotland's only veto over the UK union may be to end it, that is, by withdrawing from it.

The joint UK Westminster parliament is not itself a signatory party to the treaty. The treaty signatory parties – that is the nations of England and Scotland – are, therefore, the principals and superior parties to the treaty, not the subordinates.

The UK parliament, in this sense, would seem to be merely the appointed 'agents' of the superior signatory parties, i.e. Scotland and England. In this regard the UK is a treaty-based agreement that may be ended unilaterally and legally by either signatory party nation, much like any other international treaty-based arrangement.

The sovereignty of Scotland's people is, at any given time, held by Scotland's elected national representatives. As they represent Scotland's sovereign people and the Scottish nation, and hence represent the signatory party to the treaty, it is surely they who may revoke the treaty and withdraw Scotland from the UK union in the same way it began. It should matter less the grounds for withdrawal, of which there are arguably many. Breaches of the Treaty of Union continue to occur, the latest example being the proposed Northern Ireland 'backstop' or special customs arrangement as part of the UK's proposed Brexit 'deal', which contravenes the union treaty.

A second Scottish independence referendum has been blocked by Westminster, the latter assuming it has the power to ignore the wishes of Scotland's sovereign people. However, given the existence of the treaty, and the fact of Scottish sovereignty, a referendum may be a flawed as well as an unnecessary process to secure Scottish independence. A referendum result is not legally binding and can be ignored. A referendum assumes that Westminster would accept any Yes vote which, given the Brexit experience and Westminster's persistent rejection of that referendum result, as well as its anti-independence stance, is by no means certain. And a 'Yes' outcome in any referendum may again be prevented by Scotland's highly irregular residence-based 'national' voter franchise, also reflecting ongoing demographic change in Scotland, which invites significant external interference in Scotland's self-determination process. Moreover, any 'Yes' vote outcome may also be blocked or thwarted by external interference in other ways, such as the anti-independence activities of the British MSM, the UK Government and its agencies, and other entities. In addition, it is also the case that: *"As a matter of law, a referendum is not a required part of the process of becoming independent"* (McCorkindale and McHarg 2020).

A referendum is assumed to be democratic, as is the outcome of national elections. However, the constitutional and hence legal reality here is arguably what matters rather more than contemporary definitions or notions of what democracy may or may not be. Democracy was also of a rather different order in 1707 when Scotland's privileged nobility and other elites signed up to the union. Clearly, though, there are many ways those from outside Scotland (in rest-UK) seek to interfere in and hence influence any Scottish self-determination referendum process, which goes against UN guidelines on self-determination.

It may be instructive, therefore, for Scottish 'nationalists' to seek the opinion of a Scottish court on the constitutional and legal reality of the Treaty of Union vis-à-vis the majority of Scotland's elected national representatives' ability to unilaterally withdraw Scotland from the UK union. That is, assuming Scotland's MP's remain unsure of their sovereign 'powers'. In late 2019, some 81 per cent of Scotland's elected MP's supported independence, compared with just 61 per cent who voted to pass the Act of Union on 16th January 1707. In 2015 the SNP won 56 of Scotland's seats (95 per cent) yet these supposed 'Scottish nationalists' still turned up at Westminster, preferring to give their consent to the UK union rather than asserting Scotland's sovereignty, as they would appear to be legally entitled to do.

The 'legal authority' necessary not only to withdraw from, but to dissolve Scotland's joint UK parliament must arguably rest in the way it (i.e. the UK) was and remains constituted by Scotland; that is, through the consent of a majority of Scotland's representatives who hold Scotland's sovereignty. This needs to be, and surely can be, tested, either through assertion by Scotland's national representatives, or in a Scottish court.

Constitutionally, and in terms of sovereignty, and given the UK union treaty arrangement, Scotland (and England for that matter) remains to all intents and purposes a nation that is able to re-establish its own parliament and hence independent 'State' status at any time. The UK union arrangement, as with any treaty-based undertaking between sovereign signatory parties, only exists so long as a majority of Scotland's elected representatives agree to participate in it and give their consent to its continuance. To believe otherwise would be to deny the existence of any union, and how it was constituted, which would be to deny the existence of the Treaty and Act of Union, and which would also be to ignore the constitutional and legal basis of the UK union itself.

Of course, unionists may find the legal and constitutional reality of any such Scottish withdrawal from the UK union unsettling, however it was done. But, if pro-union supporters were ever to democratically secure a Scottish national parliamentary majority in support of union, with England or any other country, or countries, then there is nothing to stop them taking forward such a policy.

Ethnicity

The Scots may be defined as a minority ethnic group in the UK. An estimated 1.6 million Scots speakers represent a linguistic minority in Scotland. Moreover, given Scotland's rapid and uncontrolled demographic change, Scots themselves could become a minority people in Scotland, possibly by 2040, if not before.

Ethnic oppression has shifted from meaning the exercising of tyranny by a ruling group to signifying the injustice some suffer due to the everyday practices and norms of a society. Over time, oppression becomes a widespread, systemic injustice that creates systematic disparities affecting the well-being and development of individuals and groups. Ethnic oppression is essentially to do with power and oppression consists of the unequal distribution of systemic power. In Scotland, an Anglophone unionist elite wield power over Scots, and Scots-speakers in particular.

Ethnic oppression may take different forms but involves prejudice and discrimination directed at a people of the basis of their membership of an ethnic group. Ethnic discrimination against the Scots includes examples such as the public ridiculing (e.g. by the MSM, and by institutions) of Scottish people simply for speaking the ('invalid') Scots language, and the persistently negative stereotyping of Scots speakers typically played out within the dominant British cultural context amidst a supposedly 'superior' Anglophone hierarchy. The Anglophone linguistic requirement as condition of employment in Scotland whilst ignoring any Scots language imperative further reinforces ethnic oppression and ensures discrimination (against ethnic Scots speakers) leading in turn to social and economic inequalities.

> *Anely 1.6m Aye voters and 1.6m Scots spikkers in Scotlan acordin tae thon census! Langage is wha we are, oor identity, oor cultur, an hou fowk vote.*

Historically, Anglophone elites running Scotland's social institutions have considered Scots speakers to be simply speaking 'bad English' and that Scots is not a 'valid' language.

This is an ethnic and discriminatory perspective that remains relatively fixed even today within Scotland's Anglophone institutional hierarchies. Anglophone elites dominate Scotland's cultural high ground and control the linguistic 'battleground' against who they view as their linguistic and cultural inferior, that is the Scots speaker. Consequently, many Scots remain marginalised and destined to live a life of poverty and inequality, held back from socio-economic progress or achieving higher office in their own land. As Scotland's social elite structure is Anglophone dominated this means it is language which distinguishes Scots speakers from the dominant Anglophone elite hierarchy.

The existence of an Anglophone unionist elite hegemony running Scotland's social institutions is no accident; rather, an Anglophone elite is a fundamental pre-requisite of continued British colonial power and control over Scotland. This represents institutionalised ethnic oppression which ensures that Scots speakers are for the most part excluded from taking leading positions in Scotland's social institutions. This reflects cultural and linguistic imperialism as a necessary condition of trans-national nationalism, and the enculturation and hence ethnic discrimination of the Scottish minority within a UK polity.

> *Thares nae human richts for Scots. Thar's nane whaur it maiters, i.e. hou fowk spik tae ane anither. Ye'll nivver hae equalitie in Scotlan withoot a Scots Langage Act.*

A lack of opportunity and poverty are consequences of institutionalised Anglophone discrimination against Scots, and Scots language speakers in particular. The advertising of most of Scotland's professional and managerial posts primarily outside of Scotland in the London metropolitan press and hence recruitment of a mainly Anglophone elite drawn from within a larger and far more heavily populated neighbouring country amounts to ethnic discrimination in a specifically Scottish context. Thus, ethnic discrimination against Scots is a significant form of oppression prevalent in Scotland.

Ethnic discrimination and oppression of a people generates potential for 'internalized racism', also known as 'Appropriated Racial Oppression'. From this we see manifest the 'Scottish Cultural Cringe'; this relates to how some Scots negatively view themselves and their own culture and language as being 'inferior' within a British Anglophone elite hegemony context. Institutionalised Anglophone linguistic oppression instills in Scots speakers a *"schizoid element into the national psyche"* (Purves 1997); this makes Scots deny and denigrate their own language in preference to developing a false (i.e. Anglophone) persona, in the interests of personal socio-economic advancement. Ethnic oppression thus impacts the mental health of minorities and brings about the internalization of negative ethnic stereotypes. There is a lengthy history relating to the largely Anglophone promoted negative ethnic stereotypes and discrimination of Scots language speakers, not least within Scottish educational institutions at all levels, the British MSM, in industry, in government, and within the justice system.

Internalized racism and hence Appropriated Racial Oppression represent the internalization of negative stereotypes of one's own racial group. Internalized oppression is reflected in members of 'subordinate' groups experiencing greater social and material deprivation and this is clearly evident within the Scots speaking community, much less so the Anglophone community in Scotland. Scots speakers' acceptance of negative stereotypes means they do not consider themselves to be ethnically oppressed, despite the reality of their exclusion from key areas of Anglophone dominated institutional management and access to resources.

Appropriated Racial Oppression may be so deep and internal in those who are oppressed as to be rigid and unchanging. The working-class Scots speaking Scot is therefore forced to adapt his or her language to become more Anglophone in order to progress socially within the dominant Anglophone cultural and linguistic hierarchy. Those Scots who are unable to 'conform' suffer accordingly. Widespread prevalence of high levels of Appropriated Racial Oppressionhelp explain why significant numbers of Scots reject 'Scottish' identity in any meaningful sense, i.e. by voting against Scottish independence and hence blocking the creation of their own Scottish citizenship, Scottish nationality and self-governance.

In addition, there are aspects of apartheid (i.e. institutionalised racial segregation) evident in Scotland. This is characterised by longstanding and sustained Anglophone elite settler colonialism, the prevalence of private Anglophone schools and 'elite' universities which tend to 'serve' primarily the Anglophone (and now also the international elite) community and are rather less focused or interested in Scots speakers. This follows on from, and contrasts with, the largescale historic displacement and hence removal via emigration of much of the indigenous Scottish working-class Scots-speaking population over the past two centuries and more.

The dominant position of an Anglophone meritocracy in Scotland therefore serves to perpetuate and strengthen Appropriated Racial Oppression within Scots and obscures the ways in which institutionalised discrimination becomes normalised and contributes to inequality among ethnic groups. The predominant racism or ethnic 'issue' in the context of Scottish independence is not colour race, nor is it anti-English; rather, it is reflected in ethnic oppression of Scots by a dominating Anglophone elite and also through Appropriated Racial Oppression (internalized racism) exhibited by some Scots themselves. Both forms of ethnic discrimination and oppression, which oppose Scottish independence, are determined by, and hence reflect, institutionally imposed cultural and linguistic differences between the dominant Anglophone elite, and Scots language speakers.

Self-Determination

Self-determination is a cardinal principle in modern international law and recognized as an international legal right in the UN Charter. The principle of self-determination does not state how the decision is to be made and there are several ways in which self-determination has been and can be achieved. National self-determination is defined as the *"creation of national governmental institutions by a group of people who view themselves as a distinct nation (for example, because they have a common language)"*. Self-determination is the opposite of and is therefore wholly opposed to the oppressions brought about on a people through colonialism and imperialism, oppressions which Scotland arguably remains subject to politically, despite the Treaty of Union. Self-determination has come to mean the free choice of one's own acts without external compulsion or influence.

Criteria for the definition of a *"people having the right of self-determination"* was proposed during the 2010 Kosovo case. This set out key aspects of 'a people' including a common culture, ethnicity, language, identity, history and shared suffering. It is important to be clear beforehand in defining these common criteria relating to the distinct 'people' seeking self-determination, and not to confuse this with peoples holding to quite different national identities, culture, language etc.

In the context of self-determination, peace is clearly an important consideration. Peoples who remain oppressed and under colonial and imperial rule and occupation may never be fully at peace with or accept their oppression. The UN describes colonisation as *"a scourge"* on a people, which implies that colonisation is an instrument of oppression and indeed a form of punishment which often involves ethnic discrimination.

Lets hae a Scots Langage Act an lairn aw Scots bairns thair ain mither tung, as weel as thon 'administrative' English.

Critical in any national self-determination process is the need to avoid external influence affecting the outcome. This includes preventing influence by peoples and countries other than the specific 'people' seeking self-determination. British MP's from outside Scotland and successive UK Governments and their 'agencies' actively oppose Scottish independence which itself amounts to external interference. British political parties and other interests based outside Scotland also formed the 'Better Together' 'No' Campaign in 2014 to oppose independence and this also amounts to external interference and influence. There is in addition widespread British State and British MSM activity opposing Scottish self-determination. Various British institutions based inside and outside Scotland likewise openly oppose Scottish independence. All this and more (e.g. covert activity) amount to a high degree of external interference and influence in the self-determination process of the Scottish people.

A unique and irregular non-reciprocal residence-based voting franchise adopted in Scotland further serves to invite significant external interference, the latter worsened by uncontrolled demographic change. There is a recognition in all States that a 'national' voter should be a 'national' of the country in which a national vote is to take place. It should be defined well in advance of any referendum what is meant by a 'Scottish national', not least because independence creates a need to know this, i.e. who the 'nationals' of the country are. Is a Scottish 'national' simply anyone from other countries and hence people of other national identities and cultures who happen to have an address in Scotland, as the resident-based franchise assumes? Globally, national voting rights are primarily dependent on parental descent and only apply to persons from other countries when they apply for and are given citizenship of a country. However, Scotland cannot legally offer citizenship until after its independence. National voting rights globally are never normally dependent only on residence, and this appears to be a rather obvious, fundamental, and perhaps (intended?) fatal flaw in the Scottish self-determination process which materially acts to block Scottish independence. The residence-based national voting 'qualification' also means that the franchise was denied to Scots living abroad, and these are people who do hold to a Scottish identity. Most other countries afford due consideration to their nationals living abroad whereas Scotland has ignored its own people in this regard.

> *Aye, vent yer cultural anti-Scots langage racism aw ye lyke, Scots fowk are uised tae it fi yon Anglophone unionist doun-hauders.*

A referendum therefore appears a flawed process in the context of Scottish self-determination given the irregular residence-based franchise, widespread scope for external interference, plus the fact that a referendum is not a legal requirement for independence anyway. Moreover, Westminster cannot necessarily be relied on to legislate for a 'Yes' result in a referendum. The referendum question used is also 'questionable'. Ideally Scotland should have a question similar to the Brexit 'withdrawal' question reflecting the reality of a signatory party revoking its own treaty, e.g.: *"Should Scotland remain a member of the United Kingdom Union or leave the United Kingdom Union?"*. The UK Government is in any event blocking another referendum on Scottish independence, assuming it has the power to do so, which rather ignores Scottish sovereignty and the fact of a Treaty.

Decolonisation has always been the firm ground on which the right to self-determination of a people was applied and Scotland seems little different in this regard given the way the country is and has been treated politically, over centuries. The simplest way to secure independence would seem to be, as it always has been, for the majority of Scotland's democratically elected national representatives to assert Scottish sovereignty and to withdraw Scotland from the UK union. There would seem little point in a country continually voting in a majority of nationalists if these representatives then aye refuse to assert independence.

> *Fowk micht haver - awthing uised tae be e'en mair thrawn in Scotlan afore thon SNP wis in 'pouer'; tho A doot it.*

If Scotland's representatives remain unsure of their sovereign power they might test the legality of this and, subject to a positive court ruling, then legally put Scotland's constitutional withdrawal from the UK into effect via the re-establishment of Scotland's own reconstituted sovereign parliament. If such unilateral withdrawal action is rejected by the courts this implies that Scotland is deemed to hold only the status of a colony. This would imply that the Treaty of Union is therefore deemed (by the courts) to be rather meaningless, if not entirely void. No doubt a court would need to give reasons for any such decision. Any appeal may be made to the International Court of Justice, not least given that a UK court may be viewed as a further reflection of colonial rule and oppression.

> *Englis isnae ma mither tung.*

A further, perhaps final, option thereafter to secure independence is to lobby for Scotland to be *Listed* with the UN as a colony seeking decolonisation. A democratically elected 'nationalist' Scottish Government should be able to do this, and to endeavour, via the relevant UN Committee for Decolonisation, to invite international support in this regard. The UN may then be called upon to assist in a properly organised referendum process, if required, which should more adequately respect the rights of the Scottish people to self-determination, and avoid any further external interference, in an effort to end *"the scourge of colonisation"* and secure Scottish independence.

CHAPTER 13: STRATEGIES FOR INDEPENDENCE

Withdrawal Strategy

A democratically elected majority of Scotland's national representatives should initiate Scotland's withdrawal from the UK union as soon as possible. A majority of Scotland's national representatives may assert Scottish sovereignty and revoke the Treaty of Union, as it began.

The British State may or may not wish to contest Scotland's representatives' right, as signatory party to the Treaty of Union, to withdraw the sovereign nation and people of Scotland from the UK union. Should this be contested, the courts may be asked to opine on the matter.

If there remains a dispute, then the matter may be taken to the International Court of Justice. The ICJ would then seek to settle the matter in accordance with international law by giving advisory opinion.

Decolonisation Strategy

If a sovereign Scotland were for some reason deemed unable to legally withdraw from the UK union, this would mean that Scotland does not have full sovereign or political control and is therefore considered by law as a territory or colony of the British State[119].

Scotland's democratically elected representatives may then approach the United Nations with a view to having Scotland 'Listed' as a colony to be decolonized.

With UN support, Scotland may then, if required, undertake to hold a referendum on independence, which would also be a referendum on ending 'the scourge' of colonization.

Any referendum voting franchise would need to first, using established criteria, define the Scottish 'people' seeking self-determination, to ensure there is no undue external interference and influence of the result, as was arguably the case in 2014.

Similarly, there should be no external interference or influence permitted from any actors or organisations (e.g. MSM, government, politicians, agencies, corporations etc.) from outside Scotland in any Scottish self-determination referendum process.

Scots Language Strategy

Scotland's cultural liberation, the protection of Scottish national identity, and the objective of equality in society, depends on a Scots Language strategy. This strategy requires a Scots Language Act.

The Scots language has to be made the national language of Scots. English should be seen as an 'administrative' language, not as a 'superior' language.

A key requirement is to teach the Scots language in schools at all levels, and at universities, in addition to English.

All peoples from other nations seeking to work in Scotland should have some knowledge of the Scots language. This is especially important in education, in social institutions, and at higher managerial levels generally.

ANNEX I: THEORETICAL AND EMPIRICAL DIMENSIONS OF THE FRAMEWORK

CULTURE	Cultural Imperialism (Tomlinson); Cultural Colonialism Cultural Assimilation/Cultural Domination (Spiers) Cultural Hegemony (Gramsci) Scottish Cultural Cringe (Beveridge & Turnbull); Cultural Inferiorisation (Fanon) Dislocated Culture (Burns); Clandestine Culture (Fanon) Illusion of Culture (Gaughan); National Cultural Inheritance (Henderson) Deferential Civic Culture (Almond & Verba) Enculturation (Bourdieu and Passeron)
LANGUAGE	Linguistic Imperialism (Phillipson) Language Functions (Robins) Indigenous Languages (Maser) Language Death (Harrison; Lipski) Linguistic genocide (Phillipson & Skutnabb-Kangas) Sapir–Whorf hypothesis (Anderson & Lightfoot) Language Subordination (Lippi-Green); Colonial Alienation (MacKinnon) Verbal-Deficit Perspective (Bernstein) Language Symbolism (Wittgenstein; Spiers) Language as Determinant of National Identity (Madeiros)
DEMOGRAPHICS	Demographic Displacement Ethnic/racial division of labour www.scotlandscensus.gov.uk www.nrscotland.gov.uk/statistics National Identity Perceptions (Tilley et al.; Curtice; Bond)

	Genocide Elitist Scotland Report (gov.uk)
COLONISATION	External Control over Language, Leadership, Land Scots fed 'British' Symbolic Myths (Dorling) Anglophone Elite Control; 'Colonial Alienation' (MacKinnon) Self-Colonisation; Colonized Mentality (Fanon) Features of a Colony (Baird): Administrative Power; Occupation; Economic Exploitation Internal Colonisation; Ethnic Division of Labour (Hechter) Colonial Oppression of Scots is Ethnically (i.e. British) Driven (Hunter) Independence is Decolonisation (UN; Hallas) Scots Speakers Viewed by Anglophone Elite as Subaltern People (Gandhi; Small) Colony and its People Remain Under-Developed until Independence (Hechter)
NATIONALISM	National Identity & Language is Decisive (Triandafyllidou) Scots seek Self-Determination Nationalism and Anti-Colonialism Nationalism (Velychenko) UK 'Union' is Trans-national Nationalism (Hochman) Civic Nationalism - only possible post independence (Nash; Bond) Criteria to Define 'A People' is Essential (UN; ICJ) Identity and Ethnicity Key Determinants (British Attitudes Survey) British Nationalism/British Exceptionalism (Hassan; Pettigrew;

	Dorlng)
INSTITUTIONS	The Establishment (Barcan; Fairlie) Social Institutions & Oppression (Mandela) Social Exclusion (Green) Anglophone Unionist 'Establishment' (Tibbetts) Ethnic Discrimination (Audit-Scotland; Elitist Scotland? Report) The Scots 'dialect switching virtuosi' (Aitken) Appointment of a 'foreign' Anglophone elite 'National' Allegiance?
CONSTITUTION	Treaty of Union 1707 (Riley) Signatory Party may withdraw from Treaty-Based Union (ECJ) Claim of Right/Scottish Sovereignty rests with the Scottish People Referendum Flawed; Not Essential legal requirement; External Interference; Open Franchise; Doubtful Ratification Scotland is Principal to UK Treaty, not Subordinate, Right to Choose/Claim of Right Scotland's only UK Veto is Withdrawal via Majority of Scotland's MP's Test Scotland's Legal Withdrawal in Court (or ICJ/Murray) - Refusal Confirms Colonial Status, not Equal Partner
ETHNICITY	Non-Scots 'Nationals' Blocking Scottish Citizenship/Scottish Nationality is anti-Scottish Scots Language Oppression (Fanon; Deutsch) Unequal Power Distribution, Anglophone Elite Marginalize Scots Speakers (Bivens; Rangel)

	Schizoid National Psyche (Purves) Scots Speakers Self-deprecation and Fear - 'Cringe' (Prilleltensky & Gonick) Appropriated Racial Oppression/ Internalized Racism (Jones; Krieger; Rangel) Anglophone Meritocracy (Thompson & Neville) Scots Speakers / Anglophone Segregation and Displacement Scottish Independence is Identity and hence Ethnic/Linguistic Determined
SELF-DETERMINATION	Self-Determination is a Cardinal Principle in International Law (UN; McWhinney) Criteria to Define 'A People' includes Ethnicity, Language etc. (UN; Uriel) Self-Determination is Decolonisation (UN) Scottish Independence 'fits' on all Theories of Secession (Miller) British/Rest-UK Interference in Scottish Self-Determination contravenes UN rules Residence-Based Franchise Irregular/ Incoherent + not Reciprocal, Distorts Vote Scottish 'Nationals' Need to be Defined prior to referendum, e.g. Parental Descent 'Civic Nationalism' (Bond) Subjugation and Oppression are Grounds for Secession (Supreme Court of Canada)

BIBLIOGRAPHY

Aitken, A. J. (1976, 2015) The Scots Language and the Teacher of English in Scotland. In †A. J. Aitken, ed. Caroline Macafee, 'Collected Writings on the Scots Language'. http://medio.scotslanguage.com/library/document/aitken/The_Scots_language_and_the_teacher_of_English_in_Scotland

Aitken, A. J. (1981) The good old Scots tongue: Does Scots have an identity? In E. Haugen, J. D. McClure and D. Thomson, eds., Minority Languages Today. Edinburgh University Press: Edinburgh. 72–90.

Almond, G. A. and Verba, S. (1963) The Civic Culture. Little, Brown and Company: Boston, MA.

Anderson, S. R. & Lightfoot, D. W. (2002) The language organ: linguistics as cognitive physiology. Cambridge University Press: Cambridge.

Anderson, M. (2015) Migrants in Scotland's population histories since 1850. In, National Records of Scotland (2015) Scotland's Population – The Registrar General's Annual Review of Demographic Trends, 2015. 161st Edition. United Kingdom Statistics Authority. Chapter 11, 79-106.

Anfara, V. A. and Mertz, N. T. (2015) Theoretical Frameworks in Qualitative Research. Sage Publications: Thousand Oaks, California.

Audit Scotland (2016) Audit of higher education in Scotland's universities. http://www.audit-scotland.gov.uk/uploads/docs/report/2016/nr_160707_higher_education.pdf

Baird, A. J. (2013) Scotland's universities are virtually overrun by non-Scots, 14 Feb 2013 http://www.scottishreview.net/AlfBaird61.shtml

Baird, A. J. (2013A) The wishful thinking behind the funding of research in Scotland, 5 Sept 2013 http://www.scottishreview.net/AlfBaird112.shtml).

Baird, A. J. (2017) Does Brexit vote underline Scotland is not a country, but a colony? Newsnet, July 5. https://newsnet.scot/archive/brexit-vote-underline-scotland-not-country-colony/

Baird, C. (2019) Today we have printed the secret oil report that EVERY Scot must read. https://www.thenational.scot/news/17461382.today-we-have-printed-the-secret-oil-report-that-every-scot-must-read/?ref=mr&lp=6

Bambery, C. and Kerevan, G. (2018) Catalonia Reborn: How Catalonia took on the corrupt Spanish state and the legacy of Franco. Luath Press: Edinburgh.

Barcan, A. (1993). Sociological Theory and Educational Reality: Education and Society in Australia since 1949. UNSW Press: Sydney.

Bernstein, B. B. (1971) Class, Codes and Control: Volume 1 – Theoretical Studies Towards A Sociology Of Language. Routledge and Kegan: London.

Beveridge, C. and Turnbull, R. (1989) The Eclipse of Scottish Culture. Polygon: Edinburgh.

Bhabha, H. K. (1994) The Location of Culture. Routledge: Abingdon, Oxon.

Bivens, D. (1995) Internalized Racism: A Definition. Women's Theological Center. https://www.racialequitytools.org/resourcefiles/bivens.pdf

Bolaffi, G. (2003) Dictionary of race, ethnicity and culture.

SAGE Publications Ltd: London.

Bond, R. (2000) Squaring the Circles: Demonstrating and Explaining the Political 'Non-Alignment' of Scottish National Identity. Scottish Affairs, no. 32, Summer.

Bond, R. and Rosie, M. (2010) National Identities and Attitudes to Constitutional Change in Post-Devolution UK: A Four Territories Comparison. Regional & Federal Studies, Volume 20, Issue 1. https://doi.org/10.1080/13597560903174931

Bond, R. (2015) National Identities and the 2014 Independence Referendum in Scotland. Sociological Research Online. https://doi.org/10.5153/sro.3797

Bourdieu, P. and Passeron, J. C., (1990) Reproduction in Education, Society and Culture, Sage Publications Inc.

British Social Attitudes Survey (2013) National Identity: Exploring Britishness. https://www.bsa.natcen.ac.uk/media/38984/bsa31_national_identity.pdf

Buie, E. (1998) Row on Scots in schools returns. The Herald, 11 December. http://www.heraldscotland.com/sport/spl/aberdeen/row-on-scots-inschools-returns-1.314971

Bunting, M. (2017) The Language of Resistance. Bella Caledonia, 18th May. http://bellacaledonia.org.uk/2017/05/18/the-language-of-resistance/

Burns, H. (2009) From theory to policy – the implications of recent research findings on health inequality. Glasgow Centre for Population Health. GCPH Seminar Series 5. https://www.gcph.co.uk/assets/0000/0484/Harry_Burns_Summary.pdf

Buttigieg, J. A, ed. (1992) Antonio Gramsci, Prison Notebooks. Columbia University Press: New York City. pp. 233–38.

Cadwallader, A. (2013) Lethal Allies: British Collusion in Ireland. Mercier Press: Cork.

Campbell, S. (2013) The bully's gospel. https://wingsoverscotland.com/tag/wee-poor-stupid/page/4/

Cantle, T. (2012) Interculturalism: The New Era of Cohesion and Diversity. Palgrave Macmillan: Basingstoke, Hampshire.

Carter, R. T. (2007). Racism and psychological and emotional injury: Recognizing and assessing race-based traumatic stress. The Counseling Psychologist, 35 (13), 13-105.

Clemetson, L. (2007) The Racial Politics of Speaking Well. http://www.nytimes.com/2007/02/04/weekinreview/04clemetson.html

Crystal, D. (1987) The Cambridge Encyclopaedia of Language. Cambridge University Press: Cambridge.

Curtice, J. (2013) Who Supports and Opposes Independence - and Why? ScotCen Social Research: Edinburgh. http://www.scotcen.org.uk/media/176046/2012-who-supports-and-opposes-independence-and-why.pdf

David, E. J. R. and Okazaki, S. (2006) Colonial mentality: a review and recommendation for filipino american psychology. Cultural Diversity and Ethnic Minority Psychology, 12 (1), 1-16.

David, E. J. R. (2008). A colonial mentality model of depression for filipino americans. Cultural Diversity and Ethnic Minority Psychology, 14 (2), 118-127.

Davidson, N., Liinpaa, M., McBride, M., and Virdee, S. (Eds) (2018) No Problem Here: Understanding Racism in Scotland. Luath Press: Edinburgh.

Deutsch, M. (2006). A framework for thinking about oppression and its change. *Social Justice Research, 19* (1), 7-41.

Devine, T. M. (2012) The Scottish Nation: A Modern History Penguin: London.

Devine, T. (2013) Carving out a Scottish Identity. https://blogs.sps.ed.ac.uk/referendum/carving-out-a-scottish-identity/

De Vries, L. and Schomerus, M. (2017) Fettered Self-determination: South Sudan's Narrowed Path to Secession. Civil Wars, 19:1, 26-45, DOI: 10.1080/13698249.2017.1342442

Dorling, D. and Tomlinson, S. (2019) Rule Britannia: Brexit and the end of Empire. Biteback Publishing: London.

Duchene, L. (2008) Probing Question: What is Lost When a Language Dies? https://news.psu.edu/story/141259/2008/02/11/research/probing-question-what-lost-when-language-dies

Edwards, D. and Cromwell, D. (2018) Propaganda Blitz – How the Corporate Media Distort Reality. Pluto Press: London.

Eichhorn, J., Paterson, L., MacInnes, J., Rosie, M. (2014) Results from the 2014 survey on 14-17 year old persons living in Scotland on the Scottish independence referendum. Future of the UK and Scotland Programme, AQMeN/ESRC. https://www.research.aqmen.ac.uk/wp-content/uploads/sites/27/2017/07/YoungScotsBriefing060614.pdf

Fabry, M. (2010) Recognizing states: international society and the establishment of new states since 1776. Oxford: Oxford

University Press.

Fairlie, H. (1955) 'Political Commentary'. The Spectator. 23 September.

Fanon, F. (2004) The Wretched of the Earth. Grove Press: New York.

First Peoples' Heritage, Language and Culture Council (2010) *Report on the Status of BC First Nations Languages*. http://www.fpcc.ca/files/PDF/2010-report-on-the-status-of-bc-first-nations-languages.pdf

Fisch, J. (2015) A History of the Self-Determination of Peoples: The Domestication of an Illusion. Cambridge University Press: Cambridge.

Franks, M. (2014) EU petition 1448/2014 and Response 590419023. http://www.europarl.europa.eu/doceo/document/PV-8-2014-07-14_EN.html#pvitem11

Freire, P. (1970) Pedagogy of the Oppressed. Continuum International Publishing Group: New York.

Gandhi, L. (1998) Postcolonial Theory: A Critical Introduction. Columbia University Press: New York.

Gibson, C. (2015) The Voice of the People: Hamish Henderson and Scottish cultural Politics. Edinburgh University Press: Edinburgh.

Glaser, B.G. and Strauss, A.L. (1967) The Discovery of Grounded Theory. Aldine: Chicago.

Grant, A. (2018) Middle class could spurn promotions in face of tax double whammy. https://www.heraldscotland.com/news/17297312.middle-class-could-spurn-promotions-in-face-of-tax-double-whammy/?action=success#comments-feedback-anchor

Grant. A. (2018A) ECJ ruling to revoke Article 50 rubber

stamped by the highest court in Scotland. https://www.heraldscotland.com/news/17311344.ecj-ruling-to-revoke-article-50-rubber-stamped-by-the-highest-court-in-scotland/?action=success#comments-feedback-anchor

Gray, A. (2012) Settlers and Colonists. In Hames, S. (ed) Unstated: Writers on Scottish Independence. World Power Books: Edinburgh.

Green, M. E. (2011) Rethinking the Subaltern and the Question of Censorship in Gramsci's Prison Notebooks, Postcolonial Studies, Volume 14, Number 4 (2011): 385-402.

Green, E. (2011a) Decentralization and political opposition in contemporary Africa: evidence from Sudan and Ethiopia. Democratization 18, 1087–1105.

Gudeleviciute, V. (2005) Does the Principle of Self-determination Prevail over the Principle of Territorial Integrity?, International Journal of Baltic Law, Vytautas Magnus University School of Law, Volume 2, No. 2 (April).

Hallas, D. (1969) Britain's Oldest Colony: A history of famine, brutality....and heroism. Socialist Worker, No. 137, 11 September. https://www.marxists.org/archive/hallas/works/1969/08/ireland.htm

Hamilton, R. F. and Herwig, H. H. (2004) Decisions for War, 1914-1917. Cambridge University Press: Cambridge.

Hassan, J. and Mitchell, J. (eds) (2013) After Independence. Luath Press: Edinburgh.

Hassan, G. (2013) A Tale of Ideologies: Scottish nationalism and unionism. Open Democracy. 12 August. https://www.opendemocracy.net/ourkingdom/gerry-hassan/tale-of-ideologies-scottish-nationalism-and-unionism

Hassan, G. (2019) Class still defines and disfigures Britain and Scotland. https://www.gerryhassan.com/tag/british-establishment/

Hay, C. (2001) Routledge Encyclopedia of International Political Economy. New York: Routledge. pp. 1469–1474

Hayes C. W., Ornstein, J., and Gage, W. G. (1987) The ABC's of languages & linguistics, a practical primer to language science, 2nd ed. National Textbook Co.: Lincolnwood, Ill, USA.

Hechter, M. (2017) Internal Colonialism: The Celtic Fringe in British National Development, 1536-1966. Routledge: Abingdon, Oxon.

Henderson, A. (2007) Hierarchies of Belonging: National Identity and Political Culture in Scotland and Quebec. McGill-Queen's University Press: Toronto.

Herald Scotland Online (2018) Pro-independence protesters clash with police in Catalonia as Spanish cainet meets in Barcelona.   https://www.heraldscotland.com/news/17314532.pro-independence-protestors-clash-with-police-in-catalonia-as-spanish-cabinet-meets-in-barcelona/

Hochman, A. (2015) Of Vikings and Nazis: Norwegian contributions to the rise and the fall of the idea of a superior Aryan race. *Studies in History and Philosophy of Biological and Biomedical Sciences*. 54: 84–88.

Holy Bible (1996) Matthew 6:24. New Living Translation. Tyndale Charitable Trust: Wheaton, Illinois.

House of Commons Library (2018) Claim of Right for Scotland. https://researchbriefings.parliament.uk/ResearchBriefing/Summary/CDP-2018-0171

Hunter, J. (1977) The Scottish Historical Review Vol. 56, No. 161, Part 1 (Apr., 1977), pp. 103-105.

Hutcheon, P. (2018) UK Government minister received briefing on suspension of SNP councillor from MoD job. http://

www.heraldscotland.com/
news/16046297.UK_Government_Minister_received_briefing
_on_suspension_of_SNP_councillor_from_MoD_job/?
action=success#comments-feedback-anchor

Hutcheon, P. (2019) BBC in 'bias' row after senior journalist criticises colleagues over indyref coverage. https://www.heraldscotland.com/news/17506742.bbc-in-bias-row-after-senior-journalist-criticises-colleagues-over-indyref-coverage/?action=success#comments-feedback-anchor

Johnson, L. (2019) Vanishing Languages. https://maptia.com/lynnjohnson/stories/vanishing-languages

Jones, C. P. (2000) Levels of racism: theoretic framework for a gardener's tale. American Journal of Public Health, 90 (8), 1212-1215.

Katzner, K. (1999) The Languages of the World. Routledge: New York.

Keating, M. and Laforest, G. (eds) (2018) Constitutional Politics and the Territorial Question in Canada and the United Kingdom, Federalism and Devolution Compared. Palgrave Macmllan: London.

Kendrick, S. Bechhofer, F. and McCrone, D. (1985) Is Scotland different? Industrial and occupational change in Scotland and Britain. In Newby, H. et al (eds), Restructuring Capital: recession and reorganisation in industrial society. Macmillan: London. 63-102.

Kerevan, G. (2019) Our Common Home – Imagining a Post Oil Scotland. Bella Caledonia. (15 November) https://bellacaledonia.org.uk/2019/11/15/our-common-home-imagining-a-post-oil-scotland/

Kirkness, V. J. (1998) The Critical State of Aboriginal Languages in Canada, *Canadian Journal of Native Education*;

Sept; 22, 1; CBCA Complete.

Knox, W. W. (undated) A History of the Scottish People. Summary of Economy and Society in Scotland 1840-1940. http://www.scran.ac.uk/scotland/pdf/SP2_10Economy.pdf

Krieger, N. (2000) Discrimination and health. In L. Berkman and I. Kawachi, (Eds.), Social Epidemiology. (pp. 36-75). Oxford University Press: Oxford.

Kuper, S. and Symanski, S. (2014) Soccernomics. Nation Books: New York.

Leask, D. (2018) Sadness and pride as the Forth leaves the Clyde and heads south for the Falkland Islands. http://www.heraldscotland.com/news/homenews/16039987.sadness-and-pride-as-the-forth-leaves-the-clyde-and-heads-south-for-the-falkland-islands/?action=success#comments-feedback-anchor

Lederman, N. G. and Lederman, J. S. (2015) What is a Theoretical Framework? A Practical Answer. Journal of Science Teacher Education, Vol. 26, Issue 7, pp. 593-597, November. https://link.springer.com/article/10.1007%2Fs10972-015-9443-2

Lehner, S. (2007) Subaltern Scotland: Devolution and Postcoloniality. In B. Schoene (Ed.), The Edinburgh Companion to Contemporary Scottish Literature. Edinburgh University Press: Edinburgh.

Lippi-Green, R. (1997) English with an Accent: Language Ideology and Discrimination in the United States. Routledge: New York.

Lipski, J. M. (2008) Varieties of Spanish in the United States. Georgetown University Press: Washington DC.

Lipsky, S. (1987) Internalized Racism. Rational Island: Seattle.

Littlejohn, S. (2002) Theories of human communication. Wadsworth Thomson Learning: Belmont, CA, USA.

Lorimer, W. L. (1983) The New Testament in Scots. Canongate: Edinburgh.

MacKinnon, I. (2019) Education and the colonisation of the Gaidhlig mind. Bella Caledonia. 3rd December. https://bellacaledonia.org.uk/2019/12/03/education-and-the-colonisation-of-the-gaidhlig-mind/

Mandela, N. (1994) Long Walk to Freedom. Vol. II. 1962-1994. Little, Brown & Company: London.

Mangler, M. (2019) British Science Festival: Brexit, a fairer future? https://www.britishscienceassociation.org/blog/british-science-festival-brexit-a-fairer-future

Maser, C. (2011) What is Lost When a Language Becomes Extinct? https://chrismaser.wordpress.com/.../what-is-lost-when-a-language-becomes-extinct/

Maxwell, J. (2014) It is unionists, not nationalists, who are obsessed with identity. https://www.newstatesman.com/politics/2014/07/it-unionists-not-nationalists-who-are-obsessed-identity

McAlpine, R. (2016) Say it loud, we're Scots and we're proud… fighting against our cultural cringe. http://www.thenational.scot/comment/robin-mcalpine-say-it-loud-were-scots-and-were-proud-fighting-against-our-cultural-cringe.18556

McArdle, H. (2019) Doctor's leaders: Scotland's medical schools must have much higher intakes – and a greater share of Scottish students. https://www.heraldscotland.com/news/17981746.doctors-leaders-scotlands-medical-schools-must-much-higher-intakes---greater-share-scottish-students/

McCorkindale, C. and McHarg, A. (2020) Constitutional Pathways to a Second Independence Referendum. UK Constitutional Law Association. January 13.https://ukconstitutionallaw.org/2020/01/13/chris-mccorkindale-and-aileen-mcharg-constitutional-pathways-to-a-second-scottish-independence-referendum/

McCrone, D. and Bechhofer, F. (2008) National identity and social inclusion. Ethnic and Racial Studies, 31 (7): p.1245-66. [doi:10.1080/01419870701704677]

McIntosh, L. (2015) Majority of Scottish born voters said 'yes'. The Times. March 27. https://www.thetimes.co.uk/article/majority-of-scottish-born-voters-said-yes-z7v2mmhc8nt

McKenna, K. (2018) The SNP's social diktats are a betrayal of the Yes movement. https://www.heraldscotland.com/news/17768476.kevin-mckenna-snp-39-s-social-diktats-betrayal-yes-movement/

McLean, I. and McMillan, A., (2009) Self-determination. The concise Oxford dictionary of politics. Oxford: Oxford University Press.

McWhinney, E. (2007) Self-Determination of Peoples and Plural-Ethnic States in Contemporary International Law: Failed States, Nation-Building and the Alternative, Federal Option. Martinus Nijhoff Publishers: Leiden, Netherlands.

McWhinney, E. (2008) Declaration on the Granting of Independence to Colonial Countries and Peoples. United Nations Audiovisual Library of International Law. https://legal.un.org/avl/ha/decolonization.html

Medeiros, M. (2017) Refining the Influence of Language on National Attachment: Exploring Linguistic Threat Perceptions in Quebec, Nationalism and Ethnic Politics, 23:4, 375-390,

DOI: 10.1080/13537113.2017.1380457

Miller, D. (2019) Is Self-Determination a Dangerous Illusion? Polity: Cambridge.

Muehlmann, S, (2008) 'Spread Your Ass Cheeks': And Other Things That Should Not Be Said In Indigenous Languages, *American Ethnologist* 35, 36.

Murray, C. (2019) The Alex Salmond Fit-Up. https://www.craigmurray.org.uk/archives/2019/08/the-alex-salmond-fit-up/

Murray, C. (2019A) London Will Never Give Independence – We Must Take It. 20th December. https://www.craigmurray.org.uk/archives/2019/12/london-will-never-give-independence-we-must-take-it/

Murray, C. (2020) J'accuse. 30th March 2020. https://www.craigmurray.org.uk/archives/2020/03/jaccuse-2/

Nash, K. (2001) The Blackwell companion to political sociology. Wiley-Blackwell: Oxford.

National Records of Scotland (2015) Scotland's Population – The Registrar General's Annual Review of Demographic Trends, 2015. 161st Edition. United Kingdom Statistics Authority.

National Records of Scotland (2017) Mid-Year Population Estimates Scotland, Mid-2016. United Kingdom Statistics Authority.

Nettle, D. and Romaine, S. (2000) Vanishing Voices: the extinction of the world's languages. Oxford University Press: Oxford.

Pettigrew, M. (2016) 'Red, white and blue unionism: An ideological nationalism of its own'. http://

www.judecollins.com/2016/12/red-white-blue-unionism-ideological-nationalism-mark-pettigrew/

Phillipson, R. (1992) Linguistic imperialism and linguicism. Oxford University Press: Oxford.

Phillipson, R. and Skutnabb-Kangas, T. (1994) Linguistic Genocide. In Valodas Politika Baltijas Valstis/Language Policy in the Baltic States. Krajumu sagatavojis. Latvijas Republikas Valsts valodas centrs: Riga. 140-150.

Porter, M. E. (1998) The Competitive Advantage of Nations. Macmillan: New York.

Prilleltensky, I. & Gonick, L. (1996) Polities change, oppression remains: on the psychology and politics of oppression. Political Psychology, 17, 127-148.

Prodanovic, K. (2013) The Silent Genocide: Aboriginal Language Loss FAQ. www.terry.ubc.ca/2013/10/16/the-silent-genocide-aboriginal-language-loss-faq/

Purves, D. (1997) A Scots Grammar. The Saltire Society: Edinburgh.

Rangel, R. (2014) The Appropriated Racial Oppression Scale Development and Initial Validation, Unpublished PhD Dissertation. Graduate School of Arts and Sciences, Columbia University, USA.

Ravitch, S. M. and Riggan, M. (2017) Reason and Rigor: How Conceptual Frameworks Guide Research. Second edition. Sage: Los Angeles, CA.

Riddoch, L. (2013) Blossom: What Scotland Needs To Flourish. Luath Press Ltd.: Edinburgh.

Riley, P.W.J. (1978) The Union of England and Scotland. Manchester University Press: Manchester.

Roberts, A. (2018) Churchill: Walking with Destiny. Penguin

Books: London.

Robertson, J. (1997) Tebbit urges poll on independence. The Sunday Times. February 16. https://wingsoverscotland.com/from-the-archives-11/

Robertson, J. (2014) BBC bias and the Scots referendum. https://www.opendemocracy.net/en/opendemocracyuk/bbc-bias-and-scots-referendum-new-report/

Robins, R. H. (1964) General Linguistics: An Introductory Survey. Longmans: London.

Ross, D. and Smith, G. D. (1998) Scots-English English-Scots Dictionary. Lomond Books: New Lanark.

Ross, D. (2008) Scotland: History of a Nation. Lomond Books: New Lanark.

Russell, M. (2019) Brexit and Scotland. Public Meeting, Victoria Halls, Selkirk. 5th Sept. https://newsnet.scot/news-analysis/scotland-and-brexit/

Schiller, H. (1989) Culture, Inc.: The Corporate Takeover of Public Expression. Oxford University Press: Oxford.

Scott, A. (2019) Scotched Nation: Will they let Scotland walk away? Twa Corbies Publishing: Dundee.

Scottish Government (2019) Scotland's right to choose: putting Scotland's future in Scotland's hands. https://www.gov.scot/publications/scotlands-right-choose-putting-scotlands-future-scotlands-hands/

Scottish Parliament (2019) Referendums (Scotland) Bill. https://www.parliament.scot/S5_Bills/Referendums %20(Scotland)%20Bill/SPBill46S052019.pdf

Settle, M. (2018) David Linden's Scots accent proves too much for his parliamentary colleagues. https:// www.heraldscotland.com/news/16991993.david-lindens-scots-accent-proves-too-much-for-his-parliamentary-colleague/?action=success#comments-feedback-anchor

Shaw, P. (2001) Language and Identity, Language and the Land, BC Studies, no. 131: 39-55.

Silver, P. (1983) Educational Administration: Theoretical Perspectives on Practice and Research. Harper & Row: New York.

Small, M. (2019) Scotland as Subaltern Nation in a World of Madness. Bella Caledonia. (19 October). https://bellacaledonia.org.uk/2019/10/19/ scotland-as-subaltern-nation-in-a-world-of-madness/

Smith, A. (2010) Nationalism: Theory, Ideology, History. Polity: Oxford.

Speight, S. L. (2007) Internalized racism: One more piece of the puzzle. *The Counseling Psychologist*, 35 (1), 126-134.

Spiers, D. (2019) Education after Wittgenstein: A Causal-Cultural Theory of Refence and Meaning. Unpublished PhD Dissertation, Trinity College Dublin.

Stevenson, A. and Waite, M. (eds) (2011) Concise Oxford English Dictionary. Oxford University Press: Oxford.

Swanson, I. (2010) General Election is a vote on independence, say the Tories. Edinburgh Evening News. February 13. https:// wingsoverscotland.com/from-the-archives-10/

Tappan, M. B. (2006) Reframing internalized oppression and internalized domination: from the psychological to the sociocultural. *Teachers College Record, 108 (10)*, 2115 – 2144.

Taylor, J. (1990) Relationship between internalized racism and marital satisfaction. *Journal of Black Psychology*, 16 (2), 45-53.

The Coalfields Regeneration Trust (2019) Economic and social conditions in the former coalfields of England Scotland and Wales.   https://www.coalfields-regen.org.uk/wp-content/uploads/2019/10/The-State-of-the-Coalfields-2019.pdf

The Social Mobility and Child Poverty Commission (2015) Elitist Scotland? https://www.gov.uk/government/publications/elitist-scotland

Thompson, C. E., & Neville, H. A. (1999) Racism, mental health, and mental health practice. *The Counseling Psychologist*, 27, 155-223.

Thurman, J. (2015) A Loss for Words: Can a dying language be saved? Annals of Conservation, March 30. https://www.newyorker.com/magazine/2015/03/30/a-loss-for-words

Tickell, A. (2019) Salmond legal win is failure of 'apparent bias'.   https://www.thenational.scot/politics/17343668.andrew-tickell-salmond-legal-win-is-failure-of-apparent-bias/?action=success#comments-feedback-anchor

Tilley, J., Exley, S. and Heath, A. (2004) Dimensions of British Identity, in Park, A., Curtice, J., Thomson, K., Bromley, C. and

Phillips, M. (eds.), British Social Attitudes: the 21st Report. Sage: London.

Tomlinson, J. (2001) Cultural Imperialism. Continuum: London (2nd Edition).

Triandafyllidou, A. (1998). 'National Identity and the Other'. *Ethnic and Racial Studies*. 21 (4): 593–612.

United Nations (1945) Charter of the United Nations and Statute of the International Court of Justice. https://www.un.org/en/charter-united-nations/

United Nations ICJ (2017) United Nations, International Court of Justice Archived 2017-02-22 at the Wayback Machine. 2010 Kosovo Case, Separate Opinion of Judge A. A. Cançado Trindade.

United Nations Sustainable Development Solutions Network (2019). World Happiness Report 2019. https://worldhappiness.report/ed/2019/#read

Unterberger, B. M., (2002) Self Determination. In: Deconde, A. (Ed) Encyclopedia of American Foreign Policy. Simon and Schuster: New York.

Uriel, A. (2015) The Confused Compass: From Self-Determination to State-Determination. Ethnopolitics 14(5): 488-497

U.S. Department of Health and Human Services (2001) Mental health: culture, race, and ethnicity-A supplement to mental health: A report of the surgeon general. Rockville, MD: U.S. Department of Health and Human Services, Substance Abuse and Mental Health Services Administration, Center for Mental

Health Services.

Valentine, J. (2019) Neo-liberalism and the new institutional politics of universities. The Jimmy Reid Foundation. http://reidfoundation.org/2019/05/neo-liberalism-and-the-new-institutional-politics-of-universities-paper-now-available/

Velychenko, S. (2012) Ukrainia Anticolonialist Thought in Comparative Perspective. *Ab Imperio* (4): October, 339.

Wallace, L. (2009) What's Lost When a Language Dies? https://www.theatlantic.com/national/archive/2009/11/whats-lost-when-a-language-dies/29886/

Walter, C. and Von Ungern-Sternberg, A. (2014) Introduction. In: Walter, C., A. Von Ungern-Sternberg, and K. Abushov, eds. Self-determination and secession under international law. Oxford: Oxford University Press, 1–12.

Watson, M. (2002) The English diaspora: discovering Scotland's invisible migrants - 1945 to 2000, Scottish Economic and Social History 22: 23-49.

Watts-Jones, D. (2002) Healing internalized racism: the role of a within-group sanctuary among people of african descent. Family Process, 41 (4), 591-601.

Wightman, A. (2013) The Poor Had No Lawyers: Who owns Scotland (and how they got it). Birlinn: Edinburgh.

Williams, G. A. (1991) When Was Wales?: A History of the Welsh. Penguin: London.

Wilson, W. (1918) President Wilson's Address to Congress, Analyzing German and Austrian Peace Utterances (Delivered to US Congress in Joint Session on February 11, 1918). www.gwpda.org.

Wiszniewski, M. (2018) Grouse. Blood Sports. Land. https://bellacaledonia.org.uk/2018/11/29/grouse-blood-sports-land/#comment-445565

Wittgenstein, L. (1953) Philosophical Investigations. Blackwell: London.

Woodifield, P. (1988) Brittan remarks on evolution "unwise". The Sunday Times. November 20. https://wingsoverscotland.com/from-the-archives-12/

---

[1] https://www.gov.uk/government/speeches/pm-statement-on-priorities-for-the-government-25-july-2019

[2] John McGrath was one of the founders of the theatre company 7:84.

[3] https://dictionary.cambridge.org/dictionary/english/culture

[4] http://www.dictionary.com/browse/culture

[5] https://all-to-human.blogspot.com/2016/11/what-is-meaning-of-cultural-imperialism.html

[6] https://bellacaledonia.org.uk/2019/01/30/fugue-state/

[7] The Tory vote share in Scotland at the December 2019 UK General Election was 25.1 per cent: https://www.bbc.co.uk/news/election-2019-50766014

[8] 62 per cent of Scots voters opted to remain in the EU: https://www.electoralcommission.org.uk/who-we-are-and-what-we-do/elections-and-referendums/past-elections-and-referendums/eu-referendum/results-and-turnout-eu-referendum

[9] https://www.colinburnett.co.uk/home/the-scottish-cultural-cringe

[10] https://www.amazon.co.uk/Panopticon-Jenni-Fagan/

dp/0099558645#reader_0099558645

[11]http://www.heraldscotland.com/news/14699321.Holyrood_bids_to_fast_track_Indycamp_appeal_against_eviction/

[12]https://www.colinburnett.co.uk/home/the-scottish-cultural-cringe

[13]http://theconversation.com/poppies-are-a-political-symbol-both-on-and-off-the-football-pitch-68113

[14] https://www.youtube.com/watch?v=ThuBz6ly-ts

[15] https://www.youtube.com/watch?v=3nLGKFTH5sw

[16] https://www.un.org/press/en/2012/gashc4051.doc.htm

[17]However, polling in early 2020 suggested the pro-independence vote, post UK withdrawal from the EU, was at 52 per cent: https://scotgoespop.blogspot.com/2020/02/scot-goes-pop-panelbase-poll-on.html

[18]https://medium.com/tow-center/cambridge-analytica-the-geotargeting-and-emotional-data-mining-scripts-bcc3c428d77f

[19] www.dictionary.com/browse/language

[20] https://livingtongues.org/officers/

[21] http://www.unesco.org/new/en/culture/themes/endangered-languages/websites-and-online-resources/

[22] https://www.languageandculture.com/cultures-languages

[23] http://www.education.com/reference/article/culture-language/

[24] http://www.wsj.com/articles/SB10001424052748703467304575383131592767868

[25] http://anthro.palomar.edu/language/language_5.htm

[26]https://www.listenandlearn.org/blog/what-do-we-lose-when-a-language-dies/

[27] https://wingsoverscotland.com/not-too-wee-and-not-too-poor/

[28]http://www.open.ac.uk/scotland/news/new-course-makes-scots-language-accessible-all

[29]https://www.gaidhlig.scot/bord-na-gaidhlig-statement-on-the-audit-scotland-section-22-report/

[30]https://www.gov.scot/publications/12-languages-implementation-findings-2019-local-authority-survey/

[31]https://www.bing.com/videos/search?q=espa%c3%b1olizar+a+los+ni%c3%b1os+Catalanes&view=detail&mid=59856F04EFCF930B1A4159856F04EFCF930B1A41&FORM=VIRE

[32]https://www.abdn.ac.uk/elphinstone/resources/northeast-scots-language-board.php

[33] https://www2.palomar.edu/anthro/language/default.htm

[34] http://www.bing.com/search?q=language+culture&src=IE-SearchBox&FORM=IESR02

[35] http://www2.warwick.ac.uk/study/undergraduate/courses/languageculturecommunication/

[36] This does not include all Scottish emigrants who embarked on ships to destinations outside Europe, only those included in the returns to the Board of Trade.

[37] http://sociology.iresearchnet.com/sociology-of-race/ethnic-or-racial-division-of-labor/

[38] https://www.nrscotland.gov.uk/statistics-and-data/statistics/statistics-by-theme/population/population-estimates/mid-year-population-estimates/mid-2016

[39] https://www.nrscotland.gov.uk/statistics-and-data/statistics/statistics-by-theme/population/population-estimates/mid-year-population-estimates/mid-2016/list-of-tables

[40] https://www.un.org/en/genocideprevention/genocide.shtml

[41] In the early 1980's the author himself joined thousands of other Scottish migrant workers on buses leaving Glasgow's George Square heading for building sites on the continent, such was the dearth of job opportunities in Scotland.

[42] https://www.scotlandscensus.gov.uk/1921

[43] https://www.scran.ac.uk/scotland/pdf/SP2_1Education.pdf

[44] https://www.nrscotland.gov.uk/statistics-and-data/statistics/stats-at-a-glance/registrar-generals-annual-review/2014

[45] https://www.nrscotland.gov.uk/statistics-and-data/census/2001-census/results-and-products/reports-and-data/key-statistics-for-settlements-and-localities-scotland

[46] https://www.statista.com/study/22783/scottish-independence-statista-dossier/

[47] http://www.scotlandscensus.gov.uk/news/census-2011-release-2a

[48] https://ianhamiltonqc.com/

[49] http://www.scotlandscensus.gov.uk/ods-web/area.html

[50] https://www.holyrood.com/news/view,under-18s-to-get-free-bus-travel-in-scotland-after-ministers-reach-budget-d_15173.htm

[51] https://www.thesun.co.uk/news/2099502/white-british-population-has-fallen-by-more-than-half-in-just-20-years-in-parts-of-uk-as-country-becomes-more-segregated/

[52] https://www.theguardian.com/uk-news/scotland-blog/2016/mar/17/a-new-dawn-for-land-reform-in-scotland

[53] https://www.ons.gov.uk/economy/nationalaccounts/

balanceofpayments/bulletins/uktrade/june2019

[54] https://www.sustainablegrowthcommission.scot/

[55] https://www.gov.scot/policies/economic-growth/scottish-national-investment-bank/

[56] https://www.scotsman.com/whats-on/john-cleese-criticises-half-educated-tenement-scots-866627

[57] https://legal.un.org/avl/pdf/ha/dicc/dicc_e.pdf

[58] https://www.gov.uk/government/speeches/the-smith-commission

[59] https://www.dictionary.com/browse/colonialism

[60] https://www.collinsdictionary.com/dictionary/english/colonialism

[61] https://www.thefreedictionary.com/colonialism

[62] http://www.oilofscotland.org/MccronereportScottishOffice.pdf

[63] http://robertburns.org/works/344.shtml

[64] https://www.bbc.co.uk/programmes/p019dncn

[65] https://www.scotch-whisky.org.uk/insights/international-trade/

[66] https://uk.worlddutyfree.com/ukm_en/whiskies/single-malt-scotch.html

[67] The Scottish Government commitment is to invest just £2bn over 10 years or an average of £200m per annum, which is unlikely to improve Scotland's export potential much. https://www.gov.scot/policies/economic-growth/scottish-national-investment-bank/

[68] http://www.un.org/en/events/righttodevelopment/pdf/rtd_at_a_glance.pdf

[69] https://sociologyguide.com/basic-concepts/Social-Institutions.php

[70] https://www.gov.uk/government/organisations/civil-service/about/our-governance

[71] All civil servants in Scotland are technically part of the UK civil service and are employees of the Crown. The Scottish civil service terms of employment state: "Your employer is the Scottish Ministers, as agent of, and acting on behalf of, the Crown. As a Crown employee you are part of the UK Civil Service."

[72] https://www.theguardian.com/politics/2020/mar/23/alex-salmond-acquitted-of-all-charges-in-sexual-assault-trial

[73] https://www.scotlandscensus.gov.uk/education-0

[74] https://povertyinequality.scot/poverty-scotland/

[75] https://weegingerdug.wordpress.com/

[76] Former Labour MSP Kezia Dugdale was appointed to head up Glasgow University's 'John Smith Centre'.

[77] https://universitydiary.wordpress.com/2013/02/19/higher-education-and-academic-migration/#comments

[78] https://www.fiscalcommission.scot/about-us/who-we-are/

[79] https://www.heraldscotland.com/news/17629158.bbc-lacked-in-depth-knowledge-during-scottish-independence-referendum/?ref=mrb&lp=25

[80] https://www.scotsman.com/arts-and-culture/books/alasdair-gray-attacks-english-for-colonising-arts-1-2694368

[81] http://minedu.fi/en/frontpage

[82] 'Anschluss' is the idea of grouping all 'German' peoples into one nation-state, which may be comparable with the idea of grouping all 'British' peoples into one nation-state. 'Anschluss' is defined as a unifying political union, which is effectively what the UK is: https://www.thefreedictionary.com/Anschluss

[83] http://www.pol.ed.ac.uk/people

[84] http://www.pol.ed.ac.uk/people/postdoctoral_and_research_fellows

[85] https://www.historicenvironment.scot/about-us/who-we-are/our-board/board-members/

[86] https://www.bbc.co.uk/news/uk-scotland-scotland-politics-45770801

[87] https://www.britannica.com/topic/banning-South-African-law

[88] https://www.holyrood.com/news/view,independence-camp-protesters-lose-legal-battle-against-eviction_12139.htm

[89] https://en.wikipedia.org/wiki/Education_Directorates

[90] http://www.strath.ac.uk/engineering/navalarchitectureoceanmarineengineering/ourstaff/

[91] https://www.scotslanguage.com/Scots_publications/A_Scots_Grammar

[92] The Laws in Wales Act 1535 (A.D. 1535 Anno vicesimo septimo Henrici VIII c. 26)

[93] https://www.supremecourt.uk/cases/uksc-2019-0192.html

[94] http://curia.europa.eu/juris/document/document.jsf?text=&docid=208385&pageIndex=0&doclang=EN&mode=lst&dir=&occ=first&part=1&cid=252944

[95] http://www.legislation.gov.uk/aep/Ann/6/11/part/6

[96] https://www.un.org/en/sections/issues-depth/decolonization/index.html

[97] Perfidious Albion is a pejorative phrase used within the context of international relations diplomacy to refer to alleged acts of diplomatic sleights, duplicity, treachery and hence infidelity (with respect to perceived promises made to or alliances formed with other nation states) by monarchs or governments of the UK (or England prior to 1707) in their pursuit of self-interest. https://en.wikipedia.org/wiki/Perfidious_Albion

[98] See, for example, the play 'Hansard' written by Simon Wood. https://

www.tatler.com/article/simon-woods-hansard-play-national-theatre

[99] https://bdsmovement.net/colonialism-and-apartheid/summary

[100] https://povertyinequality.scot/

[101] https://en.wikisource.org/wiki/
United_Nations_General_Assembly_Resolution_1514

[102] *See:* Clause 3 of the Atlantic Charter reads: "*Third, they respect the right of all people to choose the form of government under which they will live; and they wish to see sovereign rights and self government restored to those who have been forcibly deprived of them*". This became one of the eight cardinal principal points of the Charter, all people had a right to self-determination.

[103] http://www.un.org/en/sections/un-charter/chapter-i/index.html

[104] https://www.un.org/dppa/decolonization/en/about

[105] https://www.dictionary.com/browse/national-self-determination

[106] http://www.un.org/en/decolonization/

[107] https://www.bing.com/videos/search?q=BBC+journalist+Alan+Little%27s+comments+on
+independence&view=detail&mid=B169C8EC5A42DDE874D5B169C8EC5
A42DDE874D5&FORM=VIRE

[108] https://en.wikipedia.org/wiki/Right_of_foreigners_to_vote

[109] https://www.regjeringen.no/en/topics/elections-and-democracy/den-norske-valgordningen/the-norwegian-electoral-system/id456636/

[110] https://smartexpat.com/denmark/how-to-guides/moving/becoming-an-expat/voting

[111] Response to the author from Cabinet Secretary Michael Russell MSP dated 22nd December 2019.

[112] The UN did not recognize the UK referendum held on self-determination in the Falklands because it involved a survey of colonists and ignored the indigenous community (i.e. their descendants), even though the latter were expelled over one hundred years previously. https://www.un.org/press/en/2015/gacol3283.doc.htm

[113] https://www.echr.coe.int/Documents/Convention_ENG.pdf

[114] https://www.bbc.co.uk/programmes/m000dqmd

[115] https://en.wikipedia.org/wiki/Self-determination#Defining_"peoples"

[116] https://fsi.stanford.edu/events/nicola-sturgeon

[117] 'Yes Minister' was a 1980's UK political satire sitcom TV programme.

[118] https://casebrief.fandom.com/wiki/
Reference_re_Secession_of_Quebec

[119] Legally, however, this would appear to ignore the acknowledged constitutional fact of Scottish sovereignty, and the legal and constitutional fact of the Treaty and Act of Union through which Scotland established the UK union.